Is The

"WORLD'S OLDEST BIBLE" A FAKE?

HOW A 19TH CENTURY HOAX AFFECTS YOUR FAITH

David W. Daniels
Artwork by Deborah Daniels

CHICK PUBLICATIONS
Ontario, Calif 91761

For a complete list of distributors near you,
call (909) 987-0771, or visit **www.chick.com**

Copyright © 2017 David W. Daniels

Published by:
CHICK PUBLICATIONS
PO Box 3500, Ontario, Calif. 91761-1019 USA
Tel: (909) 987-0771
Fax: (909) 941-8128
Web: www.chick.com
Email: postmaster@chick.com

Second Printing

Printed in the United States of America

All rights reserved. No part of this book may be reproduced, stored in a retrieval system or transmitted in any form or by any means (electronic, mechanical, photocopying, recording or otherwise) without permission in writing from the copyright owner.

ISBN: 978-0-75891-1704

Cover Art: Center art is a montage of the 823 Sinaiticus pages viewable on the *www.codexsinaiticus.org* web page. Notice the different white and colored sections. (See p. 86) The two side pages are adjoining pages of the Sinaiticus showing the contrast between the original snow-white parchment Tischendorf took in 1844, and the later stained pages that Tischendorf presented as "oldest and best."

Contents

1 Read This First.............................. 9
Did God keep His promise to preserve His word or was it hidden for centuries in obscure books, only to be revealed in the last couple of centuries? Modern research techniques reveal that at least one of these books is a fake.

2 Satan's Plan B.............................. 13
Beginning with Eve, Satan's plan was to raise doubt in God's words. In the church age, he has used every tool, from bonfires to inquisitions to stamp them out. When that didn't work, he resorted to his old technique of casting doubt, by "fixing" the Bible with a classic bait-and-switch strategy.

3 A Case in Point: Why Should We Preach Mark 16? 16
What happened when Deborah and I visited a church to hear our Greek professor deliver an Easter message from Mark 16. This is a classic example of how modern scholarship has promoted doubt instead of faith in the words of God.

SECTION I: THE BIG PICTURE

4 Separating Fact from Fiction 32
How I became suspicious that something might be wrong with the Sinaiticus. How I went from viewing it as just a messed up old manuscript that had affected all the modern versions, to realizing that it might, indeed, be some kind of a fake.

5 Telling Bibles Apart: Good Stream vs. Bad Stream 38
Simplified explanation of the two historical streams of manuscripts. How one stream preserved a trustworthy

English Bible and the other produces polluted Bibles modified to fit into a one world religion.

6 Why the NWO Hates the KJV **46**
This details how the New World Order proponents, specifically Manly P. Hall, planned to condition the world population to accept one world government and religion: the Bible must be "fixed" and the KJV must be eliminated!

7 KJV, Sinaiticus and the NWO **56**
Manly P. Hall touted the importance of the Sinaiticus, to change the Bible to fit into the one world religion and to loosen people's grip on the KJV.

SECTION II:
SINAITICUS: NOT WHAT WE WERE TOLD

8 Why You Can't Trust Sinaiticus **65**
The beginning of the evidence. Look at these defects in the Sinaiticus; especially the missing verses between 1 Chronicles and Ezra.

9 Is Sinaiticus a Fake? **69**
Learn about the color differences between the CFA and other Sinaiticus pages. And look at how some of its missing verses affect doctrines, such as in 1 John 5:7 and Mark 16:9-20.

10 Is the Sinaiticus Origin a Lie? **81**
I found historians who raised excellent questions about Tischendorf's story of how he found Sinaiticus. And see how it changes scriptures, such as Matthew 5:22 and John 7:8, affecting modern Bible texts.

11 Coloring the Truth **86**
Reexamines some of Tischendorf's narrative and tries to discover the source of the strange color differences of the pages.

12 Who Darkened Sinaiticus? **92**

More detailed examination of the history of the various sections of the Sinaiticus, leading to who could have darkened its pages.

13 Which Part is Scripture? **100**

Casts serious suspicion on Tischendorf's truthfulness and motives. Describes how impossible it is to sort through all the corrections, additions, missing sections to really know what God said.

14 Deleted on Purpose? **114**

Describes the difficulty for those who trust Sinaiticus, to determine exactly whether Mark 16:9-20 belonged in the Bible.

15 Is that Your Best Job? **123**

Reasons why the Sinaiticus cannot be one of the 50 bibles commissioned by Constantine, to be supplied by Eusebius. Describes how Constantine's request for quality Bibles could not have been met by the mess that is the Sinaiticus.

16 Uniquely Bad **131**

Describes the rough draft quality of the Sinaiticus and postulates that it might have been a rush job, increasing the suspicion that it was faked.

17 How Old Is It Really? **139**

Detailed reasons why the early date of the Sinaiticus is probably wrong. We know it's not the best, but it's not the oldest, either.

18 What Did Constantine Want? **157**

More details of why the Sinaiticus and Vaticanus cannot be two of the Bibles that Constantine ordered from Eusebius.

19 Sinaiticus and the Zombie Apocalypse.......... 164
A run-down of the "scholars" and "professors" involved in validating the Sinaiticus. Includes prominent figures in the history of the Sinaiticus as well as in my own academic journey.

20 It's A Job................................. 170
Describes the huge academic and commercial effort behind the modern Bibles. Many are just in it for a career. Others, who are really dedicated to the task of providing translations, are locked into a system dominated and defined by Rome.

21 No Doctrine Affected?...................... 176
Refutes the claim that no doctrines are affected by changes based on the Sinaiticus and Vaticanus. Discusses Mark 16:9-20 and other scriptures that are left out or altered, then used by scholars to cast doubt on Christ's resurrection and ascension.

22 Prove It!................................. 185
Uses the story of Codex 2427 as an example of how a supposedly high-value manuscript was proven a fake by elaborate academic detective work. Then it shows how the same process has not been applied to the Sinaiticus to test whether it is a fraud.

23 I Trusted Them!........................... 202
My personal journey from trusting my professors, to frustration over being unable to actually view the Sinaiticus, to finally seeing it, thanks to modern technology, to my conclusion that it is a fraud, and to my trust in the KJV.

24 Three Big Mistakes of Text Critics 214
Shows how text critics ignore simple common sense, the influence of Satan, and God's power to preserve His word.

SECTION III: APOCRYPHA

25 What's in YOUR Bible? 219
Modern research and archeology continue to uncover the accuracy of scripture. However, this same careful research exposes the Apocrypha as simply fanciful fiction.

26 What's Wrong with Tobit? 229
The Apocrypha book, Tobit, is a good example of how so many of the Apocrypha books are simply folk tales. When modern research is applied, they are more fiction than fact. However, all Roman Catholic Bibles contain Apocryphal books, because they are necessary to support some of Rome's heathen doctrines.

SECTION IV:
THE BIBLE VERSION CONSPIRACY

27 The Evidence 249
Overview of 20 facts discovered in the research into the origin and importance of the Sinaiticus.

28 The Beginning to the 1800s 269
Review of the history of Bible manuscripts, from the beginning until the 1800s, leading up to the discovery of the Sinaiticus.

29 1800s to Today 290
The appearance of the Sinaiticus and the Vaticanus and their effect on modern Bible versions.

30 The Sinaiticus Smoking Gun? 299
Explanation of Simonides' claim that he was the originator of the Sinaiticus manuscript and some facts that just may prove to be a missing piece to the puzzle.

31 Conclusion **332**

The effort to "fix" the Classic English Bible led to the substitution of fake manuscripts to support the text. All the modern Bibles are influenced in some way by this bait-and-switch. On top of the resulting confusion is a plot to discredit the only Bible that was made through faithful translation of correct texts. Satan is well pleased by the wide-spread doubt in God's words.

32 Appendix A: Comparison Chart of Books Containing the Apocrypha..................... **334**

33 Appendix B: Spurgeon's Quote **346**

A profound warning by a seasoned warrior after attempting to use one of the early new versions.

1

Read This First

Would God have withheld the truth for 1800 years, only to have it show up in an Orthodox monastery in the desert? And then would God arrange for it to be stolen, first 43 leaves of it in 1844, then the rest of it, with Russian help, in 1859? And then would He have it only "released" to the public in 1862 —but not directly, only as an altered, printed copy?

Would He have His people see only a typeset text that covers up thousands of erasures, write-overs, marginal notes and optional readings? Would it be missing over 1/3 of the Old Testament? And after that, would it be mixed with fairytales like Tobit and Judith, Bel and the Dragon, Susanna, and 4th Maccabees, the non-historical, fanciful writings of men?

If the apocryphal *Epistle of Barnabas*, and the Christ's deity demoting *Shepherd of Hermas* were supposed to have been scripture, would God have held them back from His people? And to top it off, would He have then secretly added them to the ***real*** New Testament?

That's not my God. The Bible says this about my God:

"Jesus Christ the same yesterday, and to day, and for ever." (Hebrews 13:8)

And:

"God *is* not a man, that he should lie; neither the son of man, that he should repent: hath he said, and shall he not do *it*? or hath he spoken, and shall he not make it good?" (Numbers 23:19)

The trustworthiness of God is at stake. God said, recorded in three places:

"Heaven and earth shall pass away, but my words shall not pass away." (Matthew 24:35, Mark 13:31; Luke 21:33)

So when God promised that His word would never pass away, He either lied, and His words crumbled up and passed away, for over 1800 years, —or there's something wrong with this famous "oldest and best text" of the Bible.

The following has been the famous narrative about the discovery of Sinaiticus, from the 1860s until today. It has been taught in universities, seminaries and even churches.

Supposedly, a world renowned text collector and Greek expert, Constantin von Tischendorf, discovered, in a waste bin, destined for the fire, a number of Greek parchment sheets, older than any he had ever seen. He then dramatically rescued them from the flames in 1844 and took 21 1/2 sheets back to Germany and called them the Codex Friderico-Augustanus (CFA). In 1853 Tischendorf returned, but claimed he couldn't find any more sheets.

He returned in 1859 with a Russian Orthodox delegation, and gave a monk there one of Tischendorf's own printed Septuagints, and in return Tischendorf received the monk's prized possession, wrapped in a red cloth. This was the Codex Sinaiticus.

Tischendorf claimed he had the codex sent to him in

Cairo. Then he transcribed the entire text, with the help of two unnamed Germans who "happened" to be in Cairo, and one of whom just "happened" to read Greek, all completed in the near miraculous space of just two months.

Then Tischendorf, with the help of printing experts in his adopted town of Leipzig, Germany, made typeface replicas of the letters, both large and small. He decided which words should be in the text, and which should be in footnotes, and prepared and published all but the CFA, for grand exhibition in 1862.

As a result, Tischendorf received numerous accolades, commendations and honoring compliments, including by the pope himself. After that, the pope, with his Jesuit Cardinal Mai, invited Tischendorf to see the grand prize of the Vatican, Codex Vaticanus, which Tischendorf transcribed and printed in 1867.

These texts, the Sinaiticus and Vaticanus, became the basis for a new Greek text, picked by Westcott and Hort, as their basis to create new English Bible versions, such as the Revised Version of 1881, the American Standard of 1901, and hundreds of changed Bible versions ever since.

Sounds too good to be true, doesn't it?

Well, it *is* too good to be true.

In this book we will find the clues that show us that the Sinaiticus, which changed Protestant and Baptist faith forever (though it didn't change Catholic or Orthodox faith), ***is not what it is claimed to be***.

It is a fake.

And whether it was made for all the ***right reasons***, for all the ***wrong reasons***, or for ***reasons we do not yet know***, the Codex Sinaiticus, which suddenly appeared in its tattered form in 1844, is not the oldest, it is certainly not the best, and it is ***not an ancient manuscript at all***.

And, to top it all off, no one has even been allowed to do scientific tests to date the ink or the parchment.

* * *

My journey started with a simple question.

I woke up one morning and went into prayer, as I usually do. Then I heard these words: ***"What if they're fakes?"*** And I saw a mental image of Codex Sinaiticus and Codex Vaticanus.

I had thought they were counterfeits, but ancient ones, from Alexandria, Egypt. I never considered seriously that they were actually ***modern*** fakes.

A few days later, I was praying about the next video I would make for our YouTube channel, *youtube.com/c/chicktracts*. My mind was filled with one thought: Codex Sinaiticus.

I thought, "Okay, that may be good for one or two videos." I was about to be surprised by a number of hints and facts, which then became a number of videos!

A few weeks later, during devotions, the thought came to my heart: "Simple answers to even simpler questions."

And then one more event really got me started. I prayed and asked God, "What question should I ask?"

And I heard, "What color is it?"

And that was the beginning of all that you are about to read. Please, check the facts all you want. Dogged research is how I got to be where I am now, and why I wrote this book. I want you to see it and answer the question for yourself.

"Is the 'Oldest and Best Bible' a fake?"

God bless you as you read.

2

Satan's Plan B

In an earlier book, *Did the Catholic Church Give Us the Bible?*, I identified two historical streams of manuscripts that produced two kinds of Bibles. One was the wide, pure "northern stream" of thousands of documents that were all faithfully copied and translated over the centuries, culminating in the Classic English Authorized (King James) Version.

The other, "southern stream" is a mere polluted rivulet of a few manuscripts used to "update" the Bible less than two centuries ago.

Using modern research technology, new information is surfacing about the origins of manuscripts in the "southern stream," and a bold move to fake out the church, to serve a dark motive.

History is clear. From the beginning of the church, Satan has relentlessly attacked the word of God. Even the Apostle Paul had to stand up to the Judaizers. They insisted on stopping the free gospel of "grace through faith" by tying it to a system of works pushed by the Pharisees.

For fifteen hundred years after that, Bible believers were hunted like animals by a determined, counterfeit "church," trying to force its rituals of pagan bondage. It's been relatively quiet in the last couple of centuries. Do you think that

Satan sat on his hands? No, he just shifted to Plan B.

What was his new strategy? Obviously, modern civilized society would not tolerate another bloody inquisition. (Though communism and Islam bear some resemblances.) But his target was the classic English version responsible for the most dynamic missionary effort ever. How could people ever *want* to leave the most faith-building Book ever printed in English?

Tell them it needs "fixing!"

Do it through the most popular scholars, preachers and teachers. Then offer to "fix" the Bible, and get those same deceived leaders to endorse it!

This isn't a guess. This isn't a doom-and-gloom prediction. It already happened.

This book is about the most nefarious bait-and-switch scheme ever perpetrated. This plot is so monstrous that millions have already fallen from the secure faith they had in the scriptures because of it.

And that once-secure faith has been replaced by blind doubt.

That makes them the perfect dupes to be pulled into believing whatever interpretation of the Bible the "scholars" give us. But the Bible that they give us is **not** one we can trust. Instead, the scholars insist we must trust **them**. See how devious this is?

Millions more are today following blindly the perverted teaching of the prostitute "church" that astonished John when he described it in his Revelation, Chapter 17.

But there's hope.

First, like it says in the *X-Files*, "The truth is out there." And it's ripe for the picking. I'll show you where to look and verify every point I make.

Second, you will see their plan unravel before your eyes. And you will see how incredibly big and detailed it is. But it all boils down to one principle: Faith vs. Doubt.

They want you to trust them to give you an imperfect Bible that will cause you to doubt for the rest of your life.

But you will see why you can actually trust in the preserved Bible, and how the words that the scholars removed actually produce faith and confidence in God and His words.

Yes, it is late in the game. But it's not too late.

God's preserved words are still available. And now, for the first time in history, you can show your doubt-filled friends the fiendish plot to destroy their belief in God, His Bible, and the most basic of doctrines, including the deity and bodily resurrection of Christ.

Don't believe that only scholars can understand this. Since the videos behind this book went online, women with a baby in one arm and the dishes in the other have been able to learn more about this issue than all my seminary professors combined *knew*.

Their goal is becoming clear. They want a Bible so stripped of essential doctrines that the silly putty text can be molded to fit with all the writings of the other religions of the world —a one world Bible for the coming one world religion of Revelation 13.

After you read this book, you will understand the magnitude of the deception that the Father of Lies has accomplished. You will also know that there is only one English Bible, one anchor of Truth built upon the bedrock of Christ's promise to preserve His word, "till heaven and earth pass away."

3

A Case in Point: Why Should We Preach Mark 16?

My fiancée Deborah and I were so excited to visit this church! The day was Resurrection Sunday, what the world calls Easter, in the early 1980s. And this church had a special guest preacher: our Greek professor, Dr. Paul McReynolds, was going to preach the resurrection sermon!

Everything we knew about Greek in Bible college pretty much came from him. Not until I took advanced Greek at Fuller and Linguistics training with the Summer Institute of Linguistics did we learn much more than he taught us.

Before I go further, please note: almost none of the surprising statements our professor was going to make were any different from what almost any other teacher taught, or that I believed, for that matter. And *some* of those beliefs *I still held*, up until *December 2015* when the Lord prompted me in prayer with *four life-changing words*.

Please understand. We loved Dr. McReynolds. We shared our years at Bible college with him. I loved the privilege of helping a tiny bit with his Greek interlinear. He wasn't a villain. He wasn't trying to mess up our faith. He was trying to deal as best he could with all that *he'd* been taught. And he taught it to us, the *next generation*.

A Case in Point: Why Should We Preach Mark 16?

But I'm sure he ***didn't*** know, and ***still may not know***, things that are just *lately* coming to light.

He is the one who taught me how our modern critical Greek texts are built upon Westcott and Hort's critical Greek text. And their critical Greek text was built upon the foundation of Constantin Tischendorf's printed Greek texts of Sinaiticus and Vaticanus, as well as Tischendorf's 8th edition of his Greek New Testament.[1]

I never found Tischendorf's 8th edition Greek New Testament, until just lately.[2] But that's okay. He died before Vaticanus could alter the basic structure of his "critical Greek edition," anyway. It took Westcott and Hort to build in both Sinaiticus **and Vaticanus.** (That's for another book.)

But I tried to get ***every other good Greek reference book*** that our professor suggested "for proper Greek study." We all had the United Bible Societies 3rd edition Greek New Testament. Then I got Fritz Rienecker's *Linguistic Key to the Greek New Testament* as soon as it was available. And then, of course, I had to get Metzger's *Textual Commentary on the Greek New Testament*.

Dr. McReynolds was the go-to guy on Greek, and a nice guy. What could be better? So when Deborah and I heard that he would be preaching at a church near my home, on Resurrection Sunday, we were excited and made sure we were there.

---

1. See, for example, *The New Testament in the Original Greek: Introduction, Appendix*, by Brooke Foss Westcott and Fenton John Anthony Hort (Cambridge: Macmillan and Co, 1882), p. 13.

2. Now, of course, you can download it for free from archive.org. It's called the *Novum Testamentum Graece*, has Tischendorf's name, and each is dated as follows: Gospels, 1869; Acts-Revelation, 1872; *Ultimae Textum* (published after Tischendorf died, a complete New Testament), 1881.

But it wasn't like any resurrection sermon we had ever heard. For one thing, he told us he was going to stick to the Gospel of Mark. That sounded intriguing! Until I learned the textual critics say, against all historical fact, that Mark was the first gospel, and that the other gospels were written later. But they claim that what's in the ***other*** gospels was added ***later***, and ***didn't actually happen***.

Picture this with me. Mark 16:1-2 sets the stage: Sometime after Saturday sunset, but before Sunday sunrise, Mary Magdalene and Mary, mother of James and Joses (sounds like Jesus' earthly mom, Mary), and Salome come up to the tomb. They arrive just as the sun breaks over the horizon.

It's very dramatic. Follow with me, right out of the text. Mark 16:3-7:

> And they (Mary Magdalene, Mary and Salome) said among themselves, Who shall roll us away the stone from the door of the sepulchre? And when they looked, they saw that the stone was rolled away: for it was very great. And entering into the sepulchre, they saw a young man sitting on the right side, clothed in a long white garment; and they were affrighted. And he saith unto them, Be not affrighted: Ye seek Jesus of Nazareth, which was crucified: he is risen; he is not here: behold the place where they laid him. But go your way, tell his disciples and Peter that he goeth before you into Galilee: there shall ye see him, as he said unto you.

Now look at verse 8:

> And they went out quickly, and fled from the sepulchre; for they trembled and were amazed:

A Case in Point: Why Should We Preach Mark 16?

neither said they any thing to any *man*; for they were afraid.

They had reason to be afraid! Women's testimony wasn't believed. They had no proof of what happened. And they'd just gone to an opened tomb, with no guards outside, and no body inside! And they had just seen an angel of God! On top of that, they were the ***only witnesses*** of all this!

How would you like the police to question ***you*** at this point? The body is missing, and ***you're*** on the scene. So they fled. Makes sense to me.

What happened next?

Our professor that Sunday morning was telling this congregation about what he said was "the oldest manuscript," Codex Sinaiticus. He said something like this:

> There are …some very, very significant omissions to this early manuscript. And it ends, uh, with an expression about the women. It says, 'For they were afraid.' And you see there's lots of space for them to go on. But he doesn't know of any other ending. And they supplied these different endings because they didn't like a Gospel ending, ***'For they were afraid.'***

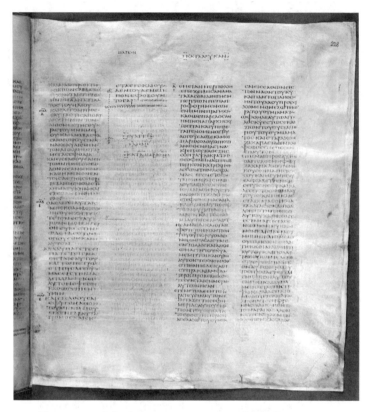

Figure 1 - Mark 16:9-20 missing from Sinaiticus

But if they'd read carefully, and I've done this, and looked through this, the word 'phobeomai,' which is the normal word for phobia, or fears, um, in Mark, more often has the idea of standing in AWE of something. And if we see that, then we can see this is an appropriate ending for the gospel of Mark. They were in AWE at what they had seen, that Jesus was no longer there. Um, and that's uh, at

> least that's my interpretation and my explanation.
> Hm. Later on, there are, as I said, two different
> kinds of endings that are here, okay. Earliest manuscripts do not have those verses in them.

So our Greek professor, who was colorful and vibrant and alive, left us without any resurrection appearances of Christ. The women left the tomb after they saw an angel, wouldn't talk to anyone, and they were afraid… or, "in AWE…"

The End.

Deborah and I walked out of that Sunday service so confused. It was Resurrection Sunday, with no resurrection. It just stopped with the women fleeing the empty tomb. Dr. McReynolds didn't even refer to Matthew or Luke or John for what happened after that. He did as he said, and stuck to Mark's gospel —as it is found in the Sinaiticus. That has stuck with me from that day to this.

Some of you will ask me, "How can you *remember* what he said *30 years ago?*" That's because I wasn't quoting something from 30 years ago. I was quoting him when he said it again, in September 2015, on video.

Let's take apart what he said and see whether it makes sense. Were the women *"afraid"*, or were they *"in awe"*?

In 16:8 it said "they trembled and were amazed, neither said they any thing to any man." Why didn't they? Because they ***were afraid***.

I can prove to you that Mary Magdalene wasn't all joyful and "in awe." Look at what John wrote, himself —and he was ***there*** that day, and ***knew*** Mary Magdalene.

John 20:10-13:

> Then the disciples went away again unto their own home. But Mary[3] stood without at the sepulchre weeping: and as she wept, she stooped down, *and looked* into the sepulchre, And seeth two angels in white sitting, the one at the head, and the other at the feet, where the body of Jesus had lain. And they say unto her, Woman, why weepest thou? She saith unto them, Because they have taken away my Lord, and I know not where they have laid him.

Mary Magdalene doesn't sound in AWE at all. ***She sounds sad***, because she doesn't know ***who*** took Jesus' body away, or ***where*** it is. Mary's not thinking about Jesus being ***resurrected*** this morning. ***That's why she's weeping.***

Look at John 20:9:

> For as yet they knew not the scripture, that he must rise again from the dead."

Jesus said a lot of things that the disciples didn't understand. This was one of them.[4]

John 20:14-15:

> And when she had thus said, she turned herself back, and saw Jesus standing, and knew not that it was Jesus. Jesus saith unto her, Woman, why weepest thou? whom seekest thou? She, supposing him to be the gardener, saith unto him, Sir, if thou have

---

3. This is Mary Magdalene. See John 20:1.
4. See how Martha misunderstood about Jesus raising the dead in John 11:23-26. Other places are Mark 9:32; Luke 9:45; and John 12:16.

A Case in Point: Why Should We Preach Mark 16?

borne him hence, tell me where thou hast laid him, and I will take him away.

Here Mary Magdalene clearly still doesn't get it. ***There's no body***. That's ***all*** she knows. Not even angels appearing can change that for her. She asks where Jesus was laid, so she can take His body away again. She doesn't understand why someone would move His body!

Verse 16: "Jesus saith unto her, Mary. She turned herself, and saith unto him, Rabboni; which is to say, Master." Not until she has ***seen the risen Lord Jesus for herself*** does she stop weeping and being sad!

So no, they were ***not*** in awe. They were afraid. Not a suitable ending for Mark's gospel. Look at Mary Magdalene. Not even angels appearing gave her hope. ***Only Jesus' body risen from the dead made her stop weeping.***

Mark's Gospel was never supposed to stop at 16:8. That's why out of 620 Greek Mark 16s in existence, 618 of them ***have verses 9-20***. That's 99.677% of Greek manuscripts that have Mark 16 that have verses 9-20.

Only two defective manuscripts are missing them: Codex Sinaiticus and Codex Vaticanus.

Even in Matthew 28:5-10, first the angel says to the women, "***Fear not***," then in verse 8 it says they departed quickly "with fear and great joy," and then in verse 10 Jesus Himself says, "***Be not afraid.***" Face it. They were ***afraid***. But the appearances of the risen Lord and Saviour, Jesus Christ, are what made them NOT afraid.

It just doesn't make sense without the resurrection appearances of Jesus. As God had Paul write: 1 Corinthians 15:17 "And if Christ be not raised, your faith *is* vain; ye are yet in your sins."

And yet these crucial words at the end of the gospel of Mark *are* missing, from only these two Greek manuscripts: Codex Sinaiticus and Codex Vaticanus. I'll show you more about what happened to Mark 16:9-20 in a later chapter.

But I didn't only transcribe the words my professor said in that videoed lecture from September, 2015. I also wrote down, word for word, what Dr. David Matson, a former top student, now a professor at my Bible college, added. But instead of simply quoting him, let me tell you what he said, in a different way.

What if I could show you how he was able to poke holes in the doctrine of Christ, with just two missing Greek words in Mark 1:1? Here it is in the King James Bible; 12 simple words:

Mark 1:1 "The beginning of the gospel of Jesus Christ, the Son of God;"

Figure 2 - The page of Sinaiticus showing Mark 1:1-35. Verse 1 is enlarged in Figure 3 below.

A Case in Point: Why Should We Preach Mark 16?

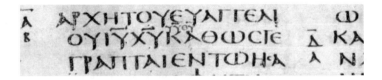

Figure 3 - Mark 1:1 close-up

In the Sinaiticus it reads, "The beginning of the gospel of Jesus Christ."

$$\overline{IY} = \text{"of Jesus"}$$
$$\overline{XY} = \text{"of Christ"}$$
$$\overline{IY}\ \overline{XY} = \text{"of Jesus Christ"}$$

That capital "IY" with the bar over it means "of Jesus." The capital "XY" with the bar over it means "of Christ." That's called in Latin, *"nomina sacra,"* "sacred names" form. But if you look carefully at Figure 4, you can see extra *nomina sacra* between the lines.

Figure 4 - Extra abbreviations between the lines

Those look like capitals "YY" with a bar over it and "O with a line through it –a theta, and a Y" with a bar over that.

$$\overline{YY} = \text{"of Son"}$$
$$\overline{\Theta Y} = \text{"of God"}$$
$$\overline{YY}\ \overline{\Theta Y} = \text{"(of) the Son of God"}$$

The "YY" is huiou, "of Son" and the "theta Y" is theou, "of God."

$$\overline{IY}\ \overline{XY}\ \overline{YY}\ \overline{\Theta Y}$$
= "of Jesus Christ, the Son of God"

"Well, there you go," someone will say. "You've got the whole verse there: The beginning of the gospel of Jesus Christ, the Son of God." Not quite. Scholars are divided over whether the "the Son of God" really belongs there.

What if the guy who wrote Mark 1:1 in Sinaiticus didn't really believe Jesus was eternally God? What if he believed Jesus was made the Son of God, say, at His baptism?

Our professor's prized student, the PhD who graduated the same semester I started Bible college, made a great case for this theory. Only Dr. Matson did it by asking the question, "Is that what the original gospel taught?" Watch this. And remember, this isn't original to me. I learned it from him!

Let's take a look at Mark 1:4-5: "John did baptize in the wilderness, and preach the baptism of repentance for the remission of sins." So step 1: John preaches baptism of repentance to get your sins forgiven.

Mark 1:5: "And there went out unto him all the land of

A Case in Point: Why Should We Preach Mark 16?

Judaea, and they of Jerusalem, and were all baptized of him in the river of Jordan, confessing their sins."

So step 2: All these people from Judaea are getting baptized, confessing their sins. The point is, they were getting their sins forgiven.

Mark 1:9 "And it came to pass in those days, that Jesus came from Nazareth of Galilee, and was baptized of John in Jordan."

What does this mean?

I'll quote what the professor said at this point.

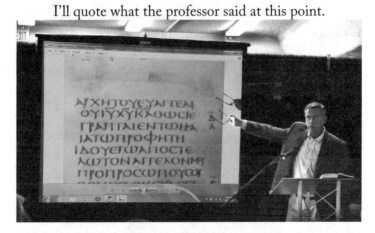

Figure 5 - Screen capture of the lecture

But first you need to know that "redactional" means that a later editor rewrote and changed the story.

> Dr. Matson said, "Now don't run over to Matthew, and pull Matthew's little redactional scene there, where Jesus and John have a discussion about this. ***Mark has no discussion***. Jesus is baptized. What might be the implication of that? ***Is Jesus one of***

these sinners? I thought He was the Son of God. No, Mark hasn't told you He's the Son of God, if that's not there [the "huiou theou," Son of God]. And so He's baptized. And then the voice comes out of the heavens. And what does the voice say? Now for the *first time*, 'You are My Son.' **Ahh**! Is He adopted? Does He *become* the Son of God at that point? Is He *now* sinless from *that* point on?

Wow. They spent the evening telling how the Sinaiticus is the oldest Greek manuscript of the New Testament. Then they told how in many ways, it's the best, even though, as Dr. McReynolds said: "This is probably the most corrected or added-to manuscript I am aware of."

Think about the people at this lecture in my old Bible college. Everyone there recognized the scholarship and accomplishments of the two doctors.

They were given a lot of ifs to think about. *If* the Sinaiticus is the oldest and best, *If* the Sinaiticus truly represents the original text the best, *If* the Sinaiticus ***wasn't*** supposed to say "the Son of God" in Mark 1:1...

Then maybe Jesus was *not* the pre-existing, eternal Son of God. Maybe He was only ***adopted*** as God's Son at His baptism!

This is called ***Adoptionism***.

Dr. Matson implied that Adoptionism *may* have been a legitimate, original Christian belief.

So not only are they questioning a simple "issue of textual criticism," whether the words "the Son of God" belong in the text. That also makes them question whether the Bible *"in the originals"* taught that Jesus was only adopted as God's Son at His baptism, after His sins were forgiven, at 30 years

A Case in Point: Why Should We Preach Mark 16?

of age!

That's what happens if you remove those two words, "huiou theou," four words in English, "the Son of God," from Mark 1:1.

And *all* of this is *only* possible if we trust the Codex Sinaiticus!

As I watched this, it hit me: everyone who believed in Sinaiticus, which they have probably only seen for the first time that night, and his explanation for the text, could never simply read Mark 1:1 and believe it again. There would always be that nagging doubt.

Yea, hath God said 'Son of God'?

Or is it just "The beginning of the gospel of Jesus Christ," with no "Son of God"?

It's not a small thing. It's a humongous thing. And it not only affects your faith. It also affects the faith of everyone you teach these lies to.

And it all started from just one thing: They believed the Sinaiticus was genuine. Then they believed the ever-changing rules taught them by text critics, as to whether a reading belonged there or not.

If they placed their faith in Codex Sinaiticus, a manuscript that has no record of even existing until about 1844, they now have their faith in the God of the universe and His promise to preserve His words slowly ebbing away.

Does that sound like something God would do?

Within a few minutes this prize student, now a PhD, whittled down the faith in everyone who listened to him. These are students, former students, and ministers. And *he just gave every reason*, based on his unqualified acceptance of Sinaiticus, or at least of Metzger's *Textual Commentary* and its notes, ***for his listeners to have a crisis of faith, and to now believe that Jesus was NOT the eternal, preexistent Son of God in Mark's Gospel.***

And believe it or not, he called this the "extremely practical side of textual criticism"! To him, this is supposed to answer the question of what a pastor should preach next Sunday. And this is supposed to help that pastor answer the question, "Why are these words in brackets in (or missing from) my Bible?"

Tell me, what is "practical" about poking a hole in the faith of his viewers and students in the eternal Son of God? ***And this is in my Bible college! And why shouldn't they believe him? He's the professor, of course! He's the expert!***

At the same time, Dr. Matson was the *first* professor I've heard who ever admitted this:

"Little, tiny, corrections can make a big ***difference***. I've heard people say, 'Well, you know, all these textual variants, they don't affect any ***doctrines*** of the faith.' Oh yes, they ***do***. (Chuckle.) They ***do***. So we need to be aware of them."

Everything I've been telling you in videos and in books, it's all coming true. I saw the beginnings of this, as a student, and in that church on Resurrection Morning, over 30 years ago!

What were they trying to prove?

What they proved to me is ***why*** someone changed those verses ***in Sinaiticus***. Whoever manufactured the Sinaiticus wanted you ***so*** confused about something so central to your faith as who Jesus really is, that you had to run to a priest — or a "professor," a replacement priest— to tell you what you can and cannot believe.

This same guy lifted up the Roman Catholic New

A Case in Point: Why Should We Preach Mark 16?

American Bible, which puts brackets around "Son of God" in Mark 1:1, to say it didn't really belong. Does this sound like what the Lord wants, doubts about what He said?

No! These are corrupt contradictions, and Sinaiticus is filled with them. Face it. The Sinaiticus is a *faith destroyer*.

If you've watched my vlogs (video blogs,) you know that for 17 years I've not trusted Sinaiticus. But, as recently as a year and a half before writing this book, I still believed the whole story about the origin and discovery and meaning of Sinaiticus.

Then, late 2015, I was in prayer and I heard those four words: *"What if they're fakes?"* In other words, what if Sinaiticus and Vaticanus weren't from the 350s AD, and were actually fakes, created by someone else?

That is what launched 7 months of reading, discovery and vlog making. I've shared the results with my viewers, one step at a time, almost as fast as I discovered them.

What did I discover? Sinaiticus is clearly a fake, probably from around the 1840s. Vaticanus couldn't have been made before the late 400s, and Erasmus thought it was made or modified after the 1430s. You can see it for yourself later in this book.

Anyone who trusts Sinaiticus or Vaticanus is stuck with nothing but contradictions of text and of doctrine.

God does *not* make or support a contradictory text. If you have a contradictory text, you have the *wrong text*. Get rid of it! If it was your Bible, it should *not* be your Bible *anymore*! That Bible has proven itself *not* to be God's holy and preserved words.

Get the faith-building, doubt-destroying, hope-bringing, devil-defeating holy preserved words of God in English, the King James Bible.

SECTION I: THE BIG PICTURE

4

Separating Fact from Fiction

I must be up-front with you: This is a book about liars.

And they are not just liars. They are, as my kids would say, "lying liars who lie." These people seem to live and thrive on lies. They get their money, their power, and their reputation from lies. You remember how the Lord Jesus said, "… all they that take the sword shall perish with the sword".[5] Ultimately, liars will meet the same fate.

But to get you to believe their lies, they must manipulate you. There is an oft-repeated fact about manipulators: They are persuasive when you listen to them. They use your friendship, gifts to you, sweet words and the most convincing stories, to get you to believe them.

But that is not how you deal with a manipulator. There is a simple rule: Don't believe what they *say*. Look at what they *do*. Always look for verifiable material. Always ask questions like, "Can this be verified?" "Who can verify this?" "Is

---

5. Matthew 26:52

the person trustworthy who is verifying this? And how do I know?"

Always look for second and third verifications. This is very scriptural.

The Lord Jesus said it:

> But if he will not hear *thee, then* take with thee one or two more, that in the mouth of two or three witnesses every word may be established.[6]

It was an excellent safeguard against simple false accusation.

> Against an elder receive not an accusation, but before two or three witnesses.[7]

And it was definitely important to prevent execution of the wrong person.

> At the mouth of two witnesses, or three witnesses, shall he that is worthy of death be put to death; *but* at the mouth of one witness he shall not be put to death.[8]

So if we have one witness against someone, that is a suspicion. If we have two, that is a theory. But if we have three good witnesses, then we can say we might have a fact fairly well established.

I believe that is the fairest way to approach finding the truth, even in a sea of liars. And that is what we just may have found, in the matter of Constantin Tischendorf and what really happened in the "discovery" and actual age and origin of the Codex Sinaiticus.

---

6. Matthew 18:16
7. 1 Timothy 5:19
8. Deuteronomy 17:6

Sinaiticus, as you will see, is the so-called ancient Bible that has changed almost every single modern Bible, and the unifying document behind the movement toward a one-world Bible.

For the last 30 years I had been willing to believe Tischendorf's story. But when confronted with Brother Chris Pinto's video series on the Bible, "A Lamp in the Dark," "Tares Among the Wheat," and the newest, "Bridge to Babylon," I found Tischendorf's testimony suddenly brought into question. And I was not totally prepared for that. I needed verification.

So I wrote back and forth with Chris, who pointed me to some information I had not read before, including a book I had to import from Greece! But I didn't want to make a mistake. If you look in the first edition of my book, *Answers to Your Bible Version Questions,* you will see that I actually repeated Tischendorf's story, as best as I found it, repeated all over, and of course, by Tischendorf himself. That was before so much new information became available. But it was perfectly in line with what my professors told me.

So I had no reason to change from my original position about Tischendorf's story. But because of what facts I could group together out of the complicated story that Chris told in his "Tares Among the Wheat" film, I came up with a basic theory, that I had no clear facts for, but which seemed to fit the facts I was finding out.

I was in the position of the fictional character Spock in *Star Trek VI*, when trying to explain the seemingly impossible: "We have no evidence, only a theory, which happens to fit the facts."

Things changed in late 2015. As people began to note,

when I started to make vlogs about Codex Sinaiticus, I began to encounter some facts I could not refute. As future President John Adams stated: "Facts are stubborn things; and whatever may be our wishes, our inclinations, or the dictates of our passion, they cannot alter the state of facts and evidence."[9]

But here's the problem. I came across two completely contradictory things. On the one hand, Tischendorf had a sterling reputation, and was regarded as one of the most brilliant scholars of the 19th century.

But on the other, Tischendorf's story about how he got hold of the Sinaiticus had numerous contradictions. *The simplest questions yielded the most uncomfortable answers!* As the fictional Sherlock Holmes stated: "You know my method. It is founded upon the observation of trifles."[10]

Little things, like:

"What color was Sinaiticus?"

"How was it found?"

"How many pieces are there?"

"Where were they?"

These questions led to other, also basic questions:

"Who else was there when this happened, to verify it?"

"What did they say happened?"

"Can we trust them?"

Ah, that is the question! Who can we trust? As I began to study more, especially with the help of researcher Steven Avery, who had found many documents that I had

---

9. "Argument in Defense of the Soldiers in the Boston Massacre Trials," Stated by John Adams, December 1770.

10. "The Bascombe Valley Mystery," by Sir Arthur Conan Doyle.

been struggling to find, I started to realize that somebody, somewhere, had to be lying!

And these were not little lies, though they may have started small. *Somebody had to be in high places to get away with it.* And that somebody had to have *not been questioned* to some extent, or have some pretty heavy-hitters on his side, to get the kind of defense he would need, to get away with this lie.

And the liar —believe it or not— turned out to be Constantin Tischendorf himself! That seemed impossible! Sure, I had a theory. But it doesn't mean I was ready to abandon the story I had set to pen in my own book, regarding the wastebasket story, or the age of the Sinaiticus!

But more things kept coming to light as I read and researched about the King James and the so-called New World Order, or NWO. I found that a high-level occultist, with massive political and religious connections, hinted that something occurred beyond what meets the eye in 1844 that was intended to change the Bible forever and eliminate King James believers.

By the way, the only Bible thing that happened in 1844, was that Tischendorf supposedly "discovered" the Sinaiticus. That, in itself, made me want to sort fact from the fiction.

As author Arthur Conan Doyle famously wrote through his character, Sherlock Holmes:

> It is an old maxim of mine that when you have excluded the impossible, whatever remains, however improbable, must be the truth.[11]

This book is like a detective story. We are sorting through history to find the liars, and the truth that they are hiding. And I

---

11. "The Adventure of the Beryl Coronet," by Sir Arthur Conan Doyle.

have to be very careful.

It is so easy for someone to find all the fault in his neighbor, when he himself has the same faults. God spoke through the Apostle Paul:

> Therefore thou art inexcusable, O man, whosoever thou art that judgest: for wherein thou judgest another, thou condemnest thyself; for thou that judgest doest the same things.[12]

So I don't want to do things in such a way that I make one side *all good*, and the other side *all bad*. As Jesus said: "Why callest thou me good? *there is* none good but one, *that is*, God."[13]

So I am not trying to find someone to be the "man in white," and the rest all bad. I want to go where the evidence leads me, even if they *all* are bad. Again, as Jesus said: "Judge not according to the appearance, but judge righteous judgment."[14]

So we ***have*** to judge. But we also have to be fair.

So you be the judge. Am I being fair? Am I treating both the evidence, and the characters, fairly? Or am I making a mountain out of a molehill? You judge. I'm just going to give you the facts as well as I can, and the theory that best seems to fit those facts.

---

12. Romans 2:1
13. Mark 10:18
14. John 7:24

5

Telling Bibles Apart: Good Stream vs. Bad Stream

In my book, ***Did the Catholic Church Give Us the Bible?*** I describe in detail the two streams of manuscripts behind the KJV and the modern versions. Here is a simple way to understand and explain these streams.

The Bible says of a bishop, that he must be "apt to teach" in 1 Timothy 3:2. And 2 Timothy 2:24 says, "And the servant of the Lord must not strive; but be gentle unto all men, ***apt to teach***, patient," which are all very important to God.

Would you like to know a simple method by which you can teach the main points about God's preserved words and the Devil's counterfeit Bibles? It's as easy as those same three letters that I read of: "apt": A, P, and T.

The first thing everybody needs to know is that ***there are two streams of Bibles.*** They flow from two cities: one north of Israel, in Syria; and the other southwest of Israel, in Egypt.

Telling Bibles Apart: Good Stream vs. Bad Stream 39

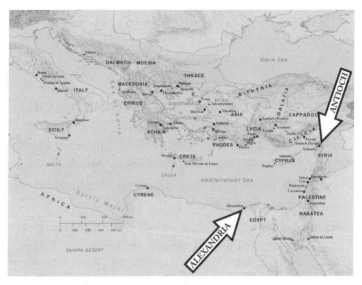

Figure 6 - Map showing Alexandria and Antioch

The ***two cities*** are: ***Antioch*** of Syria and ***Alexandria***, Egypt: ***A*** and ***A***. At Antioch were the ***Apostles***, and people the Apostles ***approved***.

But at Alexandria were ***Apostates***, who went ***against*** the ***Apostles'*** teaching. They had their own ideas of what they thought the Bible should say.

Two Cities:

A: Antioch: Apostles   **A:** Alexandria: Apostates

Can you tell I used to be a Kindergarten teacher? But hey, it works!

Now P. *The Antioch stream **preserved** the words of God. They wanted to **protect** the exact words that God said.*

*But the Alexandrian stream **polluted** the words of God with subtle changes to line up with some of their pagan philosophies.*

They didn't change all the words, just enough to *pollute* the stream of God's words by taking some of them away and adding other words they wanted, their own opinions.

Two Streams:

P: Preserved   **P**: Polluted

But ***what exactly was preserved or polluted?***

Many people make a mistake at this point. They think it was only the ***words*** that were ***preserved*** or ***polluted***.

Not at all. Two things were perverted, not just one. The first you already know. That's **T**, the *Text*.

God started by giving His words by inspiration to the Apostles and other inspired believers to write.

> All scripture is given by inspiration of God, and is profitable for doctrine, for reproof, for correction, for instruction in righteousness: That the man of God may be perfect, throughly furnished unto all good works.[15]

In John 14, Jesus told the disciples that the Holy Spirit would teach them all things and bring to their remembrance everything He had said to them (John 14:26).

Copies were made of that "text" to share with the spreading churches. But God wanted a world-wide gospel. The Lord Jesus said:

> But ye shall receive power, after that the Holy Ghost is come upon you: and ye shall be witnesses unto me both in Jerusalem, and in all Judaea, and in Samaria, and unto the uttermost part of the earth.[16]

---

15. 2 Timothy 3:16-17
16. Acts 1:8

Telling Bibles Apart: Good Stream vs. Bad Stream 41

So when the Bible was needed in another language, a **Translation** was made creating a new **Text** in that language. Then, additional copies could be made of that new text, to spread in that language.

If there were not both, a faithful **Text** and an accurate **Translation**, people would not have what God wanted us to know. Then men could pretend to speak for God and deceive the people.

But God would never tell us that He is going to *judge us by His words*,[17] if He wouldn't also *give us, and preserve for us,* His holy words.[18]

So God first preserved His words, the **Text**. Faithful believers in the Antioch stream copied that text and spread it all over the known world.

But, the Devil also made his **Text**. Of course, when you have people who think they're too smart for God's words, they most likely won't agree with each other, either. That is why none of the **Texts** from the polluted Alexandrian stream agree with each other.

But the Devil didn't stop there. Satan has put amazing effort into changing the meaning of words, **redefining** them. That's the other **T**: *Translation*.

If a word doesn't *mean* the same thing, then the scripture changes. When the scripture changes, the doctrine changes.

So if, in Matthew 7:14, the way to salvation is not "narrow," but "difficult," that single change makes getting saved look hard, like the people who believe you must do good works in order to go to heaven.

---

17. See Deuteronomy 4:2; 12:32; Proverbs 30:5-6; Jeremiah 26:2; Revelation 22:18-19.
18. See Psalm 12:6-7; Matthew 5:18; 24:35; Mark 13:31; Luke 16:17; 21:33.

And when you read 1 Corinthians 1:18 in the King James, it looks like this: "For the preaching of the cross is to them that perish foolishness; but unto **us *which are saved*** it is the power of God."

So the preaching of the cross is the power of God to us which are saved. Right? You're either saved or lost. And the preaching of the cross marks that dividing line.

But a good number of Bibles I call "King James lookalikes" also change these words. In the King James Bible, we are either *saved* or *lost*. But in most modern versions, including the lookalikes, it says something like this: "For the message of the cross is foolishness to those who are perishing, but to ***us who are being saved*** (working for our salvation? getting saved, bit by bit?) it is the power of God."

See the difference? In the preserved King James, you are sure. You are saved. But not in these lookalikes, or most modern Bibles.

Are we "saved" (a done deal) or "being saved" (a process)? With changed-text Bibles we would have to rewrite the hymn (sung to the tune of "Jesus Paid It All"):

Jesus paid for some.

All the rest I owe.

*I am only **being saved**;*

When I'll be, I don't know.

That sounds like it belongs in a Catholic hymn book, but not a Christian one. Remember, in the Catholic religion it's actually a ***sin*** to believe you are safely saved. And yet God said through the Apostle John:

> These things have I written unto you that believe on the name of the Son of God; that ye may know

that ye have eternal life, and that ye may believe on the name of the Son of God.[19]

The *Translation* can even be changed by so-called "modernizing" of the Classical English words.

But it's that simple. The Devil didn't have only the *Text* to mess with. He can simply change the *Translation,* also.

Two Changes:

T: Text

T: Translation

Text and Translation. T and T.

Translation is when someone who knows two languages makes a copy of one into the other. A faithful "translator" (or translators) will accurately give you the same concept in both languages.

Again, faithful men in the Antioch stream did just that, making accurate Bibles in the new languages. We can check this accuracy in the dozens of languages produced by the Antioch stream.

But, we can also see gross inaccuracies in the manuscripts and copies produced by the Alexandrian stream. They were not careful to make accurate copies or translations, often making changes to reflect their personal ideas and agendas.

This is so important. I want you to understand the two important issues of changed *Text* and changed *Translation.* The majority of new Bibles have a changed Greek and Hebrew text —all but the King James lookalike Bibles.[20]

One more example is found both in modern versions and in

---

19. 1 John 5:13

20. King James lookalikes are Bibles that claim the name "King James" and use the same Greek and Hebrew texts, but which change words in various places, to "fix" or "modernize" or "make it more understandable."

King James lookalikes. They "update" the language by taking away the 2nd and 3rd person singular words, like "hast" and "hath," the "t" words. Those are there to help you tell them apart from the "y" words that are plural: "ye," "you," "your," "yours."

They change these words, and others, thinking to make it easier for you. But they subtly alter the meaning, whether they wanted to or not.

In Exodus 16:28, here is a quote from a modern version of what God said to Moses: "And the Lord said to Moses, 'How long do **you** refuse to keep my commandments and my laws?'"

"Is the Lord mad at Moses? Did Moses break the law?" That is what my young child asked, not knowing he had picked up a New King James for Bible study. He asked a good question. Written like that, you can't tell!

In the modern Bibles, including King James lookalikes (like the New King James), they remove the classic language. So you can't tell the difference between singular and plural "you."

But in the King James, it is plain and simple. "Ye" is plural, and only plural. "Thee" and "thou" are singular, and always singular. Simple, right?

So Exodus 16:28 really says, "And the Lord said unto Moses, How long refuse *ye* to keep my commandments and my laws?" See? "Y". It's plural! So the Lord was upset with ***the people***, not with Moses. That makes perfect sense.

In the New Testament, Jesus told Nicodemus: "Marvel not that I said unto ***thee***, *Ye* must be born again." (John 3:7) He was speaking directly to Nicodemus (thee), but everyone (Ye) needed to be born again, not just Nicodemus.

So the ***Text*** and the ***Translation*** are both very important.

Now you see the importance of the difference between the two streams of Bibles through history.

So let's review! Remember to be an "apt" (ready and able) student of the word: A, P, and T.

Two Cities:

A: Antioch: Apostles   **A:** Alexandria: Apostates

Two Streams:

P: Preserved   **P:** Polluted

Two Changes (what Antioch Preserved, but Alexandria Polluted):

T: Text   **T:** Translation

They have different origins.

They have different purposes.

And while most Bibles are based on different Greek and Hebrew ***texts***, all of them have different ***translations*** from the wording and meaning of the King James. Now you can be "apt to teach" someone the difference between Bibles, using those three letters: A, P, and T.

These two streams not only describe past history, but the future, as well. We will find out that the polluted Alexandrian stream started being tapped again, this time to create one world Bible for one world religion. And proof of this comes from the most unlikely source: an occultist of the 20th century, while discussing a New World Order.

6

Why the NWO Hates the KJV

Now that the world is "getting smaller" because of global companies, global communications, and global wars, many are beginning to talk openly of a New World Order, politically, economically —and spiritually. The secret is out. World leaders discuss the "NWO" as if it's the next phase in our political and economic evolution.

But what about the spiritual? World leaders know that without religious unity, the other two won't work. Only in the last decades has evidence surfaced, revealing what has been cooking behind the scenes for a couple of centuries.

Since religions are essentially centered on books (or a book), world religious unity depends on making those books agree —or at least, making them not disagree. Generally, this is not a problem, since many religious writings cover similar teachings.

However, two books stand out: the Bible, and possibly the Qur'an. The contents of the Qur'an are contradictory enough that both the popes and the Islamic leaders are starting to get together, on the basis that they both worship the same God. After all, they say, Jesus Himself is one of Islam's Major Prophets.

So that leaves the Bible. But if the Bible (or one of them)

is the main stumbling block to instituting the one world religion that they want, shouldn't we find, somewhere, a plan to take it down? Would Satan sit on his hands, knowing about this obvious road block to his grand scheme?

I am about to show you details found in old and new books, journals and newsletters that we would not ordinarily get to see. Only modern research technology has recently made them available. And praise God, some of the people, both alive and dead, have let the cat out of the bag:

> And it was given unto him to make war with the saints, and to overcome them: and power was given him over all kindreds, and tongues, and nations. And all that dwell upon the earth shall worship him, whose names are not written in the book of life of the Lamb slain from the foundation of the world. If any man have an ear, let him hear.
>
> —Revelation 13:7-9

One day there is going to be a world-wide government, over every kindred, tongue and nation. And there will be a world-wide religion, where most people on earth will worship a man. The only ones who won't worship him are those who are, or are going to be, saved. And he will have a way to deal with them. A New World Order is coming.

What Is the New World Order?

People love to talk about the New World Order. They throw that term around all the time: New World Order, or NWO, for short.

What is it?

In the simplest form, it is two things:

1. It's a world *without* God.

2. It's a world ***without reminders*** of God.

One person who really got deeply into the concept of the New World Order was an occultist[21] named Manly Palmer Hall, or Manly P. Hall. Want to know what the King James Bible has to do with the New World Order? This guy let out some amazing secrets.

Manly P. Hall wrote books on all sorts of mystery religions. Forty-seven years after he wrote a book on Masonry, he was made an honorary 33rd degree Mason.

In addition, U.S. President Franklin Delano Roosevelt, a 33rd Degree Mason, loved Hall and his occultic, NWO teachings. *This guy had some major connections.*

Figure 7 - Manly P. Hall

But even I was surprised by a quote that a brother in Christ sent me. Take a look at what Manly P. Hall said.

---

21. By "occult" I mean the belief that by finding hidden information you can say secret words, do ceremonies or use special knowledge to get the power you want.

Notice all those dots to indicate missing parts? It doesn't inspire confidence in a quote to find a whole lot of information missing. Do the parts of seeming "sentences" really fit together? I had to know.

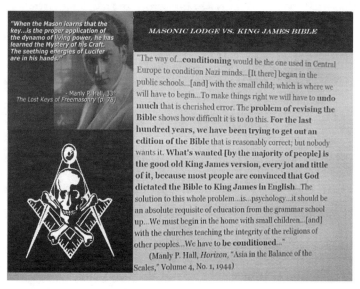

Figure 8 - The internet meme I saw

I needed the whole quote in order to see what was missing. But I couldn't find it online —at least, not in complete form. Of all that Manly P. Hall had written in his lifetime, it was interesting to learn that this was one of the few of his publications not openly spread across the internet.

As you can see, the article was called "Asia in the Balance of the Scales." It was printed in his own magazine, *Horizon: The Magazine of Useful and Intelligent Living*, the Spring, 1944 issue. But all I could find of it were a few words here and there. Clicking each link would open a small rectangular scan of a few of the words as they originally appeared on the page in a tiny graphic. This is called "snippet view." But by searching for a few words at a time, overlapping from sentence to sentence, I was able to piece together the vast majority of what Manly P. Hall wrote in that 1944 article.

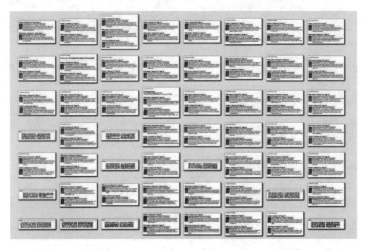

Figure 9 - These are a few of the snippets I found.

I ended up with 215 snippets, which recovered 6,000 words of the original article —enough to answer my question.

Here's what I found out.

In April of 1944, over a year before the USA dropped two nuclear bombs over Japan (so World War II was still going on), Manly P. Hall was thinking about how to construct a new world order.

Here are his words. I've been careful to keep his statements in context:

> In the next ten years we will have to ***rebuild a world civilization***. I hope for some psychologists

and even philosophers to be among those appointed to administer this problem. Without them we are just going to get into more trouble. We will first perhaps try to ***make a great world plan***. We will sit at a council table and figure how to iron out the troubles on the earth.

World problems will not be solved except by creating a solution up through and out through the people themselves; and so, no postwar program can be successful unless at least three and probably five generations of social conditioning goes with it.

The way of that conditioning would be the one used in Central Europe to condition Nazi Minds. There the circulation of an ideology began in the public schools, began with the small child; which is where we will have to begin, and educate not only our own people but the peoples of the world. And we will have to have five generations of the consciousness concept of democratic cooperation before we can create a world capable of mental and emotional tolerance.

It has to be done. It could start with a postwar international planning commission devising a world concept of education, a world concept of internal relationships. Teaching it would have to start in the first grade of the public schools.[22]

---

22. "Asia in the Balance of the Scales" by Manly P. Hall in *Horizon: The Magazine of Useful and intelligent Living*, Vol. 4, No. 1, Spring 1944, pp. 11-12. Emphasis mine.

Then Hall talked about undoing the error-filled thinking that people cherish. Look what he *claims* is error-filled thinking:

> To make things right we will have to undo much that is cherished error. ***The problem of revising the Bible*** shows how difficult it is to do this. ***For the last hundred years*** we have been trying to get out ***an edition of the Bible that is reasonably correct***; but nobody wants it. What's wanted is the good old ***King James version, every jot and tittle of it***, because most people are convinced that God dictated the Bible to King James in English.

Okay, never mind that he totally made up a false teaching to slam the King James Bible-believers. Note what he said:

> "For the last hundred years *we* have been trying to get out an edition of the Bible that is reasonably correct..."

Who is "we"? He says "we," and Hall is an occultist! Who was he involved with?

And what did "they" do to the Bible, from the 1840s-1940s?

What does an occultist, who doesn't believe the Bible, have to do with fixing the Bible?

Aren't you just a bit suspicious? Remember this. We will come back to it in a later chapter.

But let's say he gets rid of the King James Bible. What would he put in its place?

These are his words, not mine:

> The solution to this whole problem which has been given to us is the basic science which we now call

> psychology, and which has been evolved in the last
> fifty years. Psychology is the first systematic effort
> to analyze human thinking. ... and psychology can
> be the basic science of human tolerance....

Psychology from grade one and teaching "tolerance." Sound familiar?

It sounds like today, doesn't it?

So why pick on Christians?

If you ***want*** a new world order, Hall is right. You need people who are ***conditioned*** for that world government from childhood, like the Nazis conditioned German kids.

For this kind of "tolerance," you need people who will "go with the flow," and "follow the tides," so to speak. But Christians are like buoys. They're big, bright markers. And a buoy is always ***anchored to something***.

Bible-believers, according to Manly Hall, are anchored to ***the jot and tittle of the King James Bible***. But Manly P. Hall needs to "free" you from the King James, or you won't follow his New World Order.

In his *Students Monthly Letter, Fourth Year, Letter No. 12*, he has this to say about what he wants to "free" the Bible-believer from and to.

From "The Secret Doctrine of the Bible: The Revelation of St. John, Conclusion," page 8.

> "Examine several editions of the Christian Bible, as
> for example, ***compare the King James version with
> the modern revised edition*** and a recent publication,
> *The Bible as Living Literature*. Consider the poly-
> glots, and get a parallel Greek-English text. You

will make many interesting discoveries. ..."

"We will *discover numerous errors and alternative renderings,* and *slowly recover from the infallibility complex* from which so many orthodox Bible readers seem to suffer. Read the Vulgate, the Septuagint. ..."

"You will see the uselessness of picking phrases to pieces and trying to think in terms of 'jots and tittles.'"

Oh, I get it...

You will be "free" to consider the larger issues —you know, like joining his New World Order.

You see, it doesn't matter what they "free you" TO. All that matters to them is what they GET you FROM: The King James Bible: God's holy and preserved words in English.

Trust God's holy words, or free yourself to be a slave to the new world order.

Take your pick.

I don't want to go from Bible to Bible, from version to version. I want to know what God said, and to stick with it. I want my life formed around God's words, not to form a Bible around my preferred lifestyle.

And I definitely don't want a diluted, perverted, one world Bible that will help persuade Christians to join one world order, or one world religion, to worship a man.

So here was the first NWO connection I found to mention the King James Bible. But was that all there was to it? Somehow force everyone to accept a new Bible? He already said their last attempt to do it didn't work, so far.

Did Satan hang up his hat? Or did he have another plan in mind?

You know the truth. Satan works his lies from many angles. Not only does he want to switch Bibles, he also wants to change the one you have without you noticing, until you are far away from a strong "biblical faith," while still labeling yourself a "Bible-believer!"

"It's just a different translation," people say. Who would suspect people of tampering with the Holy Bible? But that is exactly what happened.

7

KJV, Sinaiticus and the NWO

It was near the end of World War II, when the well-known occultist Manly P. Hall and those working together with him, decided there was something wrong with the world. Things had to change.

Let's look again at the startling statement he made in the spring of 1944:

> "To make things right **we** will have to undo much that is cherished error. The problem of revising the Bible shows how difficult it is to do this.
>
> For the last hundred years **we** have been trying to get out an edition of the Bible that is reasonably correct; but nobody wants it.
>
> What's wanted is the good old King James version, every jot and tittle of it, because most people are convinced that God dictated the Bible to King James in English.

I asked the question, "Who is '**we**'?" Let's take that apart right now. And while we're at it, we'll see what the Sinaiticus might have to do with it.

By "**we**," it seems that Hall is referring to some very high-up people in the occultic and political world. These people were the intelligent leaders who were to create a New World Order. That was the focus of his 1944 article, *Asia in the Balance of the Scales*. And with "friends" like 33rd degree Masonic President Franklin Delano Roosevelt and other leaders, Hall probably felt able to pull it off.

In most of the article, *"we"* refers to the West as leaders in global peace. But there are certain statements that seem to go a step beyond that. Look at these specific quotes from the same article.

> In the next ten years *we* will have to ***rebuild a world civilization***. I hope for some ***psychologists*** and even ***philosophers*** to be among those appointed to ***administer this problem***.

> **We** are thinking now of a world ***police force***…

> **We** will first perhaps try to make ***a great world plan***.

> **We** will sit at a council table and figure how to iron out the troubles on the earth.

> The way of that ***conditioning*** would be the one used in Central Europe to condition Nazi Minds. There the circulation of an ideology began in the public schools, began with the small child; which is where *we* will have to begin, and educate not only ***our*** own people but the peoples of the world.

> And *we* will have to have five generations of the consciousness concept of democratic cooperation before *we* can create a world capable of mental and emotional tolerance.

Let's count the generations after World War II.
- 1946-64 were the Baby Boomers. That's one.
- 1965-early 80s were Generation X. That's two.
- Mid-1980s-early 2000s were the Millennials or Generation Y. That's three.
- Mid-2000s to now are Generation Z, the fourth generation.

So how are we doing? We are pushing "mental and emotional tolerance" and "democratic cooperation" through psychology and philosophy, from kindergarten. There's a whole lot of conditioning going on!

In fact, MTV recently asked one thousand 13-14-year-olds which of the proposed names they wanted their generation to be called. The majority of them wanted to be called "The Founder Generation." These teenagers, born after 9/11, supposedly "have a stunningly intuitive sense of the changing times they've been born into, and the huge opportunity that lies ahead to make new history."[23]

What do "founders" do? They abandon the old and start something new.

Guided by whom? Who are their teachers? Look around you.

We are barreling toward one world government, by Manly P. Hall's own standards. And we're already in Generation Four.

But Hall had a problem with a certain group of people. What did he say was wrong with them?

---

23. See the MTV Press Release, "MTV Asks Post-Millennial Generation to Name Itself" at http://thepub.viacom.com, December 2, 2015.

> What's wanted [by them] is the good old King
> James version, every jot and tittle of it…

How did his "*we*" try to pry the King James out of people's hands?

> For the last hundred years *we* have been trying to
> get out an edition of the Bible that is reasonably
> correct…

Occultist Hall wrote these words in 1944. What started 100 years earlier, in 1844? In 1844, according to text scholar Constantin Tischendorf, he began to acquire Greek parchment pages that ultimately were named, "Codex Sinaiticus."

As you will see, this is the document behind all modern Bibles and Bible-doubting footnotes.

Are we sure Hall meant the Sinaiticus? Let's check. Manly P. Hall definitely wrote strongly in favor of the Sinaiticus. Here are two powerful quotes I pieced together from snippets of that same 1944 magazine:

> The Codex Sinaiticus is a manuscript of the 4th
> Century of about the same date as the Codex Vaticanus…. This manuscript is one of the great books
> of the world…

> … it is ***sufficiently important to justify considerable revision*** of our popular conception of the Scriptural writings…[24]

—In other words, they can use Sinaiticus to justify changing the Bible and our thinking about the Bible.

---

24. *Horizon: the Magazine of Useful and Intelligent Living,* Spring, 1944, p. 62.

PRS Journal, Volume 5, 1945, p. 62
and *Horizon, the magazine of useful and intelligent living,* Spring, 1946, p. 62

62	HORIZON Spring
selves in readiness to set out with their dromedaries for Cairo on the 7th, when an entirely fortuitous circumstance carried me at once to the goal of all my desires. "On the afternoon of this day I was taking a walk with the steward of the Convent	"The manuscript was presented to the Emperor of all the Russias by the Archbishop and the monks in 1869; the Emperor paid nine thousand roubles (three hundred and fifty pounds) to the Archbishop and the monks in acknowledgment of the gifts. The Archbishop wrote
in the neighborhood, and as we returned towards sunset he begged me to take some refreshment with him in his cell. Scarcely had he entered the room, when, resuming our former subject of conversation, he said: 'And I, too, have read a Septuagint' —i.e. a copy of	'to Doctor Tischendorf (July 15, 1869), You know that this famous Bible manuscript has now been presented to the exalted Emperor and Autocrat of all the Russias as a testimony of our and the Sinai Monastery's eternal gratitude.' " After the Russian Revolution the
the Greek translation made by the Seventy. And so saying, he took down from the corner of the room a bulky volume wrapped up in a	Codex Sinaiticus was purchased by the British Museum for the sum of one hundred thousand pounds, (Slightly under half a million dollars).
red cloth, and laid it before me. I unrolled the cover and discovered to my great surprise not only those very fragments which, fifteen years before, I had taken out of the	Part of the amount was raised by popular subscription. The manuscript was displayed in a large case, and at the side was a box for donations toward the purchase price.
basket, but also other parts of the Old Testament, the New Testament complete, and, in addition, the Epistle of Barnabas and a part of the Pastor of Hermas."	The Codex Sinaiticus is a manuscript of the 4th Century of about the same date as the Codex Vaticanus. In fact, Doctor Tischendorf believed that one of the four scribes who wrote the text also
In October 1859, Doctor Tischendorf, after many adventures and delays, was able to secure the Sinaitic Bible as a loan, and on the 19th of November he brought it with him to Russia and placed it in the hands of Czar	wrote part of the Vatican manuscript. The Codex is of folio size with four columns to the page in Greek. There are many corrections dating from the 6th and 7th Centuries. This manuscript is one of the great books of the world, and
Alexander II. This monarch was so amazed and delighted that immediate steps were taken to publish an exact facsimile for the use of the scholars of the world. The production was under the personal supervision of Doctor Tischendorf.	although it was discovered long after the publication of the now universally accepted King James version of the Bible, it is sufficiently important to justify considerable revision of our popular conception of the Scriptural writings. It was only an act of providence,
The worthy doctor's own story of his monumental discovery ends in 1862, but other information is available in substance as follows:	accomplished through the instrumentation of Doctor Tischendorf, that one of the most precious manuscripts in Christendom was not burned as worthless trash. The most celebrated of the lost arts

Figure 10 - Page 62 of Hall's *Horizon* magazine constructed from snippets from the internet. Notice highlighted quotes.

Here is more, from his *Monthly Letter* of April 1st, 1935:

> Of importance to students of occultism is the fact that the Codex Sinaiticus contains many passages suppressed from the published Gospels. These passages in many cases greatly alter the significance of the text.[25]

And what did he think of the King James? In *The Students Monthly Letter*, Fourth Year, No. 5, he complained:

> This enthusiastic jot and tittle worshiper will insist that the words of the King James version are the very words of God Himself.

And in his *Monthly Letter* of November 1st, 1934, he wrote:

> ...the King James version of the Holy Bible. This translation teems with error and is hopelessly unreliable from a scholastic viewpoint, yet popular acceptance has caused this mis-version of holy writ to come to be recognized as infallible so that the religious public would now reject a correct translation. In fact, it has already shown its attitude in the matter by refusing a revised edition. For over 300 years, erroneous theological notions have been circulated, deriving their authority from the King James translation of the Bible.[26]

So let's add it up.

---

25. *A Monthly Letter Devoted to Philosophical and Spiritual Problems*, (Los Angeles: The Phoenix Press), writing from New York on April 1st, 1935, p. 4.
26. *A Monthly Letter, Devoted to Spiritual and Philosophical Problems*, by Manly P. Hall (Los Angeles, CA: The Phoenix Press, Nov. 1, 1934), "Some Philosophical Fragments: Supplement to Students Monthly Letter," p. 6. I cleaned up the spelling and punctuation a bit.

1. This occultist, Manly P. Hall, wanted a New World Order.

2. Only two things stopped this new "mental and emotional tolerance:" the thinking of the people and the King James Bible.

3. In 1944, people in general trusted that the King James version was the words of God Himself translated into English. So that's *not* a new idea, regardless of what we may have been taught.

4. The Codex Sinaiticus, with extra words (maybe referring to the *Epistle of Barnabas* and *Shepherd of Hermas*, or maybe to the Apocrypha?) offered hope, as a new occultic-friendly Bible, "of importance to students of occultism." (Those are Halls' words, not mine.)

5. He stated two goals. Goal Number One was to condition people's minds over five generations. Those born post-9/11 are Generation Four.

6. And Goal Number Two was to pry the people's jot-and-tittle Bible-trusting hands away from the King James Bible. And the Sinaiticus was the Occult world's answer to that problem.

7. This is what Hall said would move people to "recover from" the "infallibility complex" about the Bible, especially the King James Version.

Are we saying that trust in the Sinaiticus, and in the Bibles derived from the Sinaiticus, is a step toward occultic and New World Order thinking?

That's what this occultist said, not me. I'm just putting it all together.

So if you trust the King James Bible as God's preserved

words in English, guess what? By Hall's standards, YOU are "intolerant" and a hindrance to one world government. You are a threat to the "harmony" that the globalists are hoping to create.

Each Bible that is made from or trusts the Sinaiticus, is not "just another Bible." It is another doorway to losing trust in the King James, and being open and tolerant toward the New World Order. At least, that's what a top occultist (who communed with world leaders) said.

We can't hide from this. This is the elephant in the living room. We cannot avoid it.

Do you want to be a part of the New World Order? Then don't trust your King James Bible. All I can say is, there must be some pretty spiritual things in the KJV to get occultists and NWO people so riled up about it.

If for no other reason, that's a huge motivation to get a King James, pray to God for understanding, and put our trust in its holy words.

Do what you want. But for over 17 years, that's what I've done. And despite all my years of training and study, I have never regretted that choice.

Please take this decision seriously. It is bigger than you can imagine.

* * *

So now we have covered this angle from the perspective of the NWO. They want to bring about their New World Order, by getting Bible students to:

- Switch to the Sinaiticus, and to Bibles derived from it.
- Switch from the preserved, apostolic Antioch stream of Bibles to the polluted, apostate Alexandrian stream.

- Accept Bibles modified a word at a time, with subtle changes in the meaning of the text, so quietly that nobody would notice their doubts forming.
- Ultimately drop the King James Bible and faith in its words, in favor of a One-World-Order-friendly book.

Now let's focus on the Sinaiticus itself. What is it? What is the story behind it? Is there anything special about it, that both the New World Order and the occultic world seem to have a stake in it? And what does the biblical Whore of Babylon, the Roman Catholic system, have to do with it, if anything?

In short, can we trust the Sinaiticus?

SECTION II: SINAITICUS: NOT WHAT WE WERE TOLD

8

Why You Can't Trust Sinaiticus

You know that document that's used to make those major changes in modern Bibles, the Codex Sinaiticus? What if I could prove to you that you *cannot* trust it? What if I could prove it to you, using their own materials, and asking questions a third grader could understand? Would you be interested?

Dr. McReynolds, my Greek professor in Bible college, once told about how he assigned everyone in a group to copy the Gospel of John.

What would your professor think, if he got one paper and it read like this: "Jesus saith unto him, I am the way, the truth, and the life: no man cometh unto the Father, but by me." Then it went on to say, "And the brethren immediately sent away Paul and Silas by night unto Berea: who coming thither went into the synagogue of the Jews."

Did you catch it? That's John 14:6 followed by Acts 17:10. So he just skipped over 24 chapters of the Bible. But his job was to copy just John. What kind of grade would he get? An "F," right? Would your teacher trust him to copy another book of the Bible, for his personal use?

What if that guy says, "Oh, I grabbed a Bible. I guess it was missing a few pages, but I just copied what was in front of me." Would that be a good excuse?

I can hear the teacher now. "Didn't you notice anything different as you read the text? Weren't you reading it as you copied it? You have to PAY ATTENTION!"

Exactly.

What if I could show you that the main scribe (writer) of the famous Codex Sinaiticus did exactly that, the guy called "Scribe A"? Let me show you what really happened.

Figure 11 - Sinaiticus, showing 1 Chronicles 19:17 to Ezra 9:9

Why You Can't Trust Sinaiticus

Walk through this with me. It's very simple, if we take it slowly. On the same page, in the same column, he skipped from 1 Chronicles 19:17 to Ezra 9:9. It sounds like this in English:

> 1 Chronicles 19:17: "And it was told David; and he gathered all Israel, and passed over Jordan, and came upon them, and set the battle in array against them. So when David had put the battle in array against the Syrians, they fought with him. Lord our God, and extended mercy upon us in the sight of the kings of Persia, ..."

What?

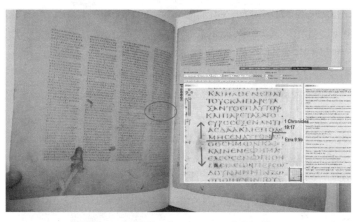

Figure 12 - The location of the skip

And good ol' Scribe A just continued on his merry way, copying Ezra and finishing the book! He didn't even notice that he skipped from the middle of one book to the middle of a sentence in a completely different book!

Let me remind you: Scribe A is the same guy who penned

most of the Sinaiticus. That's why he's called Scribe A! Scribe A also left out the story of Jesus and the adulterous woman in John 8:1-11. And, Scribe A took away "Joseph" and added "his father" in Luke 2:33, making Joseph Jesus' father, instead of God the Father! And there are many other changes and missing words. Do you trust Scribe A, now? Did he pay attention? Could he even read Greek? If he were just a calligrapher, and not able to read Greek, it might explain the huge error in making such an obvious blunder. Of course, it could just be that he was doing a rush job and didn't check his own work.

How can you trust ANY of the strange readings of the Sinaiticus when it also changes doctrines of who Christ is and what He did for you? Are we to pay no attention to the messed up Old Testament by the same guy?

I said I'd make this simple, so let me just say this: ***I CANNOT TRUST THE SINAITICUS.***

CAN YOU?

Remember, if you cannot trust Sinaiticus, then you cannot trust a multitude of changes in almost every Bible in the world, including new translations by Wycliffe, SIL and the United Bible Societies, in any language.

I know what I trust: the preserved words of God in the King James Bible.

9

Is Sinaiticus a Fake?

All modern non-King James Bibles, and all modern Bible-doubting footnotes, including doubting footnotes in King James and New King James Bibles, are based upon two supposedly ancient Bibles: the Sinaiticus and the Vaticanus.

What if one of those two pillars, Codex Sinaiticus, is a fake?

Let me clarify:

When you open most modern Bibles to 1 John 5:7-8, the words of the Godhead, "the Father, the Word, and the Holy Ghost: and these three are one," *it's missing*. Why? Largely because it's missing in the Sinaiticus. That helped tip the balance against those important words.

When you turn to Mark 16:9-20 in most modern Bibles, it's got a note, a thick line, a separate heading and/or a footnote that says it doesn't belong; don't trust it. Why?

Out of ***620 manuscripts that contain Mark's gospel, 618*** of them have those verses. That's *all* 600 minuscules (with lower case letters), *all* 15 uncials (with upper case letters), and ***three of five*** codices (the plural of codex, "big books").

Only two of the 620 leave out those verses: The Sinaiticus and the Vaticanus. And both of them were only made public in the decade before Westcott, Hort and others started the move to completely change the Bible.

Sound suspicious? Believe it or not, there is a hidden agenda in all of what you are about to read. But for now, let's look closer at the Sinaiticus.

Researcher Steven Avery contacted me in early 2014 and let me look at an amazing thing. He told me that they had put the Sinaiticus —what we have of it— online!

I was so excited! And the various pieces, from wherever they are stored, are digitally "together," so to speak, so you can turn from page to page!

Steven asked me to look at a particular section. As you will see later, two sections of the Sinaiticus were removed in 1844. The guy who said he discovered those pages was Constantin Tischendorf.

In 1844, he wrote to his family that some materials had… let's say, "come into his possession."

He decided to take them to Leipzig University Library, where they still are today. He gave them as a gift to Frederick Augustus II of Saxony, who paid for his trip, and those two sections were named Codex Friderico-Augustanus in his honor (CFA, for short).

Figure 13 - Frederick Augustus II of Saxony reigned from 1836-1854.

Section one includes: 1 Chronicles 11:22 - 19:17; 2 Esdras 9:11- 23:31; Esther 1:1 - 10:3; and Tobit 1:1 - 2:2.

Section two includes: Jeremiah 10:25 - 52:34; and Lamentations 1:1 - 2:20.

Is Sinaiticus a Fake? 71

Figure 14 shows the first page of the first section of the 43 folia called the CFA. It starts at 1 Chronicles 11:22.

Figure 14 - The first page of the first section of the CFA, starting at 1 Chronicles 11:22

Figure 15 displays a page at the end of the first section of the CFA, containing Tobit 1:7 - 2:2.

Figure 15 - CFA middle page, Tobit 1:7 – 2:2

And Figure 16 shows the last page of the second section of the CFA pages, which ends at Lamentations 2:20.

Figure 16 - CFA, ending at Lamentations 2:20

Tischendorf published a typeset facsimile of what was in the CFA, 43 leaves, 86 pages, in 1846. (See Chapter 14, Deleted on Purpose, for explanation of codex book design.) He kept all the details of where and how he got them a complete secret for years.

Nine years later, in 1853, Tischendorf went back to the Sinai

Peninsula, to St. Catherine's, a monastery run by Russian Orthodox monks. Details are sketchy about that visit.

Then somehow, in 1859, when Tischendorf came back for a third visit to St. Catherine's Monastery, paid for and authorized by Tsar Alexander II of Russia, with Russian government aid (in other words, money), he managed to return with something he called "Sinaiticus."

Tischendorf took the remains of the Sinaiticus to St. Petersburg. And in 1862, Tischendorf published a typeset replica of all but the CFA as the Codex Sinaiticus.

Eventually, the British bought it from the Russians and placed it in the British Library, where it is today. But the CFA remains in the Leipzig University Library.

Here's where it gets a little strange. Starting in 2009, digital images of all the known pages of the Sinaiticus became available to view online. So anyone could view undoctored photographs of every known page, for the first time.

In early 2014, Steven Avery asked me to look at these photos, especially the CFA pages. I told him "I am not sure what I could contribute, though I don't mind looking."

So I just looked at the CFA and other Sinaiticus pages, back and forth, over and over, for hours.

Steven gave me a hint that perhaps someone whitened up the pages of the CFA. So I was looking to see if there was evidence of this.

But what I found was even stranger: someone had ***darkened the rest of Sinaiticus!***

When you put the pages side by side, on one side the CFA and on the other side pages of Sinaiticus now held by the British Library (BL), it looks really funny. Take a look.

Is Sinaiticus a Fake?

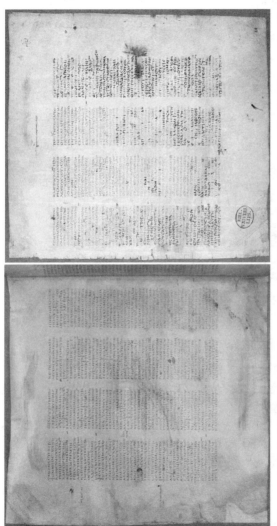

Figures 17 & 18 – British Library page (BL), ending at Jeremiah 10:25 compared to the beginning of the second section of the CFA, starting at Jeremiah 10:25

Photos have been adjusted in black and white, to show the differences you can easily see in color. We recommend you view the originals at *www.codexsinaiticus.org*.

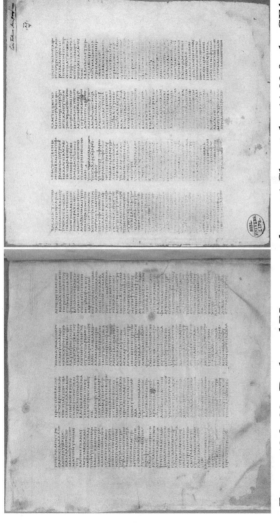

Figures 19 & 20 - Darkened BL pages, ending at 1 Chronicles 11:22 & the CFA starting at 1 Chronicles 11:22, showing a white background color.

Photos have been adjusted in black and white, to show the differences you can easily see in color. We recommend you view the originals at *www.codexsinaiticus.org*.

Is Sinaiticus a Fake?

Then, when the CFA ends and the BL starts again, the color shifts back from white to stained. (See figues 19 and 20.)

The rest of the Sinaiticus totally reminds me of coffee stains in my seminary books, except that it looked more watery. At one point it seemed like someone brushed the stain out over the page. Then after that, on the next pages, the color kind of leveled out, without the massive streaky look. But it still has that darker or more yellowed color.

Why would anyone darken the rest of the pages, after the CFA was removed?

It gets creepier.

It turns out that two different guys visited the monastery to see this manuscript among others, after Tischendorf took the CFA away. And one of them wrote about it. Porfiry Uspensky, a Russian bishop, visited St. Catherine's in 1845.

He said all of it was WHITE! But look at the background color of the parchment of Figure 20. Then compare that to the background in Figure 21 in the book of *Barnabas*, for instance, after Tischendorf got hold of it:

78 *Is the 'World's Oldest Bible' a Fake?*

Figure 21 - *Barnabas* **4:5 – 5:5. This page from Barnabas is an example of how the rest of Codex Sinaiticus is darker than the CFA.**[27]

Does this look white to you? As I told Steven Avery, it looks like coffee stains, tea stains, tobacco juice stains — something like that. Some pages are lighter than others, for sure. But none seems as white as any pages of the CFA. For

27. Photo has been adjusted in black and white, to show the differences you can easily see in color. We recommend you view the originals at *www.codexsinaiticus.org*.

a comparison of all the pages of the combined Siniaticus see Figure 22.

I smell a con.

I have books on forgeries and stuff, but Steven checked the 1800s for how they made books look old. Guess what they used? Coffee, tea, stuff like that!

But *why* would anyone take a valuable, pristine, lily-white ancient Bible and make it look old, rotten, and without covers? Yes, Sinaiticus allegedly didn't even have a cover.

Here's something that will really make you think.

When you accept the Alexandrian manuscripts, led by the (allegedly) "oldest and best" Sinaiticus and Vaticanus, you also accept the Alexandrian scholars who wrote them.

When you accept the scholars who wrote them, you say good things about their judgment and their Christianity.

So a Roman Catholic can come up to you and say something like this:

"I see you are using an Alexandrian Text."

Yes.

"That's the one *we* like. Where's the rest of it?"

What?

"You have *most* of the Bible, but you forgot the rest of it. You know, *you* call it the Apocrypha. *We* call it the Deuterocanonicals. Same thing."

"What do you mean?"

"Well, EVERY Alexandrian codex has a Greek Old Testament and a Greek New Testament, but it also has the Apocrypha in the Old Testament. Your Bible is missing the Apocrypha. You said you trust the Alexandrians, so go all the way. Put it back in. And if you put it in, you will believe in Purgatory, like we do."

In 1966, the United Bible Societies, as I proved in my book, ***Why They Changed the Bible: One World Bible for One World Religion*** (2014), agreed to do just that. They have been adding in the Apocrypha in Bible translation projects, all around the world.

And the Roman Catholic can say to you,

"Now we can all agree on one Bible. One world Bible, for one world church!"

So now we see that *someone* darkened Sinaiticus. So now we come to the next questions: ***Who did it —and why?***

Our list of suspects is rather limited. Wait till you reason it out for yourself in the next chapters.

10

Is the Sinaiticus Origin a Lie?

Have you ever believed someone, even for 30 years, and suddenly found out that he lied? And not just to others, but to you, his friend? And not just to you, but to his own brother and wife? It's devastating. It's astonishing.

This is something like what I felt when I learned the truth about Constantin Tischendorf, the guy who gave us the Sinaiticus, supposedly the oldest Bible in the world, the one they used to justify so many changes in modern Bibles.

Want to learn what I found out? I have two books —one was translated in 2013[28] and the other came out in 2015.[29] I got a digital copy. They are pro-Tischendorf, no doubt about it. But between them, they showed me that what Tischendorf claimed about how he got the Sinaiticus —that I even passed on in my earlier book— couldn't possibly have happened.

In a book that he wrote three years before he died, he told about how he found the Sinaiticus manuscript. He was in a monastery library in the Sinai desert, surrounded by shelves of printed and handwritten books. He said:

---

28. *The Bible Hunter: The Quest for the Original New Testament* by Jürgen Gottschlich (London: Haus Publishing Ltd, English translation 2013).
29. *Constantine Tischendorf: the Life and Work of a 19th Century Bible Hunter* by Stanley E. Porter (NY: Bloomsbury, 2015).

> I looked through them one by one. In the middle of the library, however, there was also a large basket containing the remains of damaged manuscripts. When I proceeded to examine this, Kyrillos the librarian remarked that its contents had twice been thrown into the fire. This, therefore, was the third filling, which to all appearances was destined for the same end.
>
> I could not fail to be astonished when I removed a number of very large parchment sheets of Greek script whose palaeographic appearance led me to conclude that they were of the greatest antiquity.

(Palaeographic means ancient writing. A Palaeographer is someone who deciphers and transcribes ancient writing.) And a bit later he wrote:

> The basket's destiny rendered it possible for the smaller, loose batch of leaves, 43 of them, to be surrendered to me at my request.

So there are four main points I want you to note, from Tischendorf's own hand, in his own book (1871): There was a large basket with remains of damaged manuscripts. Kyrillos the librarian told him that the last two basketfuls were thrown into the fire. This basketful was the third filling, put there to be burned. He got to take 43 leaves (later called the Codex Friderico-Augustanus,), because they were just going to be thrown into the fire.

What if I told you that ***all four*** of these points were bold-faced lies? Let me make it simple. On the very next page, Stanley Porter explains. That large basket wasn't a wastepaper basket. For centuries, as Tischendorf knew, those baskets were the way you store parchment, all over Europe and the East. Monks did not throw parchment into the fire. Parchment is nothing but thinly-scraped animal hide, which burns badly, and it would stink up the place!

Besides, parchment was valuable. Papyrus can get old and fall apart. Parchment is, according to Gottschlich, "almost imperishable." They didn't destroy it. They reused it! You know how? They scraped or washed off the old words and wrote on new words. Then it was called a "palimpsest." And Tischendorf knew this, as well!

Tischendorf, it turns out, became famous among palaeographers when he deciphered a Bible palimpsest, Ephraemi Rescriptus! So this couldn't have been the third filling, waiting to be burned, at all! So he didn't get the 43 snow-white leaves, the CFA, because it was just going to be burned!

But that leads us to a fifth lie. Tischendorf lied about what Kyrillos the librarian said! He couldn't have said that they were burning parchment. He couldn't have said two other basketfuls of parchment were burned. He couldn't have given snow white CFA to Tischendorf to save it from the fire!

But that is not all I found out. One night, reading Porter's book, I learned that Tischendorf wrote letters with parts of this story, to his older brother, to others, and to his future wife! What kind of man would lie to everyone he knew?

Look, I thought Tischendorf made some pretty big mistakes. But I **never** thought the story of how he got Sinaiticus was a lie. And if that is a lie, what else is?

Do you know what depends upon Sinaiticus? Matthew

5:22, taking out "without a cause," making Jesus a sinner for being angry at the moneychangers. What tipped the balance for removing those words? The Sinaiticus.

John 7:8, changing "I go not up yet unto this feast" to "I go not up to this feast," changing "not yet" to "not," making Jesus a liar to His brothers. Even the Vaticanus has that one right. But the Sinaiticus is the reason that it was changed in 22 modern Bibles. Making Jesus a sinner, and Jesus a liar, from the Codex Sinaiticus.

This "Find of the Century," as they called the Sinaiticus, changed Tischendorf into a superstar overnight. Scholar Philip Schaff in his 1883 *Companion to the Greek New Testament,* talked about Tischendorf's:

> …personal vanity and over-fondness for his many
> and well-earned titles (covering ten lines on the
> title-pages of some of his books), and twenty or
> more decorations from sovereigns which were dis-
> played in his parlor.[30]

That included, by the way, honorary doctorates from Oxford and Cambridge and a commendation from the pope. None of that fame and fortune could be the motivation for lying for thirty years to everyone he knew about the origin of the Sinaiticus, could it?

I found this out from his other new biography. In 1866, four years after he published Sinaiticus, Tischendorf said these words:

> But we have at last hit upon a better plan even
> than this, which is to set aside this textus receptus

---

30. *A Companion to the Greek New Testament and to the English Version* by Philip Schaff (NY: Harper & Brothers, 1883), p. 261.

> altogether, and to construct a fresh text, derived immediately from the most ancient and authoritative sources. [31]

Who's "we"? And did he really mean to "set aside" the preserved Bible, the Bible of the persecuted believers, in English the King James Bible, and the Bible of his own Lutheran church? Yes, he did. Brothers and sisters, this is no small thing. Remember, every modern Bible and their Bible-doubting footnotes, including those in many copies of the King James, and every Bible translated by Wycliffe Bible Translators and SIL and the United Bible Societies, in every language, around the world, is largely based upon the changed text in Sinaiticus.

---

31. See *Constantine Tischendorf: the Life and Work of a 19th Century Bible Hunter* by Stanley E. Porter (NY: Bloomsbury, 2015), p. 120.

11

Coloring the Truth

Sometimes the simplest questions give us the most interesting answers!

Codex Sinaiticus is the Greek text that tipped the balance of the world's Bible text scholars away from the King James and Bibles like it, to something called "the critical text." It became one of the most important and most studied manuscripts of all time. It even has its own web page!

So we should be able to ask simple questions and get simple answers. Right? Let's find out! Here's a child's question: What color is Sinaiticus? The answer will bring you an ***embarrassing*** surprise.

First, I've got to thank Jack McElroy, author of the amazing book, ***Which Bible Would Jesus Use?*** for sending me his own Sinaiticus facsimile to check out for myself.

Let me sum up the story. In the 1800s, Constantin Tischendorf went out to discover ancient Bibles. The nobleman who helped pay for the trip was King Frederick of Saxony. So Tischendorf went down to the St. Catherine's monastery in the Sinai Peninsula, and brought back two sections, 43 leaves, he grabbed or cut out of an Old Testament. Then he gave those as a present to King Frederick, and named them after him.

Coloring the Truth

People who finance your trip expect things like that.

Right around that time, 1844-45, a couple of guys, including a high-level religious official named Porfiry Uspensky, saw the rest of the document and described it as "white." Uspensky cut out a few pieces and took them back with him. And people later went to Germany and saw Frederick's leaves for themselves: snow white! 15 years later, Tischendorf came back with 347 other leaves. He (and a couple unnamed helpers), held onto them a couple of months in Cairo.

Now, in the 19th century, people were really into finding ancient documents. Sometimes they paid good money for them. So you can bet that faking documents to make them **look** ancient was a huge business. They would stain the documents to make them look darker, and change the ink so it would look lighter. Then they'd rough up the paper or parchment, and voila —a brand-new ancient document.

Well, after those two months with Tischendorf in Cairo, he let others see this Sinaiticus. And guess what? It wasn't snow white anymore! It was stained and darkened, and the whole thing looked old, now. What happened to the color?

But that's not all. Today, there are leaves of Sinaiticus kept in several libraries: in the Egyptian peninsula, in Russia, in Germany, and the 347 that ended up in England, as well.

But a few years ago, a number of scientists decided to use the Internet to bring them all together into one, 823-page Sinaiticus, more complete than anyone has ever seen, with high-definition photos. They even used color bars to calibrate the pictures, so they are color-accurate.

88 *Is the 'World's Oldest Bible' a Fake?*

Figure 22 - Montage of all 823 pages of Sinaiticus[32]

Here are all 823 pages in a single picture. You will notice that, even at this size, you can tell that some pages are quite differently colored. That difference is between the pages

---

32. Photo has been adjusted in black and white, to show the differences you can easily see in color (see cover for full-color image). We recommend you view the originals at *www.codexsinaiticus.org*.

Coloring the Truth 89

that are Frederick's, and Tischendorf's final set. Someone is being dishonest.

But there's more. If you spend about $500 to $800 you can get a huge book with all the discovered pages of Sinaiticus. It says, "The images, taken according to agreed technical standards, were processed to represent faithfully the actual appearance of the pages." Except, they also said that they made "sensitive adjustments" because "the appearance of the parchment and ink varied somewhat."[33] And those pages all look alike.

So what color is Sinaiticus?

If the scientists with their color bars are right, then there are some major color differences. But if they're right, then the publisher of this big book just might have Photoshopped the color in so it all looked the same, pretty much.

And if Frederick's pages are right, then the original color should really be white with dark letters. But if Frederick's are right, then Tischendorf's 347 leaves were intentionally stained to make the papers and ink look old.

One guy on the internet said, "You're wrong. The Sinaiticus has been tested by hundreds of people!" Nope. I checked it out and not a single test has been done on the age of the parchment or of the ink. They were set to test it in April of 2015. Then they changed the guy over the project, and suddenly the testing was canceled.

Why? What are they afraid they would find? Not the scientists, I mean —the powers-that-be. What are they afraid of finding out? That the Sinaiticus is actually not an ancient

---

33. See *The Codex Sinaiticus Reference Guide* (Peabody, Massachusetts: Hendrickson Publishers Marketing, LLC, 2010), p. 5.

document after all? That it was a modern forgery that was faked to make it look old? That would explain why it's never been mentioned in any clear way, anywhere, before 1844.

But Sinaiticus is the reason modern Bibles remove the second "yet" in John 7:8, making Jesus a liar. And Sinaiticus tipped the balance so we'd have the blind man believing in the "Son of man," not the "Son of God."(John 9:35) It also took out "Lord, I believe, and he worshipped him" three verses later, in 9:38, taking away that Jesus is God, to be worshipped. Not even Vaticanus removes that.

And of course, Sinaiticus is the reason we have warning notes in the last 12 verses of most copies of the Gospel of Mark, saying we can't believe them. Could they be afraid that we would find out that they "colored the truth" all this time?

The evidence shows me that the original, handwritten Sinaiticus, no matter its age, was snow white with dark lettering. But that didn't look as old as men wanted. So men aged it. And the publishers of this very expensive book also changed the color of the pages so they would all match. I cannot think of a single godly reason why they would change it.

So it's forcing me to think that the Sinaiticus is a sham, a modern counterfeit, and that it is part of an agenda. Don't believe me? Go to www.codexsinaiticus.org and compare the pages marked LUL (for the CFA) with the pages marked BL (for the British Library). Check me out!

Of course, I have no horse in this race. I don't believe Sinaiticus is God's words. This discovery is simply more evidence that the Alexandrian stream of manuscripts is polluted with fakery as well as the omissions, discrepancies, and doctrinal distortions pointed out in my previous books and videos.

I've got nothing to lose by finding all this out. But there are people who have a great deal to lose. Modern Bible Societies and publishers translate, produce, and print almost every Bible in the world, and they teach that the Sinaiticus was a real, ancient Bible.

Of course, all this is a big part of an agenda preparing a one world Bible for the coming one world religion.

But it's not hopeless. There is the bright side: You can trust **ONE** Bible —in English, it is the King James Bible; 400+ years tried, tested and proven. And it was never "found," because it was never lost in the first place.

12

Who Darkened Sinaiticus?

As I've shown you, we know historically that the document called the Sinaiticus was changed.

You can't get around it.

Something that was snow white became dark and stained —all throughout 695 pages!

But who would do something like that? Or logically speaking, who HAD to have either done it, or been in partnership with whoever did it?

It's unbelievable, but I don't see another option. And it sheds a harsh light on my education and even some of my own assumptions. May I show you what I learned?

In the last chapter I showed you how sometime during the 1800s the huge codex (big book) we call Codex Sinaiticus was changed from white to stained and dark. Let's break that down a bit. I am indebted to researcher Steven Avery once again for his painstaking research. Look at this timeline:

In 1844-1850 all of Sinaiticus —meaning the so-called Septuagint Old Testament with embedded Apocrypha, and including the New Testament, plus the *Epistle of Barnabas* and the *Shepherd of Hermas*— every bit of it was clearly white, witnessed as white, described as white.[34]

---

34. See chart in Appendix A for more information.

The two sections (the afore-mentioned CFA) that were taken away from St. Catherine's Monastery in 1844, ultimately going to the king of Saxony, are still white, to this very day.

Then Porfiry Uspensky of Russia saw what was left of it the next year, and described it as white in 1845. Then he visited again in 1850. It was still white. He published that fact in his two books on his journeys, published in 1856 and 1857. That covers 1844 to 1850, 6 to 7 years.

And, maybe because Saxony (now called Leipzig) is right there in Germany, people saw the CFA so white and thought the whole Sinaiticus was white, as well.

We know this because, in 1910, *the Encyclopædia of Religion and Ethics: Bible in the Church* said "the Sinaitic Manuscript" was "wonderfully fine snow-white parchment."

And see this 1913 description by another writer, J. A. McClymont:

> ...Sinaiticus... was rescued from oblivion... by the famous critic, Tischendorf... and now lies in the Library of St. Petersburg. It is written on snow-white vellum, supposed to have been made from the skins of antelopes.[35]

So according to two authors, the Sinaiticus was what? "Snow white."

But there's just one problem: IT WASN'T! In point of fact, after 1859 it was actually dark. That is after Tischendorf got hold of it. How do we know that, since those later writers described it as "snow white"?

---

35. *New Testament Criticism: Its History and Results*, by James Alexander McClymont (London: Hodder and Stoughton, 1913), p. 44.

From Tischendorf himself! In 1862 Tischendorf described them as "sufflava" —a Latin word that means "yellowed." Also in 1862 Tischendorf allowed another scholar, Tregelles, to examine Sinaiticus for three days.[36] So if it were changed after that date, Tregelles would have known it.

In 1864 Frederick Scrivener, in his own book, *A Full Collation of the Codex Sinaiticus with the Received Text of the New Testament*, said "the vellum leaves" were "now almost yellow in colour"[37]

And in 1911, Helen and Kirsopp Lake photographed the Sinaiticus in color, so there was no hiding what they saw. They said "… the thicker leaves… are inclined to a yellowish tint."[38]

So people who actually saw the big part of the Sinaiticus, thought it was yellow. Those who saw it before Tischendorf had it, or only saw the CFA in Germany, said it was snow white. And the CFA, which was quickly (1844) sent to the king of Saxony, in modern Germany, was and still is white.

So why did people still think it was all white, after Tischendorf published the Sinaiticus in 1862? My thought: people who saw the CFA part in Germany, could not see the rest, all the way in Russia. They had no reason to doubt that the whole Sinaiticus looked the same. So whoever saw the snow white CFA assumed it was all white. But those who saw the rest of the Sinaiticus that Tischendorf spent all that

---

36. *A Full Collation of the Codex Sinaiticus with the Received Text of the New Testament* by Frederick H. Scrivener (Cambridge: Deighton, Bell and Co., 1864), p. xvi.

37. *A Full Collation*, p. xxx.

38. *Codex Sinaiticus Petropolitanus: the New Testament, the Epistle of Barnabas and the Shepherd of Hermas*, by Helen and Kirsopp Lake, (Oxford: Clarendon Press, 1911), p. xvi

Who Darkened Sinaiticus?

time with, assumed that all of it was yellowed and dark, with those stains.

There were two sets of people, writing about two colors of Sinaiticus, at the same time. And nobody even noticed! Not until the last couple of years has anyone put all the known pieces of the Sinaiticus together where we can see them with our own eyes.

What does this tell us? There are only so many years between when we knew the Sinaiticus as a whole was white, and when a large part of it became dark: 1844-1850: white —1862: dark.

But wait. Tischendorf got the big part of it in 1859. And remember, when he got the CFA —his story says he only got a third of what he saw. So if someone else had darkened it, Tischendorf would have known, because it was part of the pages of the Bible he got in 1859. Then he could have cried foul! "What are you doing, destroying the most ancient text of the Bible?"

But he didn't. He had to have known that the Sinaiticus was actually snow white. He himself said he saw, not just 43 leaves, but another 86! Those were part of what he brought back from St. Catherine's monastery in 1859.

That means one of two things:

1. It was darkened between 1850 and 1859, and Tischendorf knew, but said nothing about it.

2. It was darkened sometime after he got it in 1859, and he hoped no one would know it was ever white.

So either Tischendorf did it, or he knew who did, and was an accomplice. Tischendorf doesn't sound so good right now, does he?

But let's look at it from a totally different angle. How does God deal with hidden things? In Luke 8:17 and a lot of other places, Jesus said,

> "For nothing is secret, that shall not be made manifest; neither *any thing* hid, that shall not be known and come abroad."

Jesus also said in Matthew 10:27:

> What I tell you in darkness, *that* speak ye in light: and what ye hear in the ear, *that* preach ye upon the housetops.

And remember what Jesus thanked God for in both Luke 10:21 and Matthew 11:25:

> At that time Jesus answered and said, I thank thee, O Father, Lord of heaven and earth, because thou hast hid these things from the wise and prudent, and hast revealed them unto babes.

See? That is God's pattern. He reveals His truth to humble people. And then He wants everyone to know about it.

Anyone studying Tischendorf will realize he was proud and loud and kowtowed to the pope, even though he was a Protestant. It seems that Tischendorf was also seeking his own "holy grail," so to speak, called the Codex Vaticanus. He spent years doing favors for Catholic leaders, so they would write letters to the pope, to say that Tischendorf was worthy to see it.

Sinaiticus and Vaticanus have something in common. They were both allegedly under the care of monks or Catholics, and kept hidden from the common Christians for centuries —at least they were hidden until just before the major push to update the Bible in the mid 1800s.

Does that sound like the fulfillment of God's promise to preserve His words? In hidden places? In secret? Away from the people for close to 2,000 years? And the only way they could get them is to kowtow to monks or Jesuits or do favors for kings or the pope?

That's something that never sounded right to me, not even when I was told all this in Bible college. And what was the result?

In Luke 8, a woman with a flow of blood tried to just grab the hem of Jesus' garment in the midst of a big crowd. She thought she was hidden, as she asked in faith for God to heal her.

Look at verse 47:

> And when the woman saw that she was not hid, she came trembling, and falling down before him, she declared unto him before all the people for what cause she had touched him, and how she was healed immediately. And he said unto her, Daughter, be of good comfort: thy faith hath made thee whole; go in peace.

See? The woman could not be hidden from God. The truth came out, and she fell before Jesus and declared everything! It was awesome! I hope I can see the video in heaven!

And what did Jesus say unto her? "Thy faith hath made thee whole…"

Let me ask you: Did Tischendorf's alleged "discovery" bring him to his knees? Did Tischendorf fall on his face and from pure conviction before God, spread the gospel and preach Christ crucified and salvation by grace through faith for the rest of his life out of his gratefulness for such a find?

Nope. He was still proud. He was still sneaky. He, or someone he knew, darkened the Sinaiticus parts he had, to make them look old. He lied about that, even if nothing else. He engaged in intrigue to "borrow" or "buy" or "steal" the manuscripts.

Those are not the actions of a man of faith. And I cannot see God rewarding that with the "discovery of the century." But that's just me.

And it doesn't matter if it was made by Alexandrian intellectuals in 325-350, or was made from scratch in the 1800s, it doesn't bear the marks of something holy to God. It isn't based on faith. It doesn't produce faith. In fact, it spawns doubt. It doesn't lift up Christ. It lowers Christ!

The god of the Sinaiticus didn't keep his promises. But our God did. And we have the proof, with 400+ years' worth of testing: God's preserved words in English, the King James Bible.

I believe that Constantin Tischendorf did something to the text, and never admitted it. No one else around him admitted it, either.

So it may have happened before anyone of them actually saw what he had. All he had to do was NOT show the two parts together, and discredit anyone who had seen them all before 1859. And by the way, that is exactly what he did. And it worked —until just a few years ago.

But remember, even if every textual critic and teacher and even preacher in the world told you the opposite, the truth I just showed you is now coming out.

Don't be afraid. As Jesus said in Matthew 10:26,

> "Fear them not therefore: for there is nothing covered, that shall not be revealed; and hid, that shall not be known."

Listen to this: 2 Corinthians 4:2

> "But have renounced the hidden things of dishonesty, not walking in craftiness, nor handling the word of God deceitfully; but by manifestation of the truth commending ourselves to every man's conscience in the sight of God."

I can't trust the Sinaiticus. But remember, if I cannot trust the Sinaiticus, then neither can I trust almost ***any Bible on the market***, that is, except the King James or preserved Bibles in other languages.

The more I know, the more I like —no, the more I love— my King James.

13

Which Part is Scripture?

The Codex Sinaiticus was the book that tipped the balance away from the historical, preserved Bible and changed hundreds of scriptures in crucial places. Text critics have used it to cast doubt on the whole idea that Christ was raised —or divine.

They don't want me to believe something because Sinaiticus doesn't have it. So what does Sinaiticus have, that they **want** me to **believe**? Isn't that a fair question?

If you want me to release my faith in the King James Bible, and put my faith in your book, shouldn't you be able to tell me which parts to believe? Shouldn't you be able to tell me which parts of Sinaiticus are scripture, and which parts are not?

Go to your professor, your pastor, your anti-King James friend, and have him read this, study the pictures, and watch the vlogs. Then see if he or she can answer the questions I'm about to ask. They are asking you to trust a document that changed the Bible in fundamental ways. They should be able to answer some simple questions.

Are you ready?

Which writer gave us the *true* scripture? Is it Scribe A, the main writer scribe of what we have of Sinaiticus? Is it Scribe

Which Part is Scripture? 101

D, the boss corrector scribe? What about B1, who wrote the Major Prophets? What about B2, who wrote the Minor Prophets and *Shepherd of Hermas*?

This is the *Shepherd of Hermas*, which taught that Jesus was a virtuous man filled with the Holy Spirit and ***adopted*** as the Son of God at His baptism. —He was not eternally the Son of God.

That would agree with Mark in the Sinaiticus that omits that Jesus is "the Son of God" in Mark 1:1.[39]

So is the true scripture their original notes? Or is it their self-corrections? Or did it become "scripture" afterward, when Scribe D came in and corrected the first scribe?

---

39. *Codex Sinaiticus: The Story of the World's Oldest Bible* by David C. Parker (London: The British Library, 2010), p. 108.

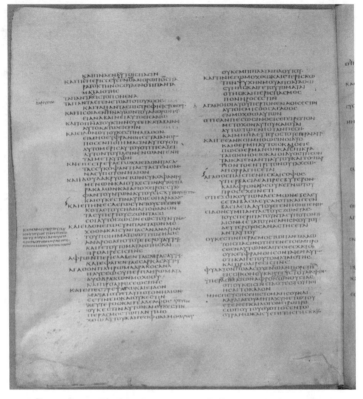

Figure 23 - Codex Sinaiticus Quire 66 Folio 1 Verso

One example is Ecclesiastes 4:3 in Figure 23. At first it was omitted. Then it was self-corrected by the scribe and put into the left margin. And there are other corrections on this page.

Which Part is Scripture?

Figure 24 - Codex Sinaiticus Quire 43 Folio 1 Recto

Take a look at Figure 24. This is the beginning of Isaiah. See all the scribbling on top? And parts of it are erased. And some is written over, and possibly corrected, by scribe D.

At what time do we stop and say, Wait! Go no further! *Now* we've got the scripture! And if *they* didn't know, then how could we know? You want *me* to place *my precious faith* in a document that has so many corrections that I can't even figure out what the final text is?

And this brings me to another important question: If I

am a faithful Christian, trying to please my Master, trying to find out what the Father wants, and I can't read Sinaiticus and figure out how to answer these basic questions for myself, then how did Tischendorf?

We have already seen that Tischendorf was an unrepentant liar. Tischendorf never told anyone, that I can find, about what *really* happened in 1844, or 1853, or 1859, when he supposedly got the Sinaiticus.

Look at what the pro-Tischendorf researchers, backed by the British Library, in conjunction with the University of Leipzig, and the University of St. Petersburg, and St. Catherine's Monastery said about Tischendorf in *Codex Sinaiticus: the Story of the World's Oldest Bible:*

Their excuse for Tischendorf's story about saving parchments from the fire: "…there are a number of ways in which Tischendorf may have been confused…" Or this one: "…he might have misunderstood what was being said," referring to what the monk told him, supposedly.[40]

And this one: "In short, although there are no grounds for believing it to be deliberately misleading, one *cannot* take Tischendorf's account at face value."[41]

You know, that's another way of saying, "Yeah, it just isn't true."

Another biographer believed that Tischendorf was precise in his reporting: "But this does not mean that his version is unquestionable."[42]

---

40. *Codex Sinaiticus* by DC Parker, p. 130.
41. *Codex Sinaiticus* by DC Parker, p. 131.
42. *Codex Sinaiticus: New Perspectives on the Ancient Biblical Manuscript* by Scot McKendrick, David Parker, Amy Myshrall and Cillian O'Hogan (London: The British Library, 2015), p. 174.

And I already showed you in *The Bible Hunter* how the author proves, in a number of steps, how everything that Tischendorf said about 1844 is impossible. [43]

If all of these guys in the Tischendorf Sinaiticus club ***can't*** tell me that Tischendorf told the truth, and if I can't look at Sinaiticus and tell you which words are supposed to be scripture, then how can I base my faith on the opinions of Tischendorf?

Do you see the problem here? The bulk of the world, with all their modern Bibles, have faith-altering and faith-destroying words, phrases, and verses —either changed or missing. And they got them from the "educated guesses" of the liar, Tischendorf? Is this like the Fox ruling the henhouse? Or the Wolf guarding the sheepfold?

Tischendorf said he was looking for God's original scriptures, to aid the Christian faith. What part of this is faith in God? All I see here are Tischendorf's guesses, which he published in his typeset facsimile.

Can any text scholars or famous preachers show me which part of this is scripture, and which is not?

---

43. *The Bible Hunter: the Quest for the Original new Testament,* by Jürgen Gottschlich (London: Haus Publishing Ltd., 2013), pp. 96-97.

Figure 25 - Codex Sinaiticus Quire 48 Folio 8 Recto

Which part of this is scripture, and which is not?

Which Part is Scripture?

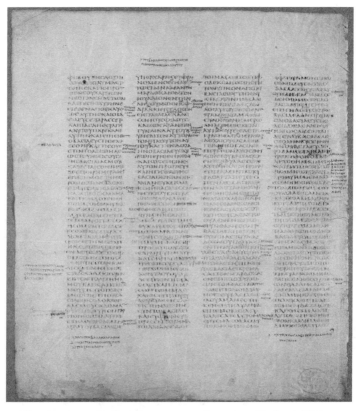

Figure 26 - Codex Sinaiticus Quire 36 Folio 8 Verso

Check it out. Look at all those changes.

How about this? Which part of this is scripture, and which part of this is not?

108 *Is the 'World's Oldest Bible' a Fake?*

Figure 27 - Codex Sinaiticus Quire 36 Folio 4 Verso

This is Nehemiah, and these are all omitted verses, written into the margin. Do they belong, or not belong? And how do you know? Or this?

Which Part is Scripture?

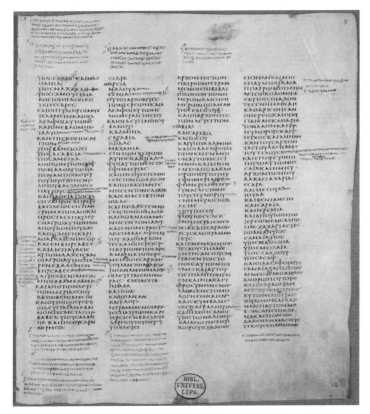

Figure 28 - Codex Sinaiticus Quire 36 Folio 4 Recto

Take a good look. Which is scripture, and which is not?

Can John MacArthur show me?

Can James White show me?

Can Charles Ryrie show me?

Can Dr. Paul, my old Greek professor, show me?

Where am I to base my faith? Is it in the Sinaiticus? Or in the liar, Tischendorf? Or in your own educated guesses about what is scripture and what is not? What are my criteria? Sinaiticus is in such bad shape.

Codex Sinaiticus is: (Are you ready for this?) missing all but four chapters of Genesis (a couple of badly weathered pieces were discovered in a secret storage area of the monastery in 1975),

missing all of Exodus,

missing all but three chapters of Leviticus,

missing all but 12 chapters of Numbers,

missing all but five chapters of Deuteronomy,

missing all but three chapters of Joshua,

missing all but seven chapters of Judges,

and it's missing all of Ruth, 1 Samuel, 2 Samuel, all of 1 Kings and 2 Kings; has parts of 1 Chronicles —twice.

How do you make a mistake like that and keep going?

And remember, it jumps from 1 Chronicles 19:17 to the middle of the sentence in Ezra 9:9 and just keeps going, without fixing it! [44]

missing 2 Chronicles,

missing the first 8 chapters of Ezra,

missing Lamentations after 2:20,

missing all of Ezekiel,

all of Daniel,

all of Hosea,

all of Amos,

and all of Micah.

So it's missing 12 entire books and most of six more, over

---

44. See Chapter 8.

Which Part is Scripture?

1/4 of the Bible books.

But of course, it has Apocrypha! It has all of Tobit, all of Judith, All of 1 Maccabees, 4 Maccabees, all of Wisdom of Solomon, And all of Sirach.

Seriously? You want me to abandon a solid foundation and a solid faith in a preserved scripture, passed down by persecuted believers, whose Bible brought about such faith it started the Reformation, and the largest missionary movement in history? Give that up for the biggest mess of pages masquerading as a Bible I have ever seen? And where nobody but a liar named Tischendorf can tell me which words are God's, and which are man's?

God said in Matthew 24:35, Mark 13:31 and Luke 21:33:

> "Heaven and earth shall pass away, but my words shall not pass away."

Maybe He didn't mean the over 1/4 of Sinaiticus that's missing.

God said through Solomon in Proverbs 30:5-6:

> Every word of God is pure: he is a shield unto them that put their trust in him. Add thou not unto his words, lest he reprove thee, and thou be found a liar.

So isn't this adding? All these notes?

Figure 29 - Codex Sinaiticus Quire 92 Folio 1 Recto

This is Quire 92, Folio 1, recto –front. You can look it up. This isn't adding? By the way, this is the *Epistle of Barnabas* that teaches baptismal regeneration.

Brothers and sisters, this is a ***con job!*** And it's only adding insult to injury to say, "Well, you have to match it up with the Vaticanus."

You're kidding. I now have to trust the Whore of Babylon to give me reliable scripture? Weren't they the persecutors of Bible-believers through history? And now you're going to believe ***their*** book, against the Bible that our ancestors in the faith died to preserve to the next generation? You're going to trust the Bible of the Inquisitors? Seriously?

Do you belong to the Reformed tradition? Read what your founders said about the Whore of Babylon. Lutheran? Read what your founders said. Baptist? You were never a Catholic, so what are you doing believing their Bible?

Do you realize that since 1966, the Catholic Church has wholly-endorsed the new critical Bibles and Critical Greek, and Critical Hebrew, and changed their Latin to match it?

I document that in *Why They Changed the Bible: One World Bible for One World Religion.*[45]

Are you going to trust the Bible that's endorsed by the guy who says he is in place of Christ on earth? And will you gladly hand over your preserved Bible to him and accept his Sinaiticus and Vaticanus?

Why ***did*** the pope commend Tischendorf for calling this mess "scripture?" Do you think that the pope had a plan —a long-term plan, and Tischendorf fit into it?

Even if Tischendorf's story was true, St. Catherine's monastery didn't preserve scripture. They abandoned it and took it apart and put it in a bin of scraps!

Porfiry Uspensky, who saw this the year after Tischendorf saw it, said the Sinaiticus was a faith-destroyer. Tischendorf arrogantly responded that Uspensky was just unable to recognize scripture when he saw it.

What do you see as a result of Sinaiticus: faith or doubt?

For example, was it to build faith or doubt that the last 12 verses of Mark were physically removed from Codex Sinaiticus? I will prove this in the next chapter.

---

45. Available from Chick Publications.

14

Deleted on Purpose?

Let's revisit Mark 16:9-20. Was this passage deleted on purpose from Sinaiticus?

"Yea, hath God said?" It's practically the motto at Bible colleges and seminaries —and some churches! I told you that I would show you more about what happened to Mark 16:9-20, that they **removed 12 verses**, and how we know they did.

Well, now is the time! I'm going to start by teaching you how a book is put together. Then I'll show you how they changed the book. You will learn what they did, which scribe did what, what the end result was, and what we can learn from that.

In a later chapter, I will build on this to show you how and maybe why Sinaiticus was faked! That's a tall order!

Shall we get started? To write a book, we start with a single sheet, like a sheet of typing paper. Then we fold the sheet in half. That makes two folia (that's Latin for leaves): folio (leaf) 1, and folio (leaf) 2. Each folio also has 2 sides.

Deleted on Purpose?

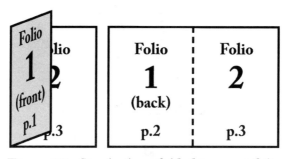

Figure 30 - Single sheet folded into two folia

I used to teach my kids in elementary school to hold a book, upright. That is the word "recto," That's the front page. To get to the other side we have to do what with the page? We "turn" it. So the back side is the verb "verso," meaning "turning." Recto, right, front. Verso, turning, back.

Verso (turning)	Recto (right)
p.2	p.3

Figure 31 - Folded sheet showing recto and verso

So we have 1 sheet, which is 2 folia (leaves), and each folio has two sides; recto, the front; and verso, the back. 1, 2, 3, 4. Four pages. So if 1 sheet is 4 pages, then 4 sheets are (4x4) 16 pages. Once we get four sheets together, we have 8 folia (leaves), and 16 pages. We call that a "quire."

Figure 32 - Example of a quire of 16 pages

The Sinaiticus is made up of quires that are supposed to be stitched together to make a large book or Codex. So Figure 32 would be 1 Quire, 4 sheets, 8 folia, making 16 pages.

So let me ask you: what happens if you are the boss corrector, and your writer makes a big mistake? If it's bad enough, it's like when a kid raises his hand and says, "Teacher? I messed up my page. Could I have another one, please?" And I would say, "Sure," and I'd hand him a new sheet of paper.

These guys who wrote Sinaiticus clearly did something like this. But if the page got bad enough, the boss corrector, also called the *diorthotes*, would get another sheet and fit it into place.

That is easy, if you put it in the middle. That's the middle sheet, folia 4 and 5, pages 7, 8, 9, and 10. All those pages are

Deleted on Purpose?

next to each other, "contiguous," so you can correct it easily. You only have to match the words up at 2 pages: page 6 to page 7, and page 10 to page 11.

But if it's on the 2nd or 3rd sheet, it's more difficult. You have to write the replacement in such a way that you can match up the end word of one page onto the beginning word of another page, four times. If the correction is on the third sheet, for instance, page 4 has to match page 5, and 6 to 7. On the other side, 10 has to match 11 and 12 to 13.

Regardless, if the mistakes are bad enough, you need a new sheet, to ***cancel out*** the other sheet. You replace the sheet completely; all four pages. So it's called a "cancel sheet." That cancel sheet has to match up with all the other pages.

In the Sinaiticus New Testament there are three sheets, (which equals 6 folia [leaves], which equals 12 pages,) where scholars say Scribe D used a cancel sheet to wipe out the mistakes of Scribe A. The 2nd sheet is the one we are interested in. And guess what? It's right in the middle of the quire! That should be easy!

Except—no. It covers from Mark 14:54 through Luke 1:56. That means that right in the middle of it is Mark 16:9-20. Does it belong, or doesn't it? Let's find out! People are curious. They want to know why Scribe D got rid of Scribe A's work, and then put in a cancel sheet that he personally rewrote.

Some people think that A wrote in verses 9-20, but Scribe D, the boss, didn't want it in. He got upset and he rewrote the entire section to get it out. Other people count the average number of letters on a line and the number of lines in a column from Scribe A, and they say that there is not enough space to include verses 9-20.

Well, let me tell you this about Scribe D. He is a perfectionist. Let me show you something he took pride in:

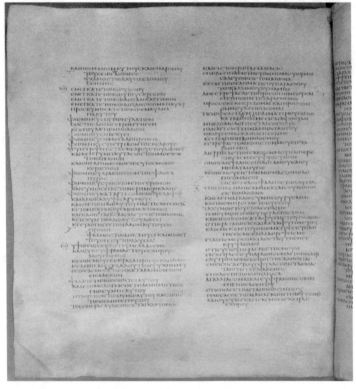

Figure 33 - Codex Sinaiticus Quire 59 Folio 7 Verso, Psalm 27:9 - 30:9

The Psalms. Isn't that beautiful? You can tell by the handwriting, the experts say, it is the same guy.

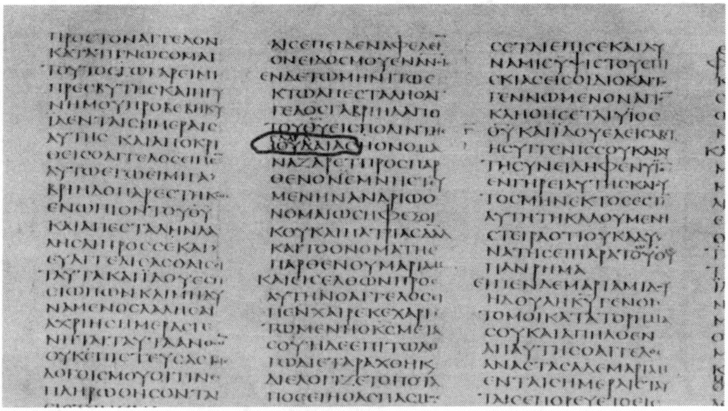

Deleted on Purpose? 119

Figure 34 - Quire 77 Folio 5 Verso, with "Judaea" rewritten as "Galilee" Luke 1:18-56

Now look at this. This is what he did on the cancel sheet. So what happened? He starts, according to the experts, by measuring space for Luke. Then he writes Luke 1, but he really compresses the letters together. On the last page he squeezes in over 200 more letters than on other pages.

And he did it emotionally, sloppily. You can tell that he's upset —and maybe under pressure. Take a look at that last page, in Luke 1:26 he actually said that the angel Gabriel appeared to Mary in Nazareth of *Judaea.* But Nazareth is in Galilee, 70 miles from Judaea. No other Bible in the world makes this mistake. He wasn't paying attention, was he?

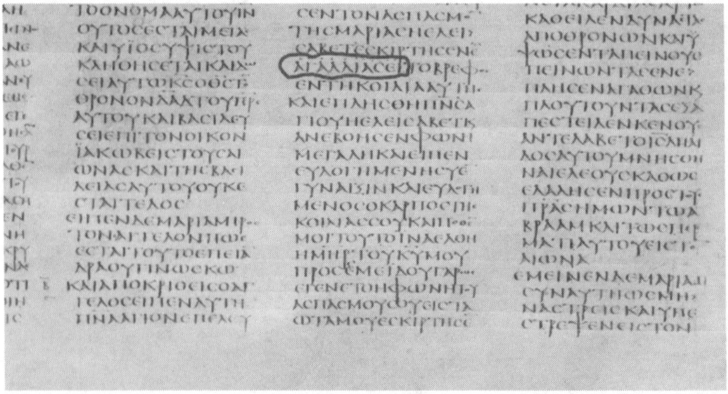

Figure 35 - Q77 F5v, with "for joy" added to Luke 1:41

Then he *added* the words "for joy" in verse 41, copying them from verse 44. No other Bible in the world adds this word at this place. But Scribe D, the corrector, did. The responsibility of a scribe is not just to get it *done*, but to get it done **RIGHT**. Look here: 14 per line, 15, 14, 17, 14. See how he's squeezing those letters in there?

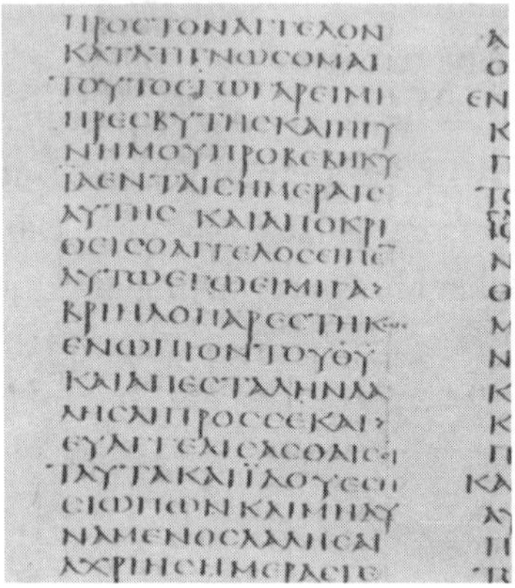

Figure 36 - Luke 1 with letters squeezed in

Deleted on Purpose? 121

Then, once he squeezed in Luke 1, he went to work, according to the experts, on Mark 14:54 through chapter 16. At one point in the beginning he actually squeezed words again. But after he noticed his mistake, he quickly went the other way. Look on the verso side. He was trying to hide the fact that he was removing verses 16:9-20, but now he had too much space!

What's he going to do? What else? Spread the letters out! So, starting at Mark 15:19, they got wider and wider, when he realized he didn't calculate right in his haste. He went way down in his letter count. See for yourself.

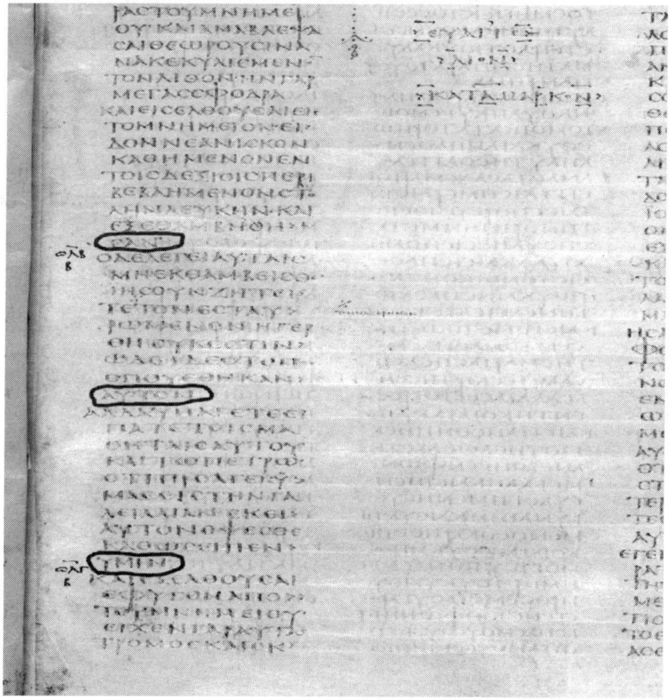

Figure 37 - Mark 16 with words spread out

There's 10 letters on one line, only 3 letters on another, and so on. Look at the count: 9, 10, 10, 5 –just one word, 10, 11, 10, 4, 10. See? Very different, isn't it? So there's a much smaller letter count per line. Then he wrote the ending to Mark, filling up a little space. But he still had almost an empty column. After such a sloppy job by this perfectionist, why didn't he just get another parchment and start over? I figure he must have been under pressure or in a hurry.

As I told you, out of 620 ancient Greek manuscripts that have Mark 16, all but two have 9-20: Codex Sinaiticus, and the Roman Catholic Codex Vaticanus. And I think Sinaiticus originally had it. Then Scribe D got upset, and wanted to (or had to) take it out. But he made a bunch of mistakes and, possibly while under a time crunch, he took out those verses.

You know the result. After Sinaiticus was published, people all over the world started writing notes in their Bibles that a part of the word of God didn't really belong. Some of you even have that note in your King James Bibles. You know why? Because the Devil wanted you to doubt, even when God's words were right in front of you. Pretty sneaky, huh?

15

Is that Your Best Job?

When I taught elementary school, I have to say that most of my kids worked well in class. I like the practice of the "One Minute Manager," to catch them doing something good, and compliment them. I'd love to tell them "You did a good job."

But with the older kids, sometimes there would be that student who turned in a paper that he clearly did not work well on. It was filled with erasures, crossing out and writing again. And it wasn't a draft —it was supposed to be a final copy!

That's when I'd look at his work, then look at him and say, "Is that your best job?"

And he'd look sheepish and say, "No, Mr. Daniels." And I'd have him do it over again.

I've told you some about the Sinaiticus, the book that changed Bible *believers* into Bible *doubters*, almost overnight, starting in the 1860s. I've told you about the perfectionist, Scribe D.

But now I'm going to show you **another reason** why I believe Sinaiticus is **not** the document the experts have made it up to be, simply by letting you see it for yourself, up-close. Then ask yourself, "Was that their best job?" You'll be amazed at what you find out.

First, look at this scripture, about the sacrifices to the Lord, which are supposed to be perfect and without blemish: Malachi 1:8: "And if ye offer the blind for sacrifice, is it not evil? and if ye offer the lame and sick, is it not evil? offer it now unto thy governor; will he be pleased with thee, or accept thy person? saith the Lord of hosts."

Now, let me ask you a simple question. If you were offering your ***very best*** to the emperor, what would it look like?

In *Codex Sinaiticus: The Story of the World's Oldest Bible*, David Parker wrote this:

> ...it has been claimed that the Codex may even have been written at the emperor's express command. The reason for this is a passage in Eusebius' Life of Constantine.

And he quotes the Roman Emperor Constantine's command to Eusebius back in the early 300s AD:

> We make known to you that you are to commission fifty volumes which are to be bound in leather, easy to read and (for convenience) portable. They are to be written by craftsmen who are both calligraphers and used to working accurately. They are to be copies of the divine Scriptures, which you well know must be available for reading in church.

At the end of all this, Eusebius wrote:

> Thus the emperor instructed. Action immediately followed word, as we sent him threes and fours in curiously worked bindings.[46]

---

46. *Codex Sinaiticus: the Story of the World's Oldest Bible* by D.C. Parker (London: The British Library, 2010), pp. 19-20.

Is that Your Best Job?

Listen to those parts very carefully. Constantine commanded 50 volumes, made how?

- To be bound in leather
- Easy to read
- Portable.
- Written by craftsmen who are (get this):
    a. Calligraphers (an artistic writer)
    b. Used to working accurately (remember that)
- COPIES of the divine Scriptures
- Available for reading in church

Let me summarize the juicy parts: Many people have said that Sinaiticus *was* one of those 50 copies. And the only pictures of Sinaiticus we ever saw in our books were beautiful, perfectly set pages of text. I think those were typeset, not the original ones. But at the very least, they didn't show you what I've been showing you. Now to the points:

1. The Sinaiticus isn't bound in beautiful leather. In fact, from the time in 1859 when Tischendorf brought it out of Egypt, it had NO covers at all! So no one could check to see if it were a beautiful, ancient bound text or a modern counterfeit.

2. Easy to read? That is only if you have a single text that you are reading. I've shown you the work of ***Scribe A with D correcting***, and the piles of ***words written into margins***, words written over other words, the erasures, etc. That is NOT easy to read.

3. Portable. Let me remind you that the facsimiles we have now of Sinaiticus are 5% smaller than real-life and they're pretty heavy. Not exactly something you can carry with you to prayer meeting.

4. Written by craftsmen who are calligraphers. That much is possible. Scribes A, B1, B2 and D did form letters that you can read.

5. But "used to working accurately"? I'm not sure you could call what they did "accurate."

Let me stop here and show you what the text of much of Sinaiticus looks like from a distance. Then let me show you close-up what is really going on.

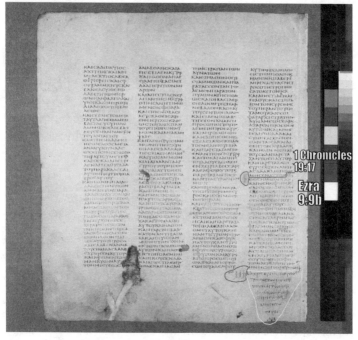

Figure 38 - Page in 1 Chronicles where it jumps to Ezra

See that upside down triangle of words? In English, it says this:

Is that Your Best Job?

> At the sign of the three crosses is the end of the seven leaves which are superfluous and not part of Esdras.

That's referring to the 19 chapters of 1 Chronicles said to be duplicated here, that I talked about in Chapter 8: "Why You Can't Trust Sinaiticus."

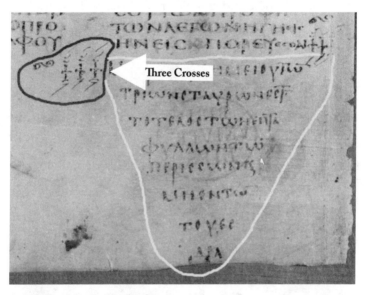

Figure 39 - Detail of page with missing section notes

There are so many wrong things here.

First, it admits that there are seven leaves —seven folia, 14 pages of 1 Chronicles – that are "superfluous," which really means "they're extra, and don't belong there." But they didn't *take them out* and *fix* them!

Second, see those three crosses at the bottom near the triangle? It says that, where the sign of the three crosses is, is the end of the seven leaves. But it's not down there. It's up above, where I drew the line.

128 *Is the 'World's Oldest Bible' a Fake?*

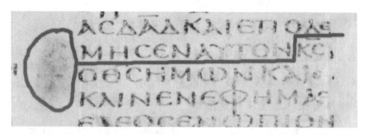

Figure 40 - Spot in text where missing section belongs

Third, look at left of that line. That circle next to it is around something smudged out. Can you see it? It's a cross! But it's not the three crosses from the note. They're down at the bottom. And there's another set on the right side of the note, as well!

So, even the ***note*** about the ***mistake*** is a ***mistake***. Yes, this is a big mistake. But there are also little mistakes all throughout Sinaiticus even in the Psalms that I told you were beautiful.

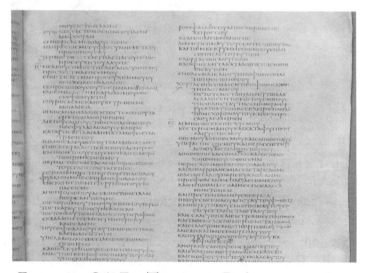

Figure 41 - Q59 F4r. This page in Psalms appears clean from a distance

Is that Your Best Job?

But they have mistakes if you look closely.

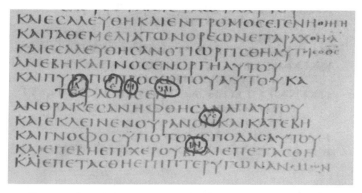

Figure 42 - Q59 F4r. Detail of page above showing inserted corrections

It doesn't matter how you slice it, or where you look. Let's face it: it's ***nobody's*** best job, not even Scribe D. And it's ***not*** a *final* job, either.

*That's why the mess called Sinaiticus is all the more surprising to me, now that people have carefully scanned every page and put it on line, so I can finally look at every page for myself. It doesn't look like the final work of any real "scribe" at all. It looks more like a messy term paper in the middle of corrections. It looks like a **draft** copy, before they knuckle down and make a **real** Bible.*

If you turned that writing in to your teacher, you'd get an F. He'd say, "Don't give me your draft. Give me your final copy."

I no longer think that Sinaiticus was one of Constantine's 50 Bibles. So why *is* Codex Sinaiticus in this messed-up condition? That gets into my conclusion, and that's for another chapter. In the meantime, aren't you glad you can simply ***trust*** what God put in plain sight?

We have God's preserved words —in English in the King James Bible. It's easy to read. It's portable. It's beautiful. It's accurate.

And best of all, *it's scripture. EVERY WORD OF IT!*

16

Uniquely Bad

In Bible College I was taught the lie that the scholars of Alexandria were the best in the world. So their copies of scripture were also the best in the world. I bet many of my readers were told that, too.

And we were told that the best examples of Alexandrian scholarship were the giant ancient books, Codex Vaticanus and especially Codex Sinaiticus. Do you realize we were told this, but we were never able to **see** Sinaiticus for ourselves? Think about what that means.

It means that not only did we have ***blind faith*** in Sinaiticus, a book we'd never seen... We also had ***blind faith*** in our professors. Faith in God is one thing, but everyone else? Remember the scripture: Romans 3:4 "...yea, let God be true, but every man a liar...." Or the paraphrase: In God we trust: all others pay cash.

I trust God. I want to trust my Bible, too. Don't you? I only want the words of God.

So if you place your trust in Alexandrian scholars, here's a heads-up. I'm about to show you some mistakes in Codex Sinaiticus, that are not found in 5,700 other manuscripts. Could Sinaiticus be the draft copy for something else? Or could it have been a rush job? Let's look at the evidence.

I'm not sure about your experience, but for me, in Bible college, seminary and about 8 other colleges and universities, I've found that the intellectuals were the *first* people to change things to suit their own opinions. The average Christians, who feared God, were way more likely to make sure they **don't** change a word of what God said.

When you fear God, you want to please Him over yourself. Not so with many scholars. Remember, it was the "scholars" who disputed with Jesus. "…the common people heard Him gladly" (Mark 12:37).

We were presented the "oldest and best," as if they had the right to change the historically preserved scriptures. And yet, we were not even allowed to see it, until just a few years ago, 2009, when it came online.

And a word of warning: don't trust the English translation you find on the Codex Sinaiticus.org website. The translation that they provide is not of the actual Sinaiticus.

So here are some mistakes in geography: Jesus came back to Nazareth of Galilee in Matthew 13:54: "And when he was come into *his own country*, he taught them in their synagogue, …"

"Country" in Greek is *patrida*. Sinaiticus changes *patrida* to *antipatrida*. Antipatris is a different city, 46 miles away from Nazareth of Galilee —in Samaria! "He was come into his own Antipatris?" That makes no sense!

Here's Nazareth, and here's Antipatris.

Uniquely Bad 133

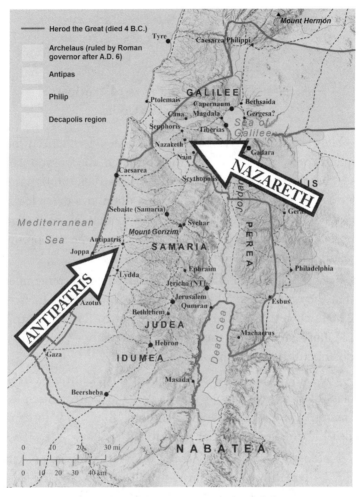

Figure 43 - Map showing Nazareth and Antipatris

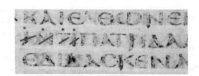

**Figure 44 - Q74 F4v, with the word "Antipatris"
(*Antipatrida*) in the Codex**

Here's that word Antipatris in the codex. I enhanced the image, here, and drew over the editor's marks so you can see them better. Note that another scribe struck through the letters "ANTI" and marked it with a dot above every letter that had to be changed. That was one way that mistakes were noted in the Sinaiticus. It's almost like someone was proofreading the text before the final edit.

Scribe A had read enough New Testament to remember that the only place you find this word Antipatris is in Acts 23:31, when the Roman soldiers brought Paul to Antipatris. He must have written these words from memory, not from a document in front of him.

You know, I made the same type of mistake in my Greek class over 33 years ago, when at first I confused "disciple," "*mathetes*," for Matthew and confused "John" and "Jordan." But I learned to pay closer attention after that.

Here's another one that ***really is*** about Samaria, in Acts 8:5: "Then Philip went down to the city of Samaria, and preached Christ unto them." That's obvious. This is the section of Acts about Samaria. Every manuscript of Acts 8:5 in the world says "Samaria"—except Sinaiticus.

Scribe A of Sinaiticus wrote "Caesarea," 24 miles away, on the sea coast. People fault the Book of Mormon for confusing Jerusalem and Bethlehem, and that's only six miles apart. This is four times as far. And remember, it's the *only* place that mistake has ever been found.

Figure 45 - Q87 F3v, Correction of *Kaisaria* to "Samaria"

As you can see, the corrector was clever. He put the three dots above the KAI of KAISARIA, then added a little MA in the middle, SA MA RIA, to make SAMARIA.

It's a great editor's mark, but I can tell you as an author — you don't want editors' marks in your final publication. The first printing of one of my early books had editors' marks in it. But unlike Sinaiticus, we fixed it.

I already told you about how it said Nazareth was in Judaea and not in Galilee, 70 miles away. That was in Chapter 14, "Deleted on Purpose."

So how about something else intriguing? In 2 Timothy 4:10, Paul wrote that the disciple Crescens had departed to "**Galatia**." That agrees with all manuscripts, except for four minuscules (that means written with lower case letters): #81, #104, #326 and #436, and Codex Ephraemi Rescriptus. These five, instead of "Galatia," say "**Gallia**" —meaning Gaul— right across the English Channel from Britain. That's over 1,200 miles off the mark!

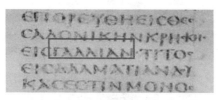

Figure 46 - Q86 F4v, 2 Timothy 4:10 "Gallia" instead of "Galatia"

Here's where it gets interesting. #81 had been examined by... Constantin Tischendorf. And Ephraemi Rescriptus had just been deciphered for the first time by... Constantin Tischendorf, in 1840-1843, one year *before* coming to St. Catherine's monastery in the Sinai Peninsula.

Could Tischendorf have had something to do with the making of the fake Codex Sinaiticus?

I tell you, the Sinaiticus is starting to look like one of two things: a rough draft, or a rush job.

If it were a book draft, the final copy would have only one 1 Chronicles, not two, Ezra wouldn't start in chapter 9, Isaiah wouldn't be all marked up, nor would Nehemiah. They would have fixed the folia from Mark 15 to Luke 1, so the words weren't all either squeezed in or spread out.

But if it were a book draft, where's the final copy? They certainly would have time for that in a monastery. They're supposed to be separated for "the Lord's work." They'd have nothing but time.

Right?

So how come we have never seen another codex like Sinaiticus, ever? Something that valuable would certainly have been kept somewhere. But there is no clear evidence of this book's existence, anywhere, before 1844.

Uniquely Bad 137

That would leave the second possibility: a rush job. But a rush job for what? What were they trying to do? Who would believe that this horrible mess of a document is a more reliable and ancient Bible than the traditional text?

Wait a minute. They ***DO*** say this horrible mess of a document is more reliable than the traditional text! Almost every Bible in the world has been ***changed to match it***, along with a few other Alexandrian-type Bibles they have found over the years. So it ***DID*** work, after all.

It's beginning to look like this document may have come into existence a short time before 1844. Who knows why a third of the Old Testament was removed? They clearly had some unknown reason for removing 1/4 of the Bible books. That will take further research.

Then someone aged the remaining Old Testament pieces, to make it look like the parts were separated or fell apart, and someone hid some of the evidence away, or reused it somehow. But remember, they got certain books of the Apocrypha, which is something they wanted.

Let me close the chapter with this:

The plot is thickening like hasty pudding. But I don't mind.

I don't have the problems that so many scholars have.

I have no position to lose at a university or college for questioning Sinaiticus.

I have no church board that will kick me off for suspecting it's not genuine, and that the Bibles made from it or using it are actually defective.

It won't hurt me if Sinaiticus goes down, along with the Bible-doubting footnotes and translations of most Bibles all over the world since the 1880s, even ones being translated by Wycliffe and Summer Institute of Linguistics (SIL) and the United Bible Societies (UBS) while I speak.

I don't trust Codex Sinaiticus, or a single reading in it.

I trust what God didn't *hide* in a corner.

I trust His preserved words through faithful, common Christians, through the centuries from the northern, Antiochian, stream, carefully translated for us in English in the King James Bible.

And I think the truth is going to sink the Titanic —the Sinaiticus.

That Bible-doubting ship, it's going down.

17

How Old Is It Really?

In my King James Ryrie Study Bible, Charles Ryrie's note on Mark 16:9-20 reads like this:

> These verses do not appear in two of the most trustworthy mss. [manuscripts] of the NT, though they are part of many other mss. and versions. If they are not a part of the genuine text of Mark, the abrupt ending at verse 8 is probably because the original closing verses were lost. The doubtful genuineness of verses 9-20 makes it unwise to build a doctrine or base an experience on them (esp. vv. 16-18).

Can't you just feel the faith in God's holy words oozing out of his commentary? Yeah, I don't, either. But that is what I was taught. And that is what millions upon millions of Christians have been taught for decades. By reading the first chapters of this book, or watching my vlogs, you already know more than almost ***all*** of those people about Codex Sinaiticus, maybe even more than Ryrie!

So many people believed and do believe, as I was taught as well, that the Sinaiticus is "the oldest complete Bible in the world." Well, you already know Sinaiticus ***isn't complete***. About a quarter of the books are missing.

But what if I could show you *proof positive* that the Sinaiticus **wasn't** written in the 300s? And maybe I could show you one reason we know it wasn't written before the mid-400s, either. What if I could prove from the Sinaiticus itself, that it isn't any older than the 1300s?

I've shown you how the "oldest and best" is not the "best." Now, would you like to see how it isn't the "oldest," either? I've told you before that the New Testament of the Sinaiticus was complete —all 27 books are in it. But there are two extra books: the *Epistle of Barnabas* and the *Shepherd of Hermas*.

Barnabas is complete. But the *Shepherd of Hermas* is in pieces. How long has it been that way? It doesn't seem like such a big mystery, after you learn what I found out.

In 1844, Tischendorf made his first journey to St. Catherine's monastery in the Sinai Peninsula.

Figure 47 - Lithograph based upon Porfiry Uspensky's description of St. Catherine's Monastery

15 years later when he talked about it, all Tischendorf said that he saw were some pieces of the Old Testament, and he

took 1/3 of what he saw, 43 leaves. That went to his patron, Frederick of Saxony.

Figure 48 - Constantin Tischendorf in 1844

But the next year, in 1845, Russian Orthodox religious official Porfiry Uspensky came to St. Catherine's. Both then and again in 1850 he saw the Sinaiticus, and wrote about it, describing it in terms that show he saw all that Tischendorf would describe 14 years later.

I and my fellow researchers, Steven Avery and Mark Michie, wanted to know *what* Uspensky wrote. But none of us knows Old Slavonic. Thankfully, a missionary to Ukraine, John Spillman, got it translated for us, from Old Slavonic, into Russian, then into English. We were pretty excited! This may be the first time this has ever been openly translated into English. Even so, I'll just point out the important parts for us now.

Figure 49 - Porfiry Uspensky

Uspensky wrote:

> The best Greek manuscripts are stored in the priors' cells [the head monks' rooms]. There are only four of them, but they are very precious for their antiquity, rarity and handwriting features, for their content, for the elegance of the beautiful faces of the saints and entertaining drawings and paintings.
>
> The first manuscript, containing the Old Testament which was incomplete and the entire New Testament with the *epistle of St. Barnabas* **and the book of Hermas,** was written on ***the finest white parchment*** in the fourth share (one sheet folded over to make four pages) of a long and a wide sheet.

Did you catch the "finest white parchment"? And did you note that he didn't say "part of *Hermas*"? Remember, he said "the Old Testament" was "incomplete," then talked about "the entire New Testament with the *epistle of St. Barnabas* and the book of *Hermas*."

I'm just summarizing. He wrote in a lot more detail than I'm giving. But it sounds to me like in 1845 and 1850, The *Shepherd of Hermas* was... or seemed... *complete*! Remember that. " ... All the sacred texts were written in four and two columns ... and so together as if one long utterance stretches from point to point."

As you have seen, Sinaiticus has either two or four columns, and all the words connect without spaces. Uspensky went on: "Such a formulation of letters ... the way of the writing of the sacred text, invented by the Alexandrian deacon [Euthalius] about 446 AD, and soon abandoned due to the many gaps between the columns on the expensive parchment, prove that this manuscript was published in ***the fifth century***."

It was strange that Uspensky spent time telling about Sinaiticus in great detail, yet Tischendorf later implied that Uspensky was ignorant. I think Tischendorf didn't want anyone to believe what Uspensky was saying. Uspensky further states that Euthalius the deacon of Alexandria came up with that way of writing in columns like you see in Sinaiticus and Vaticanus, but it was only done for a short time. And this change in formatting didn't start till at least 446 AD.

In his simple, detailed analysis, Uspensky gave evidence that Sinaiticus was no earlier than the middle 5th century! That's ***100 years too late*** to be one of Constantine's 50 Bibles decreed in 330, or to qualify as the "the oldest and best." At ***450*** AD, that puts it at the same age that people date the only other possibly ancient Alexandrian codex, Alexandrinus.

So now we know the Sinaiticus can be no older than *450 AD*.

But wait. Vaticanus was **also** made like that, with three columns instead of 4, and lots of empty space. That means Vaticanus can't be older than *450 AD*, either! So neither Sinaiticus nor Vaticanus could have been one of Constantine's 50 Bibles. And both are no older than they say Codex Alexandrinus is.

But we're not finished. Now it gets *really* interesting. Let's go back to the *Shepherd of Hermas*. Many people say the *Shepherd of Hermas* was originally composed no earlier than about 130 AD, and maybe not later than the 160s. And it was originally written in Greek. But all we had for the longest time were Latin copies.

There is a codex called Vaticanus 3848, dated in the late 1300s AD. There are a few others, of about the same date. There's the Dresden Codex, dated in the 1400s. These pretty much seem to have been made from the same Latin text.

But there is one unusual one. It's called Codex Palatinus 150, in the Vatican Library. This Palatine Codex made some changes, and clearly added more *Latin* terms so that it was different from the other translations of *Hermas*.

But no one in the West had ever seen *Hermas* in Greek, aside from small quotes out of it by proto-Catholic Church Fathers like Origen, up until 1855. In 1855, a man claimed that he came from Northern Greece, from a place called Mount Athos that was filled with 20 Eastern Orthodox monasteries. He said that he found a rare Greek copy of the original *Shepherd of Hermas*!

He got somebody to buy his copy of *Hermas*. And in 1856 it was published at Leipzig, and thus called Codex Lipsiensis.

But Tischendorf was shown it, and he had his doubts about the text. He said there was no way it could be an original form of the Greek. He said it back-translated Latin words into Greek, and gave a number of examples. That changed the date of the Lipsiensis forward to the late 1300s, the date of the Palatine Codex. That's because the Greek words were clearly based off of certain Latin words that were only in the Palatine Codex version of *Hermas*, not the others.

Then a man who claimed to be the manuscript seller's partner came forward. He said "Don't believe him. He's a con man and a forger!" It was claimed that the seller sold supposedly ancient manuscripts from 1843 to 1856. People all over Europe suddenly felt conned. They trusted this man as a scholar. He had claimed he found hidden ancient treasures on Mt. Athos. And they paid top dollar for them.

That man who sold the manuscript was Constantine Simonides.

Figure 50 - Constantine Simonides

Here's a limerick to help you remember Constantine Simonides.

There once was a man called Simonides.
With him scholars once all felt at ease.
But when he was "exposed,"
They all felt disposed
To dispose of his supposed antiquities!

The people believed the brilliant scholar, Tischendorf. People stopped believing the "brilliant forger" Simonides, But then, three short years later, Tischendorf reversed his view. Why? Because he had just come from St. Catherine's with a pile of Greek Bible parchment. And in that parchment was… the *Shepherd of Hermas*! But now, according to Tischendorf's story, it was only **part** of *Hermas*! But just as important, now Tischendorf said Codex Lipsiensis wasn't messed up after all, but was actually 1000 years older than he had previously thought!

You know why? Because the parts of the *Shepherd of Hermas* that were in the Sinaiticus were almost **identical** to the Codex Lipsiensis that Simonides sold. Once again, people believed Tischendorf. Why would he lie? And it was big of him to sort of admit that he was a **bit** mistaken before.

And they said, "Thank you! At least we know this ONE manuscript is genuine." And because of Tischendorf's endorsement of Simonides' Hermas, Simonides' reputation was at least partially restored.

Why is this story important? Because of what I am about to show you. How can we find out if what Tischendorf said was true? And at which time? Tischendorf said two opposite things. Another scholar named James Donaldson wrote

How Old Is It Really?

in 1874, saying that Tischendorf was right the first time.

Let me show you why I know the Sinaiticus is even newer than 450 AD! I've even got the photos to prove it! The best way to prove the character of a text is to see where it came from. That's why one way to group texts has been to see who repeats the same mistakes. If you have a text that makes the same changes in numerous places as another text, those two are probably related.

There are only so many copies of the *Shepherd of Hermas*. But of all of the manuscripts available in those days, only one makes the mistakes that were in Simonides' Hermas. Could those same mistakes also be in the Sinaiticus? Let's check!

Donaldson's first objection was that a lot of the words in Simonides' *Hermas* (Lipsiensis) are actually more modern Greek words, and not ones he has ever found in such abundance in any ancient Greek manuscript. These include, in Donaldson's words, "a great number of words unknown to the classical period, but common in later or modern Greek."

I'll just show you the list, both with modern Greek letters and in the Sinaiticus font. You are welcome to look for them yourself, at *www.codexsinaiticus.org*.[47]

---

47. This chart is largely derived from *The Apostolical Fathers: A Critical Account of Their Genuine Writings and of Their Doctrines*, by James Donaldson (London: Macmillan and Co., 1874), pp. 388-391.

Simonides' Hermas	Sinaiticus Greek Form
βουνος	ΒΟΥΝΟC
cυμβιοc (as wife)	CΥΜΒΙΟC
πρωτοκαθεδριειc	ΠΡΩΤΟΚΑΘΕΔΡΙΕΙC
ιcχυροποιω	ΙCΧΥΡΟΠΟΙΩ
κατεπιθυμω	ΚΑΤΕΠΙΘΥΜΩ
αcυγκραcια	ΑCΥΓΚΡΑCΙΑ
καταχυμα	ΚΑΤΑΧΥΜΑ
εξακριβαζομαι	ΕΞΑΚΡΙΒΑΖΟΜΑΙ

"The lateness of the Greek appears also from late forms; such as

αγαθωτατηc	ΑΓΑΘΩΤΑΤΗC
μεθιcτανει	ΜΕΘΙCΤΑΝΕΙ
οιδαc	ΟΙΔΑC
αφιουcι	ΑΦΙΟΥCΙ

(αφινουcιν in Simonides' Greek)

κατεκοπταν	ΚΑΤΕΚΟΠΤΑΝ
ενεcκιρωμενοι	ΕΝΕCΚΙΡΩΜΕΝΟΙ
επεδιδουν	ΕΠΕΔΙΔΟΥΝ
ετιθουν	ΕΤΙΘΟΥΝ

Figure 51a - Words that are common from later Greek[48]

---

48. The hyphen (-) is used to indicate where a word continues on the next line. The terms "ca," "s1" and "corr" refer to correctors of the Sinaiticus

How Old Is It Really? 149

Book Locations	Sinaiticus Location
Visions i.7	3:4 βουνουc
Visions ii.2	6:3 cυμβι-ω
	17:7 πρωτοκαθε-
	δριειc
	[ca: πρωτοκαθεδριταιc]
	3:2 ϊcχυροποιη-cι
	3:2 ειcχυροποιει
	20:3 ϊcχυροποιηcιν
	21:2 ϊcχυροποι-ειται
	22:3 ϊcχυροποιηcη
	25:5 ϊcχυροποι-ου
Visions iii.2	10:2 κατεπιθυμιc
Visions iii.9	17:4 αcυνκρα-cια
Visions iii.9	17:2 καταχυματοc
Mandates iv.2	30:3 εξακριβαζο-μαι

Visions i.2	2:3 αγαθωτατηc
Visions i.3	3:4 μεθιcτανι
οιδαc not found;	found 3:2 οιδα
Visions iii.7	15:1 αφιουcιν

Visions iii.2	10:7 κατεκοπταν
Visions iii.9	17:8 ενεcκιρωμενοι
Visions iii.2	10:5 επεδιδουν
Visions iii.2	10:7 ετιθουν ειc
	10:7 ετιθουν μακραν

Figure 51b - Words that are common from later Greek

Simonides' Hermas	Sinaiticus Greek Form
"beside:	
ετιθεcαν	ЄΤΙΘЄCΑΝ
εcχαν	ЄCΧΑΝ
λημψη	ΛΗΜΨΗ
ελπιδαν	ЄΛΠΙΔΑΝ
τιθω	ΤΙΘѠ
επεριψαc	ЄΠЄΡΙΨΑC
ηνοιξαc	ΗΝΟΙΞΑC
ειπαcα	ЄΙΠΑCΑ
χειραν	ΧЄΙΡΑΝ
απλοτηταν	ΑΠΛΟΤΗΤΑΝ
cαρκαν	CΑΡΚΑΝ
cυνιω	CΥΝΙѠ
cυνιει	CΥΝΙЄΙ

"And some modern Greek forms, such as
κραταουcα **for** κρατουcα, ΚΡΑΤΑΟΥCΑ
have been corrected by the writer of the manuscript.
...
ειc **is continually used for** εν
as

εχουcιν τοπον	ЄΧΟΥCΙΝ ΤΟΠΟΝ
ειc τον πυργον	ЄΙC ΤΟΝ ΠΥΡΓΟΝ

"...and peculiar constructions, as

cπουδαιοc ειc το γνωναι	CΠΟΥΔΑΙΟC ЄΙC ΤΟ ΓΝѠΝΑΙ
απεγνωριcθαι απο	ΑΠЄΓΝѠΡΙCΘΑΙ ΑΠΟ

"And we have a neuter plural joined with a plural verb,
κτηνη ερχονται"   ΚΤΗΝΗ ЄΡΧΟΝΤΑΙ

Figure 52a - Words that are common from later Greek

Book Locations	Sinaiticus Location
Visions iii.2	10:6 ετιθεcαν
Visions iii.5	13:1 εcχαν
Visions iii.10	18:6 λημψη
Visions iii.11	19:3 ελπιδαν
Visions i.1 ; ii.1	1:3 τιθω
	5:2 τιθω
	23:4 επεριψαc
Visions iv.2	23:4 ηνυξαc [?]
Visions iv.3	24:7 ειπαcα
	[ca: ειπουcα]
Visions v.[5?]	25:1 χιραν
Mandates ii.	27:1 απλοτη-ταν
	[ca: απλοτητα]
Mandates iv.1	17:3 cαρκαν
	[ca: cαρκα]
Mandates iv.2	30:1 cυνϊω
Mandates iv.2	30:2 cυνϊει
Visions iii.8	16:3 κραταουcα
	[s1, corr: κρατουcα]
Visions i.1, 2, 4; iii 7, 9	
Visions iii.9	15:5 εχουcιν το-πον ειc τον πυρ-γον
Visions iii.1	9:2 cπουδεοc ειc το γνωνε [ca: cπουδαιοc]
Visions ii.2	6:8 απεγνω-ριcθαι απο
Visions iv.1	22:5 τε κτηνη ερχοντε

Figure 52b - Words that are common from later Greek

A second proof that Donaldson gave was that there were Latin words transliterated (copied letter-for-letter) into Greek, instead of regular Greek words. When I looked at his example, I found they were all from the same verse, *Hermas* Visions 3:1, which online is listed as *Hermas* 9:4. Here is the page marked out for you:

Figure 53 - Q93 F2v. Page showing Latinized words inserted in Greek text

And here are the enhanced detail shots:

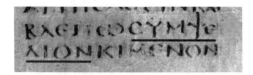

Figure 54 - Detail of "*sumpselion*" in first column

Figure 55 - Detail of "*kerbikarion,*" "*lention*" and "*karpasinon*" in the second column

Please note on the second line here, that Scribe B2 actually started writing ***kai e*** on the previous line, then forgot he wrote it, and started all over again on the next line with the full ***kai epano***. It pays to pay attention.

But now we come to ***maximum overkill***. As I said, all but one of the Latin translations of the *Shepherd of Hermas* are pretty much the same. But one stands out: the Palatine Codex 150 of the Vatican Library.

And one example above all convinced me that Simonides' Lipsiensis and the Sinaiticus Hermas both seem back-translated from the Vatican Palatine Codex: Visions ii.3. There is more than one numbering system. Online it's called *Hermas* 7:4.

154   *Is the 'World's Oldest Bible' a Fake?*

Figure 56 - Q93 F2r. Page showing mistaken term *"maximo"* for *"magna."*

As Donaldson showed, it's *supposed* to say "But say thou, behold, great tribulation cometh." In Latin, great is "magna." In Greek, great is "megale." And "thlipsis megale" is exactly the term "great tribulation" used three times in the New Testament.

But the Vatican's Palatine Codex changed **"*magna*"** to **"*maximo.*"** That's like changing "great" to "greatest." Or, Maximo could be the name of a person, "Maximus." Either

How Old Is It Really?

way, it's the wrong word. Guess what Simonides' Lipsiensis says? Maximo!

Guess what the Sinaiticus did with the Greek? It also transliterated Maximo!

Figure 57 - Detail shows the verse with the Latinized term, "*maximo.*"

In fact, in Donaldson's words, "Now we find that the text of the Pastor of Hermas found in the Sinaitic codex is substantially the same as that given in the Athos manuscript. The variations are comparatively slight."

He also wrote:

> Then there is a considerable number of passages preserved to us in Greek by Origen and other writers. The Sinaitic Greek differs often from this Greek, and agrees with the Latin translation, especially the Palatine.

And there isn't anything earlier they could have copied.

So Codex Sinaiticus is a fake, a phony, a counterfeit. It is not from 350 AD. It is not from 450 AD. And it couldn't have been made before 1350 AD.

Sinaiticus is not the best. And it is not the oldest. It is ***AT BEST***, a medieval fake. And I think that it was made, in a bit of a rush, not long before 1843 AD.

So much for Ryrie's doubting note. This takes down one of his "most trustworthy" manuscripts. And Ryrie is not the only one. This doubting note appears in most of the other modern Bibles in one way or another.

But I don't have to look for a hidden book in a monastery (Sinaiticus). I don't need Rome to give me a partial Bible, hidden by monks (Vaticanus). My God gave me His book in plain sight. The faith-building, God-exalting, sin-busting, Gospel-preaching, 400+ years tried, tested and proved King James Bible.

Don't leave Rome without it.

18

What Did Constantine Want?

Do we have the Bibles Constantine wanted? How can we know? Look at the Sinaiticus. I never could see the Sinaiticus for myself in Bible college or at Fuller Seminary in the 1980s. Almost no one could, just about anywhere, until these last few years.

Go to www.codexsinaiticus.org, click "see the manuscript," and look at it! And when you look at it, look carefully. Notice all those corrections, the missing words, phrases, verses —not in the New Testament only— but also in the Old Testament. It's all over the place! Don't take my word for it. Don't just trust me. Don't trust your professors, either. Look at the pictures yourself. Click from page to page, book to book. See it for yourself.

This is the first time non-scholars have been able to. And you have no idea how long it's going to last. Then, when you have spent some time studying it, ask yourself this: "Did the copyists believe they had the words of God?" How could they? They were marking it up and correcting it all over the place! So if *they* didn't believe they had the words of God, then why should *I* believe that they did?

Sometimes simple questions lead to powerful answers. Want to ask some questions with me? When you were growing up, did you ever say, "If I were king…"? Well, what if you were the head of a giant empire? And what if that empire had pagans and Jewish people and a bunch of different groups called Christians? How would you unite your empire?

Well, I can tell you what Constantine wanted. He wanted to unite the Roman Empire in the early 300s AD. As emperor, he was the Pontifex Maximus, the guy who sets the religious calendar. That made him the guy who had the empire united in its national holidays and sacrifice schedule.

Then, he had himself declared to be "the Bishop of Bishops," basically the first pope. That meant he could try to unite these Christian groups, as well.

In 324 AD, Constantine laid the plans for a new capital city for his empire. He picked Byzantium, the border city at the northwestern part of Turkey, on the east side of his empire. And he named it after himself, Constantinople. Six years later, in 330 AD, Constantine finished it and moved his stuff from Rome to Constantinople.

The next year, in 331 AD, he summoned Eusebius of Caesarea, his lapdog, and commanded him to get together 50 Bibles. Listen again to Constantine's words:

> We make known to you that you are to commission fifty volumes which are to be bound in leather, easy to read and (for convenience) portable. They are to be written by craftsmen who are both calligraphers and used to working accurately.
>
> They are to be copies of the divine Scriptures, which you well know must be available for reading in church." And then Eusebius wrote,"… we sent

What Did Constantine Want?

him threes and fours in curiously worked bindings.

What did Constantine want? Would you think that Constantine wanted 50 different, disagreeable Bibles? Think about it. That story is still around today. Some of you have professors in Bible college or seminary, like I did, who will tell you that Sinaiticus and Vaticanus were likely two of Constantine's 50 Bibles.

Even the "Fifty Bibles of Constantine" Wikipedia page shows images of Sinaiticus and Vaticanus. Check it for yourself. Ask yourself: Was this Constantine's grand scheme to unite his empire? With 50 Bibles that didn't agree with each other?

Does that story, that professors tell to this day, even make sense? Remember, Constantine said: "They are to be copies of the divine Scriptures…" I think he just wanted 50 copies of the same Bible. It makes sense. If I were emperor, and 50 different Bibles were sent to me, I'd say, "You didn't do your job…" and then I'd fire them. But first, I would have to ask, "So which one is the right one? Which one do I trust? Which one is the one God promised?" And if they said, "All of them," I'd say, "You mean your God can't give me just one single copy of His word that I, the emperor, can totally trust?" Who can I trust, then?

And you know what they would have to say? Trust a priest, the pope, or a scholar (or set of scholars.) They'd be telling me to put my trust in man; that I couldn't just trust in God and His words. Because if a man convinced me not to trust God, then all I'd have left to trust in would be that man! Remember, the Sinaiticus and the Vaticanus don't agree with each other. They only have two basic things in common:

1. They add the Apocrypha and other words of men, added as if they were scripture. That raises ***their*** value, but it lowers the value of actual scripture.

2. They disagree with the preserved texts which we find in the King James and other preserved Bibles. But they also disagree with each other, which means you cannot go to them, or either one of them, as your absolute authority, no matter how hard you try.

I know. I tried for years! I trusted my professors. My own doctrines began to change, and waver, as I became my own textual critic, "weighing" the various readings. To my professors it meant giving more "weight" to what disagrees with the King James and other preserved Bibles, even if there are only two of them, and less "weight" to whatever agrees with the King James, even if there are a thousand of them!

I read Metzger's discussion points: "A Textual Commentary On the Greek New Testament" and the committee's votes to rate which reading was "most likely" true. Yes, they decided scripture by voting on the readings, based on "textual criticism" and their own prejudices.

If their goal was faith, they failed, both then and now. But if their goal was never-ending doubt, they succeeded.

Remember Kirsopp Lake, the photographer of Sinaiticus? He said: "In spite of the claims of Westcott and Hort and of Von Soden, ***we do not know the original form of the Gospels, and it is quite likely that we never shall.***" He wrote that after he had photographed Sinaiticus starting in 1910!

Did the Sinaiticus lead him to faith, or doubt?

Doubt!

Let's go to another Constantine, Constantin Tischendorf.

What Did Constantine Want? 161

His college professor convinced him that he didn't have God's preserved words. So he wanted to find them somewhere hidden in a monastery.

He wrote to his fiancée, Angelika: "I am confronted by a sacred task, the struggle to regain the original form of the New Testament." He believed he had lost God's words! He said he wanted the "oldest and best." Instead he found a jumbled mess. At best he found a draft copy. At worst he found a counterfeit. And that's only if he did "find" it and didn't come up with it, himself.

Let's go back to the first Constantine. Why would the emperor want a bunch of Bibles that were not the same, that disagreed in important points, and that had piles of erasing and correcting and rewriting and notes and excuses? Does that make sense to you? If you were the emperor, and wanted to unite your empire, you wouldn't want 50 disagreeing Bibles. You'd want 50, carefully prepared, skillfully executed, identical Bibles, wouldn't you? And that's what Constantine the emperor asked for.

What was Constantin Tischendorf looking for? What did this second Constantin want? Tischendorf knew that Eusebius had written: "…we sent him threes and fours in curiously worked bindings." What could that mean? Threes and fours? It could mean:

1. Sending three or four Bibles at a time.

2. Three or four books to add up to one Bible —one for Law, one for Prophets, one for Writings and one for the New Testament.

3. Three or four Bibles to a shipping crate, or…

4. Written in three or four columns to a page.

Did Tischendorf invent the three or four column idea? He sure made it popular. I can imagine him thinking: "Let's see. Vaticanus has three columns. Maybe I can find one with four columns! In my four years of going to monasteries in Europe, I've found added or taken away words and phrases and verses. And I've written them down. Maybe I can find another, older Bible that has those same added to or taken away words and verses! I'll be famous!"

He really was trying to come up with another ancient Bible that would make him famous. Read his biographies. Nobody disputes that fact. Isn't it amazing that in that jumbled mess he called the Sinaiticus, he found exactly that? He found the same unique readings he had been discovering in various manuscripts, but in ONE —sort of— Bible! Imagine that! What a coincidence!

And he found them right after he decided there had to be one more Bible for him to find, since the others (the Alexandrinus, the Vaticanus, and the Ephraemi Rescriptus —that rewritten one that he had just deciphered,) were already well-known!

And he found them in the *first* place he went after he saw the pope and Jesuit Cardinal Mai in the Vatican the year before, in 1843 —and then raised some money. And he found them in a place so remote, that everyone would be forced to believe his own testimony, since there were no easy-to-produce witnesses to verify what he said. Imagine that!

Maybe I should start all over again and ask: "If I were a scholar and I wanted to produce a fake Bible that would make me famous, what would I do?" Maybe that will get me closer to the truth. What did Constantin [Tischendorf] want?

I am so glad I don't have to worry about whether Tischendorf was deluded, a liar, a con, or incredibly naive. I'm glad I don't have to search the ends of the earth to find the words of God hidden somewhere. God made sure His words were right here in front of me. Proverbs 17:24 "Wisdom is before him that hath understanding; but the eyes of a fool are in the ends of the earth"—or maybe a monastery in the desert.

19

Sinaiticus and the Zombie Apocalypse

I could not believe what happened this morning. There I was, walking quietly, stepping carefully, hoping that nobody would notice me as I stealthily crept by the people around me. I had no idea what I'd stumbled into. I was right in the middle of a field of zombies!

No, I wasn't dreaming. As a matter of fact, I was wide awake! I had unknowingly stumbled into a website full of New Testament textual critics! I even found the rotting corpse of one of my old professors at Fuller Seminary! And I'm sorry to say it, but this largely came to pass because of that mess of contradictions and errors known as Codex Sinaiticus.

I'm not talking about *movie* zombies. I'm talking about the *real* ones, the dry husks of people who teach in theological seminaries. I've never seen a zombie movie in my life. But this weekend I watched a review of one. And I think they get their material from theological seminaries.

I prayed for a year before I entered Fuller Seminary that God would keep me away if He didn't want me to get my Master's degree there. I visited one day and met the president's secretary, and to my surprise found out she didn't believe in Old Testament miracles!

Well, I then talked with some professors, and found out they were almost all *evolutionists!* They believed that Genesis 1-11, the basis of all Christian and Jewish belief about sin, righteousness, and judgment, was a *poem* and nothing more.

Creation scientist Henry Morris once changed my life by saying if you don't believe Genesis 1-11, you have no reason to believe John 3:16. If there was no "first Adam," then Christ can't be the "second Adam."

I only had two professors at Fuller who actually still believed the Bible. Both of them were women: Julie Gorman, who took the scriptures as literally as she could; and Dean Meye's daughter, Marianne Meye Thompson, who confided to our class the extremely controversial fact that she had found a way to actually believe the Apostle Peter wrote 2nd Peter!

Imagine that!

I had Dr. Ralph P. Martin, who said "That wouldn't hurt your faith, *would it?*" when I pointed out in front of class how his re-translating "from the beginning" in Luke 1 would make Luke not written until the 2nd century AD.

I also had Don Hagner for New Testament class. He would always read passages directly out of his Greek Critical Text, and then offer his interpretation as we went into each topic.

Well, guess what? I found a zombie munching on *Hagner's* brains on a website just this morning! I hear that zombies feed on other people's brains. One movie claimed that was how they could absorb the memories of a person. That is what I found this morning.

Some guy was making a paper about the beliefs of Don

Hagner about the Pastoral Epistles, 1 and 2 Timothy, and Titus. This article showed that after I went to Fuller, Hagner slowly started doubting that Paul wrote some of the letters in the Bible with Paul's name on them. He called them "pseudonymous"—that means "fake name." He believed that some guy used Paul's name, but wasn't Paul, and probably wrote after Paul died.

This is a real quote from the article:

> I don't get the impression that he [Hagner] has confidently changed his stance on authorship, but has edged over the line, so to speak, with the balance of evidence ever so slightly disposing him to a rather agnostic position of pseudonymity.

So professors and pastors spew out words like "pseudonymity," but say people can't understand "thee" and "thou"? Such hypocrites. Anyway, another article was about Bart Ehrman, the assistant to Text Critic Bruce Metzger, who disbelieves in the whole Bible.

Other "scholarly" papers included these doubt-producing questions:

• Could Jesus read?

• Does the gospel of Mark even teach that Jesus is God? Or is He just a human messiah?

• How Jesus became God, and whether His resurrection was historical or just "eschatological."

• Did the Council of Nicea invent the idea that Jesus was God?

• Was 1 Peter written much later, after Peter's death?

This is what I've been telling you about. It's not

"Bible-believing." It's Bible ***doubting and disbelieving.*** You see, it's ***important*** to me how Jacob felt, after he wrestled with facing his brother Esau... and how he wrestled with God the Son the night before.

It's ***important*** how Job felt, while listing out all the many things he did for the hurting people around him, before he was confronted with the Living God speaking out of the whirlwind.

And it's ***important*** that God's Son, the Lord Jesus Christ, said, "Heaven and earth shall pass away, but my words shall not pass away," in Matthew, Mark and Luke. These guys think it's fair game to debate when Jesus "became God"!

How did this start? Mark 16:9-20 is missing from Codex Vaticanus —and was changed with a cancel sheet to be missing those verses in Codex Sinaiticus. So, as it says in one Sinaiticus book, if Mark is the first Gospel written, and it doesn't contain the resurrection, maybe the other gospels and books just made it up! And they believed that lie, because Sinaiticus was supposed to be, "the oldest and best."

But you need to know this: Codex Sinaiticus was pretty much accepted as-is, no questions asked. They accepted Tischendorf's word that it was from the fourth century, 300s AD, even though his ***claiming*** that early date is what made Tischendorf a superstar. That sounds like a ***motive*** for his claiming that Sinaiticus was old, doesn't it? They have never even scientifically tested the animal skin parchment or the age of the inks!

And what did they get? To ***us***, it is a really sloppy, erased, rewritten, corrected and re-corrected, ripped apart, colored and partially hidden document. But to those who criticize the Bible, the textual critics, it's a gold mine! Everything you could ever want, to endlessly pick at, and dice and slice, and devour.

And the more you trust those zombie text scholars, the more zombie-like *you* get. Until finally, one day, you become just like them, doubting everything, and wanting to devour other people's brains, to see if there is any other way you can slice and dice the Bible!

2 Timothy 3:7: "Ever learning, and never able to come to the knowledge of the truth." And yet *the true Jesus of the Bible*, God the Son, our Lord and Saviour Jesus Christ is He "Who will have *all men to be saved*, and to come unto the knowledge of the truth." 1 Timothy 2:4.

God *never* wanted you to be a Bible-doubting scholar. There is *not a single benefit* to doubting God or His words *anywhere* in scripture. Don't catch that zombie-making virus! Like in 2 Kings 4:40, "there is death in the pot."

But Jesus said, in John 5:39-40: "Search the scriptures; for in them ye think ye have eternal life: and they are they which testify of me. And ye will not come to me, that ye might have life." Life is why Jesus came. He wants us to have *eternal life*, starting right now.

Those Bible doubting scholars, in ever-growing numbers, have justified their disbelief, starting with publishing the Sinaiticus in 1862. And all they leave behind them is a mass of either *dead bodies*, or *spiritual zombies*.

I graduated from Fuller in 1987. And gradually, the Lord delivered me from the zombie-making virus of doubt. Eleven years later, on November 30th, 1998, the Lord brought me to a fullness of faith that *He had preserved His words*, and that those words were preserved in Classic English *in the King James Bible*. 400 years, tried, tested, and proved.

And just like Romans 1:17 says, I went "from faith to faith," believing God and trusting Him more and more every day.

Don't believe Bible-doubting professors. Don't trust their doubt-inducing Sinaiticus. It's a trap to make you a spiritual zombie. Many of them are walking dead people, devouring the life out of anyone who comes too near. Give them the truth, just as you would anybody else. But don't follow them. Follow Jesus.

Matthew 8:22: "But Jesus said unto him, Follow me; and let the dead bury their dead."

20

It's A Job

On a beautiful summer's day in 1983, on a mountain hike in Washington State with my linguistics professor, he told me why he became a missionary linguist. It wasn't because he wanted to reach the people with the gospel and give them God's word. It was because he was a linguist and liked to work with languages. And Bible translation was one career where he could go somewhere neat and "do" linguistics.

In other words, for him, it's not a calling; it's a job. Where else are you going to get people to pay you to "do" linguistics research on little-known people groups, in exotic locations all over the world?

There are only so many university positions for linguists. What if you want to explore and do "new" language studies, write groundbreaking papers, and have them published in journals, and get a reputation? Or what if you just don't like the humdrum of 9-5 life? Well then, Bible translation may be right for you.

All you have to do is sign the Statements of Faith of various churches and organizations, repeat the right words, raise the money, and poof! You're off! Then when you get onto the field, you can "do linguistics" to your heart's content! And you never actually have to evangelize anyone with the gospel. You just have to do your job.

So what if they found out they were translating the wrong Bible? If they have no qualms about the other lies, this one won't bother them, either. How could anybody expect a guy who doesn't believe the scriptures to give up his or her job in defense of the truth? So, I have nothing much I can say to those people, except, "You need to get saved."

But now, what about the sincere Christians? What about the people who do live by a moral code, and try to have some integrity in their life? There are plenty of them in the midst of all this Bible translation work, as well.

Have you ever thought about how much people would have to give up, if they were to admit the truth about Sinaiticus being a fake and the Bibles made from it being perverted? What if they were to admit that God kept His promise to preserve His words through history?

Let me give you a glimpse into how big this really is. Just a few years ago I learned about the missionary linguist Karl Grebe. He trusted the people at Wycliffe/SIL (Summer Institute of Linguistics), to tell him what Greek New Testament he was permitted to use. You see, he was translating the Bible for a group in Cameroon. And they said he must use the UBS (United Bible Societies) Greek text to translate the New Testament.

Bible translators don't just translate from English. They also get some basic Greek training so they can use a Greek text and linguistic manuals provided by the agency, to help them make new Bible translations. You may not know this, but since 1966, translators have not been allowed to use the King James or the Greek Received Text, which was a foundation for the King James.

They have to use the UBS text, because the Protestants, Baptists, and Roman Catholics agreed to use just one Greek text for the sake of unity.

Grebe never planned to work with Roman Catholics, but it didn't matter what he thought. Because of that 1966 agreement, eventually he had to work alongside Roman Catholic priests, to edit Apocryphal books that are nothing more than folk tales that he didn't believe in, to be part of their Roman Catholic Bible. He had to do it. It was part of his job.

But what if he said, "No"? Then he'd be out of a job! All those decades of work in Cameroon, for what?

But also realize this: that UBS Bible text itself, that he was forced to use, was a joint text made with Roman Catholics. It had changes that differed from the preserved Bible, because of that fake Sinaiticus manuscript with all those changes favorable to Roman Catholic pagan doctrines. So it was a double-whammy. This issue of which Greek text to use clearly affects the Bible translators on the mission field and everywhere else.

But notice it also affects the modern textual scholar. Remember, it was the textual scholars who told Grebe which text to use. What if they figured out they were basing their work on a fake Greek text? Now, we have to think of the larger picture to understand the situation where we find a modern textual scholar.

He or she, like thousands of other scholars, may have spent years poring over the intricacies of textual corruption and correction, carefully analyzing the quality of ancient papyrus and vellum parchment, figuring out in what order scribes erased and corrected the text, creating theories about what was behind the many changes, and on and on. These people have a lot of interesting investigative work to do, when they work with the corrupted Alexandrian-type texts.

But if they were to acknowledge the preserved Bibles as God's words, they'd be admitting that the best text is one that is "static." It doesn't change. It is what God said in a particular language, nothing added, nothing taken away. They could study textual ***preservation***, but would have no reason to study ***perversion*** or alteration of the text. There are almost no differences of any merit in the Received Text manuscripts. So there would only be so many people who could or would be able to get a job investigating it.

The majority of highly-trained text scholars would be out of a job. And who would hire them to look at some tiny differences, when we already know what words God wanted written? It's like a forensics team analyzing a room where no crime has been committed. What good will that do? Who will pay them for that? What's the use?

So knowing that, think of this: Who would hire them if they were to openly admit they believe that God preserved His words? Or that the texts in front of them are ***counterfeits*** and unworthy of their time and effort, much less their faith. Remember who gave them their jobs.

Bible translation agencies have been bound by agreements with the Roman Catholic religion since 1966. But this is what struck me: It is much, much larger than missionary Bible translators. How many people are there, wrapped up with this corrupt Greek text? How many careers are we talking about?

There are not just linguists out on the Bible translation field. There are also linguists at home, who train those linguists to go out onto the field. And there are the support teams, the editors, and the publishers of those corrupt texts.

Then it gets larger. There are universities and colleges who employ linguistic professors, philologists (who study ancient languages and writings) and other text experts. There are Bible societies who license all the translations to the publishers, almost all of whom have agreements with Rome.

There are publishing companies who sell all the Bibles based on the counterfeit texts, and keep selling one new version after another, at least a few per year, in multiple languages.

Then there are the stores who sell those Bibles, the marketers who make the advertising for each new Bible as it comes down the pike. That's more merchandise for everyone from Amazon to Wal-Mart!

That's a LOT of money —and a LOT of jobs. But it doesn't stop there. What about the pastors? For many, their denominations or "fellowships" have stated what Bibles they can or cannot use.

Think of what would happen if the pastor suddenly held up one single Bible and said, "These are the words of God. This is the one Bible we all have to obey. No other Bible will be allowed in this congregation. They're all based on a counterfeit text."

Even with the right Bible, there could be a cost. Some people could leave. Their denomination or board could fire them. What about the youth ministers, who seem to spend a lot of time telling young people the King James is too hard, and offering up every new fad Bible to excite the youth? Same for them. Again, we are talking a lot of jobs, all over the earth.

This bait-and-switch plot began 150 years ago, to give a corrupted, counterfeit Bible, largely based on the missing and changed words of the Sinaiticus. And it has grown into a huge, worldwide deception, involving thousands, even millions of people.

But in all sincerity, I would say to all of these people: "What's more important, your standing in your job, or your standing in front of Jesus at the Judgment?"

I know that some of them, maybe many of the people I've listed, don't even **believe** in a Judgment Day. That really does not matter. God is not subject to our belief in Him. And the Judgment Day will still come, whether we want it to or not.

It may be a big coincidence, but the end-time Babylon is something that is so big, that lots of people, including believers, will be in it.

But the Lord calls them out in Revelation 18:4: "And I heard another voice from heaven, saying, Come out of her, my people, that ye be not partakers of her sins, and that ye receive not of her plagues." And it may be another coincidence, but Revelation 18 then lists all sorts of jobs and all the business that will be lost when Babylon falls. And in Revelation 18:13, that includes "the souls of men."

Your soul is very important. Don't treat this whole Sinaiticus issue lightly. If you check for yourself and find that even a few of the facts I have presented are correct, that means the entire Bible translating, producing, teaching, preaching and believing multitudes are believing lies that were placed there by someone.

Both the Bible, and the Bible translation agencies, are very specific about who that "someone" is that agreed upon those lies and placed that lying text in people's hands: The Roman Catholic System.

It's not just a job. There are souls of men on the line. Count the cost, carefully.

21

No Doctrine Affected?

The Codex Sinaiticus was the Greek manuscript that tipped the balance away from the historical, preserved Bible and changed hundreds of scriptures in crucial places. Did you know that Sinaiticus casts doubt on the resurrection of Jesus Christ?

See it for yourself!

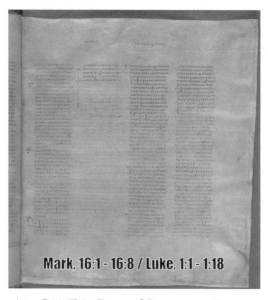

Figure 58 - Q77 F5r. Page of Sinaiticus showing gap in text missing Mark 16:9-20

No Doctrine Affected?

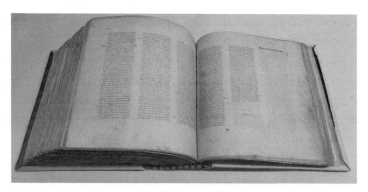

Figure 59 - Vaticanus pp. 1302-1303, showing gap in text missing Mark 16:9-20

See those blank spaces? Neither Sinaiticus nor Vaticanus in its present form contains Mark 16:9-20. Do you know what that means? For the last 150 years, to a textual critic, or a Bible-doubter, it has meant two things:

1. Jesus in His resurrected body is ***not*** in the Gospel of Mark. Textual criticism then claims that Mark is the first gospel, not Matthew. That would mean that the first Gospel did not have a resurrected Jesus.

2. They say, since Mark was the first gospel written, then the whole doctrine of Christ's bodily resurrection is ***not*** part of the ***original*** Gospel. They say it was added later, by the church! That's funny. Jesuit-educated Norman Geisler said "none of these [changes] affect any basic doctrine of the Christian faith."[49]

I think the resurrection of Christ is a pretty basic doctrine. Don't you? Want to see more of what happens when you trust the Sinaiticus, and how you can answer those critics?

---

49. *A General Introduction to the Bible* by Norman L. Geisler and William E. Nix (Chicago: Moody Press, 1968), First Printing, p. 375.

I know that it's essential to their theories that Mark has to have been written first.

Everywhere, even in Wikipedia, they will tell you that it was in the 5th century, the 400s AD, that people got the idea that the gospels should be "Matthew, Mark, Luke and John," in that familiar order. They even go on to list what they say are 5th century documents that have that order.

But what they ***don't tell you,*** *that would hurt their theory* —is that their beloved Sinaiticus and Vaticanus are *also* in the order of Matthew, Mark, Luke and John! Shh! Don't tell them I told you. Let them look it up for themselves!

But they don't stop there. What comes after the resurrection? The ascension, right? Get ready for this. The Sinaiticus and Vaticanus obviously don't have the ascension from Mark 16:19, since they remove verses 9-20. But Sinaiticus doesn't stop there. It does not have the ascension of Christ in the Gospel of Luke, either. Here is the page of Sinaiticus that has Luke 24:51.

No Doctrine Affected? 179

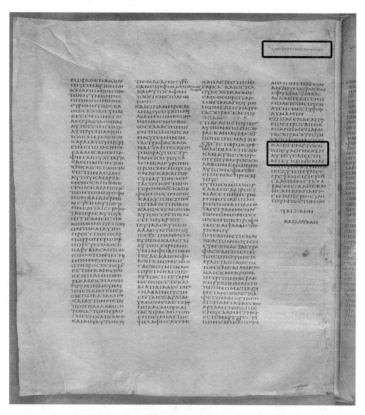

Figure 60 - Q79 F7v. Page showing missing phrase in Luke 24:51

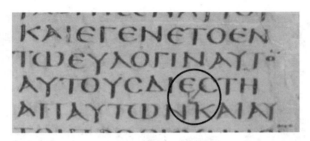

Figure 61 - Arrow showing spot for missing phrase

It says in English: "And it came to pass, while he blessed them, he was parted from them." But can you see that arrow? That refers to words at the top of the page.

Figure 62 - Missing phrase in top margin of page

They show the rest of the verse: "and [was] carried up into heaven." But you can see it for yourself that it was *not* something the original scribe wrote in the text. Someone wrote it,

No Doctrine Affected? 181

in a different ink, at the top of the page.

What does this mean? Let me ask you: once you remove Mark 16:9-20, in how many other verses of the four Gospels do you find Christ's bodily ascending into heaven? Just this one. So if Luke 24:51 doesn't belong, according to 20th century text critic C.S.C. Williams:[50] "…there is no reference at all to the Ascension in the original text of the Gospels."

It's a one-two punch! They say Mark is the first Gospel. Their Sinaiticus/Vaticanus Mark is missing the bodily resurrection. So they say the doctrine of Jesus' resurrection from the dead is a later addition.

But there is no ascension left in Mark, either. Then here in Luke 24:51, Sinaiticus is missing the ascension into heaven of our risen Saviour. So they say the doctrine of Jesus' ascension into heaven is ALSO a later addition!

Oh, and let me add that by "first gospel," they also meant that the "first gospel" was written about the year 80 AD, after the fall of Jerusalem and after most of the Apostles and eyewitnesses were dead.

Still think no basic doctrine of the Christian faith is affected? Now let's turn the tables on the text critics. Please get out a King James and look at Luke 1:1-3. It's important. "Forasmuch as many have taken in hand to set forth in order a declaration of those things which are most surely believed among us,"

Luke says that "many have" written accounts of the Gospel story. So there were Gospels —plural— before Luke wrote.

---

50. C.S.C. Williams was a textual critic and the author of the 1951 book, *Alterations to the Text of the Synoptic Gospels and Acts* (Oxford: Blackwell, 1951).

Verse 2: "Even as they delivered them unto us, which from the beginning were eyewitnesses, and ministers of the word;" Here Luke said that eyewitnesses back to the beginning ***were still alive***, and ministered the word, and passed the information to Luke and others. So they were obviously still alive for the earlier gospels, like Matthew and Mark.

But text critics like my old professor, the late Dr. Ralph Martin, said Luke was written in the ***2nd century, after they all were dead!***

Verse 3: "It seemed good to me also, having had perfect understanding of all things from the very first, to write unto thee in order, most excellent Theophilus," So Luke took it in hand to check on the story from the very first scene, talking with eyewitnesses, and to write it down in order as it happened.

So get this, these modern scholars are calling the very first verses of the Gospel of Luke a lie! Do you trust Luke, or the text critics? Now go to Acts 1:1-2. You need to see this. "The former treatise have I made, O Theophilus, of all that Jesus began both to do and teach," Nobody I've found disputes that the same guy wrote both Luke and Acts. Luke here is referring to his Gospel.

Verse 2: "Until the day in which he was taken up, after that he through the Holy Ghost had given commandments unto the apostles whom he had chosen:" Whoops! "Until the day in which He was" what? "Taken up!" Luke just told us his gospel ENDS with the ascension! Imagine that!

The original New American Standard, from 1963 until 1994, actually removed those words from Luke 24, "and was carried up into heaven," copying Sinaiticus! They may have copied the Westcott and Hort 1881 English Revised Version and 1901 American Standard Version. But that's no excuse for taking out God's words. So the Lockman Foundation translators followed the Sinaiticus on this —even though Vaticanus and Alexandrinus **and almost every other manuscript in existence** has those words! And on top of it, Luke himself **TOLD** us they were there!

Who are you going to believe, the text critics, or the author Luke himself?

Gail Riplinger pointed it out in *New Age Bible Versions*. People saw the blunder. And in 1995 an embarrassed Lockman Foundation released the Updated NAS with even more mistakes, but —they put the ascension back into Luke 24:51.

So Sinaiticus is wrong. The text critics were wrong. And someone removed those words, gutting the doctrine of Christ. I think I see Satan's claw prints.

Here's the summary:

1. Only Sinaiticus and Vaticanus remove Jesus' bodily resurrection and ascension, by removing Mark 16:9-20.

2. Only Sinaiticus —not even Vaticanus— takes away Jesus' bodily ascension into heaven out of Luke 24:51, the *only* reference to Jesus' bodily ascension in the four gospels.

3. Two of the most basic, foundational doctrines of the Christian faith, Jesus' physical resurrection and Jesus' physical ascension into heaven, are totally removed from crucial Gospel passages in the Sinaiticus.

Then unsuspecting Bible college students, the future pastors and leaders, are taught that they don't belong. Then they will teach those same Bible-doubting lies to their congregations or classes.

It's just another step in creating a Bible flexible enough for anyone to believe in: one world Bible for one world religion. This is the fruit of textual criticism. And this is the fruit of trusting Sinaiticus. If this is what the pro-Sinaiticus guys want, they can have it. I refuse to bow down.

I'm going to trust God's holy and preserved words in the 400+ year tried, tested and proved King James Bible supported by thousands of manuscripts that agree. Let them show me their doubt based so heavily on one or two confusing documents, and I'll show them my faith. And we'll see who stands on the judgment day.

22

Prove It!

I was so excited to learn Biblical Greek! I bought every Greek text and Greek help I could get my hands on. Even after I graduated Fuller Seminary in 1987, I kept buying the newest Greek helps and texts.

My Nestles 27th edition Greek New Testament was edited by people like Kurt and Barbara Aland,

Figure 63 - Barbara and Kurt Aland

Jesuit Carlo Maria Martini,

Figure 64 - Pope Benedict XVI with Jesuit Cardinal Carlo Maria Martini

and the famous Bruce Metzger.

Figure 65 - Bruce Metzger

This Nestles 27th edition Greek New Testament was the Greek text that determined almost every single translation of the New Testament done in the world today, whether Roman Catholic, Orthodox, Protestant or Baptist. No translator working with the United Bible Societies, Wycliffe Bible Translators, Summer Institute of Linguistics, or any other of hundreds of groups, was allowed to use other than this official text —that is, until the Nestles 28th edition came out in 2013!

Figure 66 - Mark 1, noting Codex 2427 references

Figure 66 is the Gospel of Mark. I've done some shading here. Take a look at the bottom of the right page. Do you see all those dark spots? That continues throughout the Gospel of Mark. We find it about every place an important textual reading is found from one source, Greek Codex 2427. It's rated Category I. I'll explain that in a minute. But that Greek text was considered so important that it could never be ignored for any change in a word, phrase or verse in the Gospel of Mark.

*So why am I telling you about this? Because... it's a **FAKE**!! What does this fake codex have to do with Sinaiticus? Its story teaches us specific lessons about how to detect a forgery. And Sinaiticus, well...*

As I said, Codex 2427 was rated Category I. Here is the description, straight from Kurt and Barbara Aland in their textbook on textual criticism, *The Text of the New Testament*:

> Category I: Manuscripts of a very special quality which should always be considered in establishing the original text (e.g., the Alexandrian text belongs here). The papyri and uncials [capital Greek letters] up to the 3rd or 4th century belong here almost automatically because they represent the text of the early period....[51]

So according to Kurt and Barbara Aland, if it is Alexandrian text, or if it was dated by someone as being 3rd or 4th century, it is almost always called Category I.

In fact, look at this! There's the last page of **2427** right there in the textbook, across from the definition of ***Category I!***

---

51. *The Text of the New Testament: An Introduction to the Critical Editions and to the Theory and Practice of Modern Textual Criticism*, 2nd Edition, by Kurt and Barbara Aland, translated by Erroll F. Rhodes (Grand Rapids, Michigan: William B. Eerdmans Publishing Company, 1987, 1989), pp. 158-159.

Prove It! 189

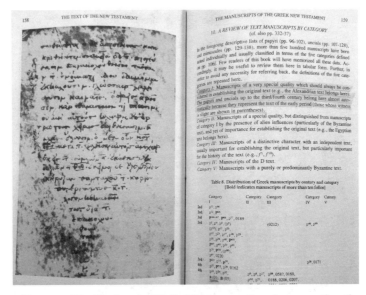

Figure 67 - Codex 2427 (left) as a textbook example of Category I (right)

Codex 2427 is a tiny codex. It has only the Gospel of Mark, along with little painted illustrations. Here is a quick look at 2427.

Figure 68 - Codex 2427

Figure 69 - Pages of Codex 2427 with illustrations

Figure 70 - Codex 2427 is a miniscule (written in lower case letters)

Here's where it gets interesting. It's dated as 14th century, 1300s, and yet it's Category I. Why is a 1300s text supposedly one of the best? Because it is almost completely the same as the text of the Codex Vaticanus —you know, the one text that, along with Codex Sinaiticus, is used to make almost all the changes in modern Bibles.

Vaticanus is an Alexandrian text. And any manuscript matching that Alexandrian text is Category I, so… 2427 is also Category I.

My professor's professor, Ernest Cadman Colwell, gave 2427 its other name. He called it "Archaic Mark," archaic, as in "oldest and best." He said it preserved a "primitive text" of the Gospel of Mark.

Figure 71 - Ernest Cadman Colwell with Edgar Goodspeed at the University of Chicago.

In Figure 71 we see him (left) with Edgar Goodspeed. Goodspeed, who made his own Bible, is the guy who acquired 2427 for the University of Chicago.

To the text scholars it seemed like some scribe in the 1300s AD had a copy of Mark that was *almost identical to Mark in Vaticanus*. Then he copied it down. But this Mark was *completely different* text from the other Greek Bibles written in the 1300s.

So, Ernest Colwell, Edgar Goodspeed, Kirsopp and Helen Lake (photographers of Sinaiticus in 1910) and Kurt and Barbara Aland, all bought into Minuscule Codex 2427. People were saying it might be the *closest thing to the original Gospel of Mark!*

Figure 72 - Kirsopp Lake in 1914

Figure 73 - Kurt Aland with pope John Paul II

Figure 74 - Barbara Aland

We know that every Bible manuscript is a copy of something. But of what? Professor Colwell wondered about that, but he never figured it out. A few people suspected it was possibly a fake. Colwell said, "Everything about 2427 was wrong."

But you saw those 2427 references in my Greek New Testament. Thinking it was fake didn't stop their agenda. They said it was one of the most important "witnesses" to the "original" gospel of Mark! It influenced their textual decisions for years!

But think about it: this codex of Mark had *something for everyone*.

For **palaeographers** (ancient writing experts), it had an unusual handwriting. It was sloppy and rather inconsistent. The experts couldn't figure out what century it belonged in, from 1300s to the 1700s.

Figure 75 - Codex 2427 colored illustrations

For art history students, it had "illuminations." That means paintings that illustrate the Gospel story. For text critics, it had words that were *like* Vaticanus, as well as words that were ***strangely different***, and even ***three sets of missing words*** that were baffling. But no one could prove if 2427 was genuine or a fake; ***until 1989***, when a chemistry professor named Mary Virginia Orna noticed that Archaic Mark had a lot of "iron" or Prussian blue pigment in the pictures. She did tests on it and proved it was so. Prussian blue!

Figure 76 - Professor Mary Virginia Orna

Why does that matter? Because Prussian blue was not around in the 1300s. It was invented in 1704, and not available for sale until the 1720s! So now 2427 could *not* be from the 1300s. It would have to be *after 1720*.

But there's more. No one could prove where it came from, called its "*provenance*," before it was found in the collection of a Byzantine collector, in Athens, Greece, after he died in *1917*.

But there was *more*. In 2006, Margaret Mitchell of the University of Chicago made high-resolution digital photos available online for the first time! Then regular people could look at the codex and try to figure out the mysteries.

Figure 77 - Margaret M. Mitchell with 2427

A few years later she asked Abigail Quandt, an expert in rare books and preservation, to restore and analyze 2427 and send it out to be tested.

Figure 78 - Abigail Quandt

These are the results:

1. The Prussian blue is not a later touch-up. Nobody retouched the manuscript. So the codex ***had*** to be made after ***1704***.

2. They also found synthetic ultramarine blue. It was only available as a pigment since the 1820s. So the codex ***had*** to be made after ***1820***.

3. The white was a zinc white. So it had to be made after ***1825***.

4. But then they found another pigment that was fluorescent, called zinc sulfide. This was part of lithopone. It was made by a special process, but not until ***1874***. So our 1300s miraculous witness to the Vaticanus was actually made when? After 1874! So much for "oldest and best."

But wait. What if they had found a really ancient manuscript and copied it? Wouldn't that be the same as if it was made in 1300? Isn't a copy of an ancient copy of Mark just as good as an ancient copy??

Then it's important that we find out what 2427 is a *copy* of! That's where Stephen Carlson comes in.

Figure 79 - Stephen Carlson

Carlson had been working on another supposed copy of Mark. He wanted a careful analysis of 2427. Back in the summer of 2005 he found out Margaret Mitchell had put the whole thing online, so he went to work.

As he did, he ultimately found three verses of Mark: 6:2; 8:11; and 14:14; where there were so many words missing that it looked like the writer accidentally skipped a whole line of text three times while copying. But it wasn't short lines, like in the Vaticanus. It was wide lines, like a modern printed book.

He thought that if he could find a book with those *exact missing words* from 2427 on one line of text, that would prove his theory and show him which book the writer copied!

Vaticanus didn't work. Too few words on a line. Westcott and Hort's text didn't work. Tischendorf's 7th and 8th editions of the New Testament didn't work.

Where was that book? And when was it made?

He went through Washington D.C. libraries, checking critical editions, like Lachmann's and Jesuit Cardinal Mai's, but no luck. In 2006 he wrote the missing words on note cards, and he checked Bibles in Jesuit Georgetown University and the Library of Congress. Nothing. Finally he went to the Catholic University of America. He went through about a dozen Bibles, and then he hit pay dirt!

He found out that it was a copy of this particular edition of the Greek New Testament, by Philipp Buttmann.

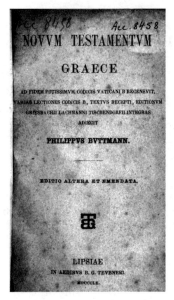

Figure 80 - Philipp Buttmann's Greek New Testament (1860)

Here's what happened. Jesuit Cardinal Angelo Mai had control over the Vaticanus for many years. He kept

Tischendorf and Tregelles from seeing it, as much as possible while he prepared his own edition for publication. It came out in 1857 and 1859. It was close, but Mai made a number of mistakes.

One guy duplicated those mistakes. He had never seen the actual Vaticanus, so he couldn't know. That man was Philipp Buttmann. He copied Mai's errors into his copy of Mark.

But he was a scholar, so he couldn't stop there. He also had about 85 other "personal choices" for the text that didn't read like either Mai or the Vaticanus in Mark. Then he published his Greek New Testament in 1860. He probably rushed it to be first.

But in 1867 Tischendorf's Vaticanus came out, and it was way better than Mai's. And nobody wanted Buttmann's mistakes. So they bought Tischendorf's Vaticanus. Buttmann's New Testament was going into the trash can of history. Except that sometime between 1874 and 1917, an enterprising forger grabbed Buttmann's copy to make his fake ancient Gospel of Mark.

We know that because he not only repeated Cardinal Mai's mistakes. He also copied 81 of Buttmann's 85 "personal choices" for the text, as well! And no other manuscript in the world had those mistakes, plus those choices. And of course, his lines matched the three sets of missing words in 2427. It was settled.

But you know, nobody had to trust 2427 in the first place, if they had followed a couple of basic rules:

1. Provenance. Where did it come from? What was it like then? How do you know? Can you prove it?

2. Chain of Custody. Prove the evidence wasn't tampered

with. Where did it go? Who had it? Can you prove it? You want to know that what you have now is what they had then.

So provenance, chain of custody, chemical tests and checking which manuscript they copied. ***Guess how many of these rules they followed for the Sinaiticus?***

ZERO!!

1. No testing. I told you how they cancelled the April 2015 tests. ***Codex Sinaiticus remains untested.***

2. No master copy. We have never found a text that is like Sinaiticus. Vaticanus may be the closest, but it has thousands of differences.

3. No provenance. Remember, despite all the stories they make up about ancient catalogs and places where it's been, they're all out of whole cloth. The first time anyone ever is documented seeing the Sinaiticus or any part of it is 1844 with the parts sent to Frederick of Saxony, then 1845 when we know Porfiry Uspensky saw everything else that Tischendorf took from there later in 1859, and maybe a bit more.

4. No chain of custody. Only a few people ever even claimed to witness when Tischendorf had the Sinaiticus. And they said he changed it and aged it, to make it look older! Imagine that.

Did I mention that I don't trust the Sinaiticus —at all?

*What can you prove about Sinaiticus? It's **almost** like someone created it out of the air, to give textual critics and palaeographers something to analyze for years on end, and make them hunger to compare it with Vaticanus. There's no **proof** of **provenance** with Sinaiticus. It's almost **poof! provenance**, as Steven Avery says.*

But with the preserved Bible, proving provenance is easy.

Prove It!

There are thousands of copies that were found ***all over*** the ancient world, just like Jesus said in Matthew 24:14: "And this gospel of the kingdom shall be preached in all the world for a witness unto all nations…"

And those copies are so close to each other, that they are designated by a single letter, for the most part: ***M*** for ***Majority***. There are ***small*** differences, of course, but those were dealt with centuries ago.

Modern scholars HATE the preserved, Antiochian stream of Bible texts. They call them "Byzantine." There are ***over 1,200*** minuscules alone! But you won't see ***them*** listed in a critical Greek text.

According to Kurt and Barbara Aland: "These were omitted to restrict the list to manuscripts with a ***significance*** for textual criticism."[52] In other words, they won't have a job if all they have are the preserved texts to work with. They need major differences.

But ***we*** don't. All ***we*** need are God's words preserved through the chain of custody of faithful Bible believers, translated perfectly into our language. In English, it's the King James Bible.

When someone tries to say their Bible is better, I just say, ***"Please, prove it."***

---

52. *The Text of the New Testament*, p. 163.

23

I Trusted Them!

When my professors in Bible college told us about the amazing "oldest and best" Codex Sinaiticus, I couldn't wait to see it for myself. They told us that the text critics had already gotten *amazing information* off of it and copied it down for us.

But I *still* wanted to see what it looked like. If they're telling you *NOT* to trust your King James anymore because of what was in a book someone found, you kind of want to *look at the book*, don't you?

Here is a description of the Sinaiticus from the 2009 book by Janet Soskice, *The Sisters of Sinai*. It sounds virtually identical to what my professors said. "It contained *all the books of the Bible* as known to the modern world, and its weight was such that one man alone could not carry it. It was clearly *the product of a professional scriptorium of the highest order....*"

Then it says, "No manuscript of the Bible was *more complete or more ancient* —the Codex Sinaiticus (as it came to be called) antedating most known copies by almost 600 years."[53]

Now as you know from Chapter 16, it's missing a good fourth of the Bible. In addition, it has erasures, rewrites,

53. *The Sisters of Sinai: How Two Lady Adventurers Discovered the Hidden Gospels*, by Janet Soskice (New York: Alfred A. Knopf, 2009), p. 100.

I Trusted Them! 203

overwriting, corrections and marginal notes. And it's not nearly as ancient as people have been led to believe.

But back to my questions in Bible college in the 1980s. Where was this magical book? How could I see it? How could I get one? I looked it up in any dictionary or textbook I could find. Here is what we were able to see of the Sinaiticus.

Here is *Introduction to the History of Christianity*.[54]

Figure 81 - *Introduction to the History of Christianity*
p. 131, showing John 21

This one says, "This page from *Codex Sinaiticus* contains the last chapter of John's Gospel." Well, you know that's John 21.

---

54. The following illustrations are from *Introduction to the History of Christianity*, edited by Tim Dowley (Minneapolis: Fortress Press, 1977, Rev. 1990, 1995 ed.), pp. 131 and 135.

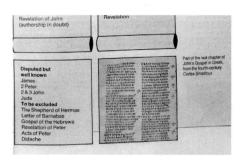

Figure 82 - *Introduction to the History of Christianity* **p. 135 showing the same page from Sinaiticus**

This page says, "Part of the last chapter of John's Gospel in Greek, from the fourth-century *Codex Sinaiticus*." Notice that they are both pictures of the ***same page!*** So far, we have seen John 21, just one page.

Now look at *A General Introduction to the Bible*, the book by Jesuit-educated Norman Geisler.[55] The same illustration is in the 1968 and 1986 editions, so I'll use the first printing.

Figure 83 - Same Sinaiticus page in *A General Introduction to the Bible***, p. 272**

55. *A General Introduction to the Bible*, by Norman L. Geisler and William E. Nix (Chicago: Moody Press, 1968), p. 272. In the 1986 edition, it's page 392.

I Trusted Them! 205

It says, "*Codex Sinaiticus opened to John 21:1-25 (British Museum.)*"

Anyone detecting a pattern? How about this one? *Archaeology in Bible Lands*.[56] What did it say in 1977?

Figure 84 - Same Sinaiticus page in *Archaeology in Bible Lands*, p. 82

It says, "Codex Sinaiticus opened to John 21:1-25 (British Museum)."

I started wondering if there was any other part of Sinaiticus to show, other than that one page. What is going on here?

Let me tell you a little story.

Diamonds were once rare and expensive. But in 1869 a diamond rush started. People began to find them all over.

According to the laws of supply and demand, diamonds should have been dirt cheap at that point.

But South African Prime Minister Cecil Rhodes, financed by the Rothschilds, got a bunch of diamond merchants together and made the De Beers Group. They stuffed their heaps of diamonds

---

56. *Archaeology in Bible Lands*, by Howard F. Vos (Chicago: Moody Press, 1977), p. 82.

into a bunch of warehouses, and only let out a few at a time.

That low supply and high demand made the price of diamonds stay high. People wanted them all the more, because they thought they were rare. But they couldn't have been more wrong.

The Sinaiticus pushers were just like this. Only they didn't hold back diamonds. They held back pages of Sinaiticus.

So just like me, the scholars heard stories and legends about the magical Codex Sinaiticus. But they never got to see it all for themselves. It stayed mysterious and someone else behind the scenes decided who could see what. Meanwhile, our teachers kept showing us its "more accurate" words, in their new official critical Greek texts, which slowly destroyed our faith.

*And more importantly for the Devil, they pried our hands off of the King James Bible and sold us a cheap, faith-destroying knock-off. They made it hard to see the Sinaiticus. So we were forced to just trust our teachers and all the scholars who **said** it was so great.*

Bye bye, Faith. Hello, Doubt.

It wasn't until 2004 that I finally got my first glimpse of Sinaiticus. And when I did, it looked like this.

Figure 85 - Tischendorf's 1862 facsimile of Sinaiticus

I Trusted Them! 207

This is an 1862 edition by Tischendorf.

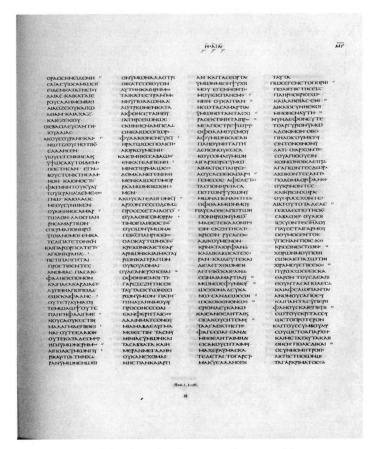

Figure 86 - Tischendorf's printed copy of Sinaiticus

This is Isaiah 1:1-27.

Do you see how neat and orderly that is?

Only that's not the actual codex. This is a "facsimile," which in 1860 meant Tischendorf made up letters for printing that looked like the letters from the Sinaiticus. And he had the fonts made in a bunch of different sizes, and quickly printed up editions of the Sinaiticus —only they were all cleaned up.

We had no idea that we had a typeset copy to look at, and not photographs of the real thing. So that was just a facsimile.

And this is the real thing.

Figure 87 - Actual photo of the same page in the original Sinaiticus

See a difference?

I Trusted Them!

Figure 88 - Close-up of the text on actual Sinaiticus page. Note the Arabic in the middle of the second column.

After seeing this close-up, can you honestly call the guys who created this mess "scribes of the highest order"?

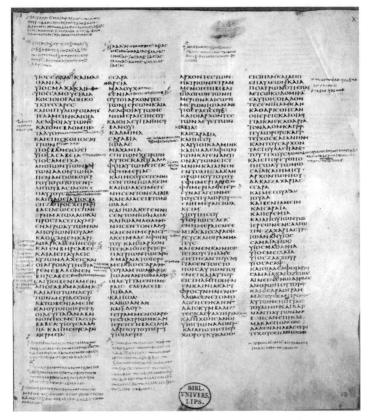

Figure 89 - Q36 f4r, 2 Esdras 21:15-22:37 in the CFA

Holding back pages like ***this*** tricked us into trusting our teachers. For all we knew, they had seen it for themselves. But maybe they ***hadn't***. Maybe ***they*** were tricked into trusting ***their*** teachers, as well!

I made such a huge mistake back then. I handed over my trust to my teachers. It should have stayed in my Bible. I think I was one of the few that had started out with a King James Bible.

I Trusted Them!

But from the very first day, the King James Bible was ***zeroed out and set aside***, in favor of ***whatever they liked*** — always based on the Sinaiticus and Vaticanus, of course.

We students, by trusting our teachers, also trusted that Sinaiticus was right when it removed words of the Bible. So we no longer had faith in verses about:

1. The story of the woman caught in adultery, John 7:53-8:11

2. The resurrection appearances of Jesus in Mark 16:9-20

3. The three Person Godhead in 1 John 5:7-8

4. The need to believe before being baptized in Acts 8:37

5. That Jesus is the only-begotten Son in John 1:18. Instead, we were taught that He was an only-begotten God. That's what the Jehovah's Witnesses teach!

Little by little our trust in basic Bible verses faded. That's why I bought all those Greek helps and critical notes. I could no longer be sure of what God said. And that wasn't because the King James doctrine was ever proved ***wrong***. Not at all! It was because I trusted my teachers, who ***said*** that the King James was wrong. I never actually ***saw*** the evidence for myself.

But now you can. After generations of people trusting the lying Sinaiticus, the evidence was finally made available to the public ***147 years*** after it was published. Since 2009, www.codexsinaiticus.org has been online. We have no idea how long it will be available. Please take advantage of it.

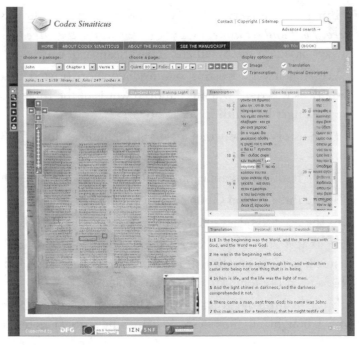

Figure 90 - Screen shot of John 1 in the Sinaiticus on www.codexsinaiticus.org

Check every picture I show you. Do what I could *not* do for over 30 years. See whether your professors and preachers are telling you the truth or not. That is my purpose in putting out the videos and this book for you to see. With all my heart, I want you to have ***FAITH***, not ***DOUBT***.

*If I had it to do all over again, I would NEVER simply trust my teachers. I would check up on **every** claim they made. It is too easy to trust a teacher. But it is hard to stand on the words of God, especially when you have to do it alone in a school, Bible college or church.*

I Trusted Them!

But as the Lord Jesus said in Luke 4:4, "It is written, That man shall not live by bread alone, ***but by every word of God.***" Guess what? Sinaiticus ***also*** took out "but by every word of God"! Those guys had no shame.

But I don't have to worry about any of that. The night I repented and came back to the Lord on August 24th, 1980, the Lord changed my life with this verse: Psalm 118:8 "It is better to trust in the LORD than to put confidence in man."

I trust every word of God, perfectly preserved and translated exactly in English in my King James Bible. Over 400 years it has been tried, tested and proved.

Accept no substitutes.

24

Three Big Mistakes of Text Critics

There are ***three really big mistakes*** that modern Text Critics make. You know, the guys who tell you what ancient, hidden manuscripts you should trust to change your Bible, because what was passed down through the ages isn't really "the Bible." They literally made up one thing, and they forget two things. See what they are, and judge for yourself:

1. Text Critics made up a rule. Then they judged the scriptures by that rule. And they didn't even get that rule *from* the scriptures. Think about this. The basic principle of Textual Criticism, "the harder reading is to be preferred," is not a rule that comes from scripture. It's exactly the opposite. God wrote things down, and had man write things down to make it easy, not hard.

Look at Luke 10:21:

> In that hour Jesus rejoiced in spirit, and said, I thank thee, O Father, Lord of heaven and earth, that thou hast *hid these things from the wise and prudent, and hast revealed them unto babes*: even so, Father; for so it seemed good in thy sight.

And God told us through the Apostle Paul in 1 Corinthians 1:26-29, what He has chosen:

> For ye see your calling, brethren, how that not many wise men after the flesh, not many mighty, not many noble, *are called*: But *God hath chosen the foolish things* of the world to confound the wise; and *God hath chosen the weak things* of the world to confound the things which are mighty; And base things of the world, and things which are despised, hath God chosen, *yea*, and things which are not, to bring to nought things that are: *That no flesh should glory in his presence.*

God doesn't reserve truth for the scholars. He makes things simple for us ordinary folks. God gave us the ability to check all things by scripture, and commanded it: In 2 Timothy 3:16, God said "All scripture *is* given by inspiration of God, and *is* profitable for doctrine, for reproof, for correction, for instruction in righteousness:" So we are to judge truth by scripture. We are to "search the scriptures" (John 5:39). But modern Bibles change even that verse, so it is not a command to search the scriptures. Ever wonder why?

God says to "Study to shew thyself approved unto God, a workman that needeth not to be ashamed, rightly dividing the word of truth," (2 Timothy 2:15). Modern Bibles change the word from "study," to "be diligent." How are you diligent with "the word of truth"? How can you be diligent with a book? You ***study it,*** of course!

Their rule, "the harder reading is to be preferred," leads you to look for and expect a text that is inconsistent, contradictory, incomplete, even grammatically incorrect. But God made His words so easy to understand, that harlots and publicans —tax collectors— could understand and get saved.

2. Text Critics forget the active presence of the Devil. If you read the writings of Tischendorf, Westcott, Hort, or even most professors, including mine, they will make it sound like everyone was basically well-intentioned. Everything was hunky dory, *but* some Christian copyists wanted to make the text a little smoother. So they smoothed things (the critics say), they harmonized things, to make the Bible read easier.

So on the one hand, your teacher will tell you, "All Bibles are generally the same. But on the other hand, they warn, "Watch out! Stay away from that King James! It's *filled* with errors!" How many of you have heard this? Bible college students, I know you have, just like I did.

But let's consider a simple fact. There IS a Devil. So, if you were the Devil, which of the two Bibles would you choose to promote? Because there *are* just two.

If you were the Devil, would you choose the one that lifts up Jesus Christ, proclaims clearly His Godhood and the Godhead, that proclaims salvation is a free gift obtainable only by faith, and the consequences, either of faith leading to everlasting life, or rejection of Christ leading to eternal damnation?

Or, if you were the Devil, would you choose to push the one that lowers Jesus Christ, makes people question His Godhood and the Godhead, that shows a mixture of works and faith in salvation (like every other religion,) and that makes people unsure of the existence of heaven and hell? If you were the Devil, which would you choose?

I think the answer is rather obvious. The King James Bible has 400+ years of fruit, bolstering faith and encouraging soul winning and repentance and holy lives.

Three Big Mistakes of Text Critics

The other Bibles have nothing but bitter fruit of a man-made gospel: doubts, disbelief, being unsure about even basic doctrines or an outright rejection of the faith, —people like Bart Ehrman. He simply followed the principles of Textual Criticism to their logical ends.

That's why modern Textual Critics have to downplay or even dismiss any activities of the Devil in the making of one of the two Bibles. Nothing could be more clear, when you put it that way, about which Bible God supports, and which one the Devil supports. That brings us to the third mistake of Textual Critics.

3. Text Critics forget the power of God. Text Critics act as if God had nothing to do with the Bible, once he handed off the originals. He inspired their production, then did nothing to preserve those scriptures after that moment.

You don't need a perfect Bible to prove that wrong. I can even prove that wrong with a Jehovah's Witness Bible. You can see God's pattern, even in the *New World Translation*. Check it by your Bible! Look at Jeremiah 26:2 (NWT):

> This is what Jehovah has said, "Stand in the courtyard of the house of Jehovah, and *you must speak* concerning all the cities of Judah that are coming in to bow down at the house of Jehovah *all the words that I will command you to speak to them. Do not take away a word*.

Do not take away a word. That is God's pattern.

Now look at Proverbs 30:5-6, Jehovah's Witness Bible. Check it in yours:

> Every saying of God is refined. He is a shield to

those taking refuge in him. Add nothing to his
words, that he may not reprove you, and that you
may not have to be proved a liar.

Add nothing to His words. That is also God's pattern. ***Even in a JW Bible*** you can see that God commands us not to take away or add anything to His words.

Now back to ***the real Bible*** in English. In Mark 12, the Sadducees questioned Jesus. Please note, the Sadducees accepted nothing but the Books of Moses: Genesis, Exodus, Leviticus, Numbers and Deuteronomy. So notice that every time Jesus answers their unbelief, he uses those books to put them to shame! It's awesome!

Sadducees were Text Critics. They denied the prophetic writings, the Psalms of David, and Solomon's books. They also denied angels and bodily resurrection. So they asked a question about the resurrection, thoroughly disbelieving that there is an afterlife.

What did Jesus answer them? Mark 12:24:

> "And Jesus answering said unto them, Do ye not therefore err, because ***ye know not the scriptures, neither the power of God?***"

The Scriptures and the power of God! That's two of the three things I listed here, and by the mouth of the Son of God, the Creator of the universe, Himself!

So don't feel bad, if the critics are against you. If you remember nothing else, please remember these two things.

1. I do not ***judge*** the scriptures. The scriptures ***judge*** me.

2. I do not ***change*** the scriptures. The scriptures ***change*** me.

SECTION III: APOCRYPHA

25

What's in YOUR Bible?

When you read the inspired and preserved words of God, they ring with the truth. When an archaeologist digs his shovel in a place the Bible *says* a city once was —he finds it, right *where the Bible says*.

Figure 91 - Ancient coin showing Cyrenius of Luke 2

When critics said Luke was mistaken, Cyrenius wasn't governor of Syria when Jesus was born… eventually historians found documentation that he was governor *twice*, not once, right when Luke said he governed.

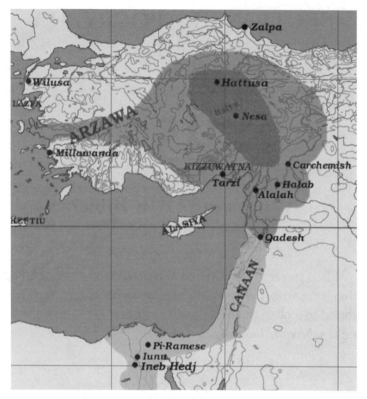

Figure 92 - Extent of the Hittite Kingdom

And when the Bible said an entire civilization existed, that has long ago disappeared, and the Bible was ridiculed for making up the Hittites, lo and behold! Now they say the Hittite kingdom was one of the *largest* in early Old Testament history!

Time and time again, God's words prove themselves true, scientifically verifiable, and ***absolutely reliable***, as they lift up God the Father and His only begotten Son, and call, ***not for works***, but for ***faith*** in the sacrifice of the Lord Jesus Christ, shedding His blood to atone for our sins, ***by that faith alone***, to be granted eternal life.

*The Bible, God's holy and preserved words, is like no other book in the world. That is why the Devil is so hell-bent to destroy and corrupt it with **man's words.***

His earliest known attempt was through Alexandria, Egypt, getting them to insert some folk tales and fiction into the Bible. Those books are known as ***Apocrypha***.

You have read so far what I learned in months of study. But as you have seen, it was mostly confined to the Codex Sinaiticus.

I started to wonder, how do the different Alexandrian Greek Bibles compare to each other? Do they all have the same books? Are they in the same order? What's in those Bibles?

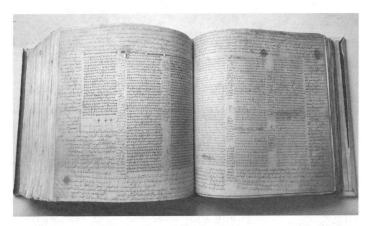

Figure 93 - Daniel 1 of Codex Vaticanus with the apocryphal legend of Susanna scribbled in the margins.

It was a lot of work to find the information, including

checking photos of the Greek in Codex Vaticanus.

Here is what I learned so you can share it with others. The Catholic religion claims the Septuagint was the *real* Old Testament. They say Jesus and the Apostles used it. And they say the Catholic Latin Vulgate was based upon it.

So what is "it"? Do *all* those Greek Old Testaments say the same thing?

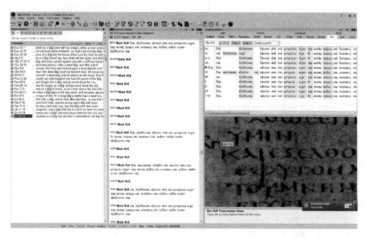

Figure 94 - Screen shot comparing Mark 16:8 in the Alexandrinus and other manuscripts using BibleWorks software

I have expensive Bible software that shows me the Greek text of Sinaiticus, Vaticanus, and Alexandrinus and of the notes of the people who edited them, as well as many other Greek texts. But it only shows me the *New* Testament of those codices! It doesn't show me the *Old* Testament.

Why? It's all one book.

Let me remind you: These codices (big books), are made

What's in YOUR Bible?

up of **more** than one part. You already know they have the New Testament. In addition, all of these codices have at least part of the Old Testament.

But there's **more** than the books you find in the **Hebrew** Old Testament. It adds **other** books that we call the "Apocrypha." The origin of the word means something that would be better stuck into an out-of-the-way drawer and forgotten about. It's basically something "better stored out of sight." That's the reason Christians called it Apocrypha and rejected any of it from being included in the Bible. There are many apocryphal writings. Are they in your Bible Version?

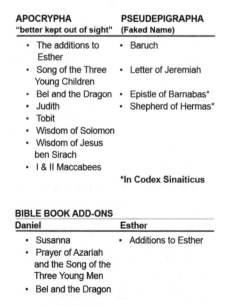

Figure 95 - Additional Apocryphal books and stories found in Old Testaments of Alexandrian Bibles

I looked for Bibles containing the "Apocrypha" today and found these versions available:

The Revised Standard (RSV) – The approved version when I went to Fuller Seminary

The New RSV (NRSV) – The approved version after I left Fuller Seminary

The English Standard (ESV) – How many of you knew they made one for the ESV? It's been out with Apocrypha since 2009.

The World English Bible – or WEB Bible

The Living Bible – It's been out since the 1970s in a Catholic Edition.

Let me break for a second and tell you something about the Living Bible that a good friend told me. I'm quoting it right off the recording I made of him:

> I was in a CBA (Christian Booksellers Association) convention in the '70s, attending the keynote session. The auditorium was filled with many, perhaps a thousand or more, Christian booksellers. They served their communities with Christian books. And [Kenneth] Taylor, [author of the Living Bible], had been invited as their keynote speaker.
>
> He stepped up to the podium. He turned and looked up at the big banner across the top of the stage that said, "People Serving People."

Figure 96 - Kenneth N. Taylor (1917-2005)

The CBA certainly felt that was laudable. After all, that's what their members do: serve their communities with Bibles and books, "people serving people."

Taylor turned and looked at the banner, turned back to the microphone, and said —actually whispered— "I have a problem with that. I have a problem with that. Because when your goal is to serve people, you will ultimately make compromise."

He went on later to say, *to whisper*, how he had lost his voice after doing the Living Bible. And with his own mouth I heard him say, "That may have been God's judgment for me tampering with His words."

The New English Bible (NEB) - 1970

The Revised English Bible (REB) - 1976

The Common English Bible (CEB) - The present approved version for Fuller Seminary - and the CEB Study Bible with Apocrypha was edited by the present Dean of the Fuller School of Theology!

The Good News Bible (GNB) from the American Bible Society – This is the text that Bible translators all over the world have with them, and that will help Protestants and Baptists translate the Apocrypha in new Bibles in all mission fields for the Roman Catholic Religion.

All of these Bibles are available with the Apocrypha added.

Then there are all the Catholic Bibles, every single one of which has the Apocrypha.

There is a sneaky move out right now to get people to put the lying Apocrypha in their Bibles. I'll go more into that in the next chapter.

But this much I will say: Everyone, from the Ecumenical to the Amish, is being pushed to put the Apocrypha in the Bible. And one of the most deceitful methods is to say, "Well, the King James Bible had the Apocrypha in it!"

I will go more into detail about the many, many problems with the Apocryphal books, but let me say this about the King James. The translators were told by the bishops of the Church of England that they had to translate the Apocrypha and put it in the new Bible. They had no choice.

But they stood firm, like Shadrach, Meshach and Abednego. They refused to put any apocryphal books in either testament, either the New or the Old. They stuck it in between the Testaments. Then they gave seven reasons for this, which I also listed in *Answers to Your Bible Version Questions.*

1. "Not one of them is in the Hebrew language, which was alone used by the inspired historians and poets of the Old Testament."

2. "Not one of the writers lays any claim to inspiration."

3. "These books were never acknowledged as sacred Scriptures by the Jewish Church, and therefore were never sanctioned by our Lord."

4. "They were not allowed a place among the sacred books, during the first four centuries of the Christian Church."

5. "They contain fabulous statements, and statements which contradict not only the canonical Scriptures, but themselves; as when, in the two Books of Maccabees, Antiochus IV Epiphanes is made to die three different deaths in as many different places."

I have to break in here. Even the Catholic New American Bible admits these massive contradictions in their note at 2 Maccabees 1:14-17:

> A different account of the death of Antiochus IV is given in 2 Maccabees 9:1-29, and another variant account in 1 Maccabees 6:1-16….

Why would the Catholic leaders include these books if they *knew* they were lies? I'll deal with that later. Back to the list.

6. "It inculcates doctrines at variance with the Bible, such as prayers for the dead and sinless perfection."

7. "It teaches immoral practices, such as lying, suicide, assassination and magical incantation."

These seven reasons explain why the KJV translators refused to mix any of this fictional Apocrypha with either the New or Old Testaments, but stuck them off by themselves, between the Testaments.

I will show you examples of these lies and false doctrines in the next chapter, when I expose the many lies and a couple of serious false doctrines in the Apocryphal Book of Tobit.

What's in *your* Bible?

Even notes in the Study Bibles show they *don't believe* what's in the Apocrypha, as well as other parts of the actual Bible.

But I know what is in *my* KJV Bible. And I believe every single word.

26

What's Wrong with Tobit?

There are many apocryphal books. But I was curious about which ones were found in the "big three:" Sinaiticus, Vaticanus and Alexandrinus. This is useful, because the modern, 21st century "Septuagint" is pretty much based on just them.

But I can never lose sight of the fact that from about 405 AD to the mid-1900s, the Catholic religion didn't push the Greek anything. During that time, they only backed the Roman Catholic **Latin** Vulgate. They told the world it was "the Bible."

The Catholic Latin Vulgate was translated into English in the Douay-Rheims Bible: the New Testament in 1582 and the Old Testament in 1609-10. But the English was so Latinized that it was almost unreadable. Then it was revised about 1750 by Richard Challoner. Today, Americans usually have the 1899 edition of the Douay-Rheims.

Catholics had to admit that the King James was very clear. So when they revised the Douay Rheims they actually ***tried to make it sound like the King James***. Then they changed the text to match the Catholic Latin Vulgate's errors, which they thought improved it.

Changing the King James, to "improve it?" Sounds familiar.

For over 360 years the Douay-Rheims was "the" Catholic English Bible, from 1610 to the 1970s. And for 1500 years, all Catholic Bibles were based upon the Roman Catholic Latin

Vulgate. But all that changed when the Sinaiticus was foisted upon the world in 1862, after suddenly being "found" in 1844.

You are about to find out:

1. What the Sinaiticus did to the Apocrypha in Catholic Bibles. And from that you will learn:

2. *Really* why the Catholics have the Apocrypha in their Bibles. Take a journey with me into the world —and book— of Tobit. Even if you have read Tobit before, you are about to understand it like you never have before.

Before I say anything else, I have to tell you something I just checked for myself. In the Preface to the Revised Standard Version are these words:

> Yet the King James Version has grave defects. By the middle of the nineteenth century [the mid-1800s], the development of Biblical studies and the discovery of many manuscripts more ancient than those upon which the King James Version was based, made it manifest that these defects are so many and so serious as to call for revision of the English translation.

So they were saying that we need a new Bible, because there is *new evidence* that was found, that will *improve* the Bible.

That is *false*! And I have *proof!*

In 1851 Sir Lancelot Charles Lee Brenton was putting together a Greek Septuagint from the Greek of Vaticanus and Alexandrinus. He also put an English translation in the column on the side.

Everything I can find assumed that Brenton translated that English text all brand-new. It does *seem* he did his own translation of the Greek books that are in the regular Bible books. I've checked in it, over the years.

But it's ***not true*** for the Apocrypha.

It turns out that Brenton found a 200+ year old translation that happened to translate very nicely the specific Greek text of the Vaticanus and Alexandrinus in 10 of the Apocryphal books and most of an 11th.

Lancelot Brenton used that other translation to translate the Greek from these Apocryphal writings:

1. 1 Esdras [1]
2. Tobit
3. Judith
4. Wisdom of Solomon
5. Wisdom of Jesus ben Sirach, or Ecclesiasticus [2]
6. Baruch (chapters 1-5)
6a. Letter of Jeremiah = Baruch chapter 6
7. The Song of the 3 Children (Theodotion's version) [3]
8. Susanna (Theodotion's version) [4]
9. Bel and the Dragon (Theodotion's version) [5]
10. 1 Maccabees
11. 2 Maccabees

[1] Only tiny changes were made where the Greek differed a bit.
[2] Chapters 31-36 in the KJVA are in the order 34-36, 31-33 in Brenton.
[3] Brenton changes v.44, omits v.45, 48, switches 54 and 55.
[4] Vaticanus doesn't have Susanna originally. It was scribbled into the margins of the beginning of Daniel. But Alexandrinus does have Susanna.
[5] The actual KJV Book of Daniel is from the Hebrew, but these Apocryphal stories (7-9) added to Daniel are from Theodotion's Alexandrian Greek and are the same as the text of the Vaticanus. I verified these with Rahlf's Septuaginta Editio Altera (2006).

That translation was made of the same Greek text, not from the Latin or any other language.

Guess which English translation Brenton used? It was the **King James** Apocrypha!

*As I've showed you, the King James translators had been **forced**, under **protest**, and **despite their seven objections**, to include the Apocrypha between the covers of the new Bible. But they **refused** to put them in either the New or Old Testaments. So they put them in their own "outcast" section —you know, the Apocrypha section, labeled **"APOCRYPHA"** on every column.*

But look at what those translators used to ***translate*** the Apocrypha! I've been checking the Greek text against the English for myself. The King James translators clearly used an Alexandrian text like the Vaticanus and Alexandrinus to make the Apocrypha —which they knew ***wasn't*** scripture.

Wait a minute! That means:

1. They ***did*** have access to an Alexandrian manuscript, and ***used*** these to translate Apocryphal books that they knew were not inspired.

2. They did have the type of text which we have in Vaticanus and Alexandrinus. But they ***rejected*** them, when they translated what they knew were the true, inspired scriptures.

So that note in the front of the RSV and other Bibles is ***FALSE.***

And I found this out for myself last night, as I compared the Greek in Tobit and other Apocryphal books to the English of the King James Apocrypha. That's why Brenton chose the KJV text for the Apocrypha of Vaticanus. He could do no better. Why translate it again?

The KJV translators had, and used, an Alexandrian text

like the Vaticanus and Alexandrinus for the **uninspired Apocrypha**. The KJV translators had, but **REJECTED**, that same Alexandrian text for any part of the inspired scriptures. And the proof is right there in Sir Lancelot Brenton's Septuagint with Apocrypha.

So the so-called "better" texts were well-known. They aren't really *new* evidence, after all, are they?

*Now let's get into the book of Tobit. You are about to see a book that **contradicts** history, geography, cartography, and chronology. This book also contradicts other books of the Bible, in theology, angelology, soteriology, **and it even contradicts itself!***

Then why is this book in so many Bibles?

One reason: because it makes you confused. And your confusion plays into the hands of the Roman Catholic hierarchy. You will need to run to a priest or some authority figure to interpret it for you. "Why are all these contradictions in my Bible? And what is this book supposed to mean?" So now you would trust Rome and her minions, and not trust that *you* can understand the scriptures.

But let me remind you: These books of Apocrypha *are not scripture*.

Shall we begin?

Why Tobit? Well, I made a detailed chart of every book that's in Vaticanus, Sinaiticus and Alexandrinus.[57] And because Sinaiticus is missing so much of the Old Testament, they only have four apocryphal books in common between them all: Tobit, Judith, Wisdom of Solomon and Wisdom of Jesus Son of Sirach, also called Ecclesiasticus.

Tobit's just the first one in order, so I started there. But

---
57. See Appendix A, A Comparison of Books with Apocrypha.

oh, what I've found in that one book! Tobit's plot has more holes than Swiss cheese. It's like a bad high school play. It has so many errors, I kept wondering who the proofreader was.

And this is true, despite the fact that there are at least ***Three different versions of Tobit,*** which we can find in English Bibles. I made a 42 page chart just to figure out *some* of the differences between them.

They are so different. It's not like a word or two was different, not affecting the truth, like in Matthew, Mark and Luke. No, it's like three different people took a whack at ***retelling*** the story around the campfire. You'll never get the same story.

Welcome to Tobit. Here are the three versions that we have clearly in English:

The first is found in the Latin Vulgate, translated into English in the Catholic Douay-Rheims and the Catholic Living Bible (for a good part of it, at least).

The second is found in the Vaticanus and Alexandrinus, which Sir Lancelot Brenton could tell matched the text in 10 books of the King James Apocrypha.

And the third is a ***wholly different text.*** It adds 1,700 words to the Greek. But it also is missing 12 verses in one place and three in another. ***That text is the Sinaiticus.*** Since the mid-1900s, the text of Tobit in modern Bibles has been shifting to the Sinaiticus version. That's amazing, because not much else matches it. The Latin Vulgate doesn't. Vaticanus and Alexandrinus don't.

Before the mid-20th century, the only other known Greek manuscript in the world that matched Sinaiticus in Tobit was in chapters 3-6, found in Manuscript 319 from Mt. Athos, Greece, dated 1021 AD.[58]

So both the *Shepherd of Hermas* and Tobit in Sinaiticus have texts that pretty much only match up with manuscripts from Mt. Athos, Greece. And that's the same place where a guy named Constantine Simonides claimed he **created** the Sinaiticus.

Could that be a ***coincidence?***

I arranged the three versions for myself in columns, in parallel, to make sure I wouldn't be making mistakes about what Tobit says, in any of the three different "campfire retellings" of the story. I will focus on errors of history, chronology, geography, and theology. But let's start at the beginning, with Tobit's problem with pride that is never criticized or corrected in the book. For more than 2 chapters, the character, Tobit, keeps bragging about his own righteousness. Like Tobit 1:3 in the New RSV: "I, Tobit, walked in the ways of truth and righteousness all the days of my life."

But Proverbs 27:2 says that bragging is wrong. "Let another man praise thee, and not thine own mouth; a stranger, and not thine own lips."

Now let's go to the story. The Jesuit editor of Tobit in the Common English Bible (CEB) Study Bible with Apocrypha wrote, "…the book has obvious errors in geography, chronology, and history."[59] In other words, whoever wrote the book

---

58. See *Tobit: the Book of Tobit in Codex Sinaiticus*, by Robert J. Littman (Boston: Brill, 2008), pp. xv-xvi. On top of all this, according to Robert Littman there are not 2, but actually 3 different Greek versions of Tobit. That's not counting any other language.

59. "Tobit Introduction" by Daniel J. Harrington, S.J., in *The Common English Study Bible with Apocrypha* (Nashville, TN: Common English Bible, 2013), p. 6 AP.

didn't know where things were, or when they happened.

All three Oxford Study Bibles with Apocrypha, the Revised Standard, NRSV and Revised English Bible, agree. At 1:4 The RSV says bluntly, "Such chronological, and other historical, difficulties make it clear that *the story is fiction…*."[60]

They're right. If you use real historical dates with the events of the book, you have huge complications and contradictions. That's why this is part of the Apocrypha, rejected as a fake by the early Christians and the King James translators. They knew that God doesn't contradict Himself.

But there are contradictions even when you ask the simplest of questions. For instance, "How old was Tobit when he died?" According to the description in 1:4, Tobit was "still a young man"[61] in 928 BC. But according to 1:2, he was taken into captivity in 722 BC, 206 years later. Then he did all sorts of good works up through 1:21, another 41 years, until 681 BC, making Tobit about 250 years old. And that's even before the story starts!

Of course, that is a huge problem, since according to Tobit 14:2 he was only 62 years old (Sinaiticus) or 58 (Vaticanus and Alexandrinus) or 56 (Latin Vulgate) at that same point! That is ***188-194 years younger*** than Tobit's age, based on 1:1-5.

So was he born before 928 BC, or in the 740s BC? They *can't* all be right. This story sounds *fake*, along with Tobit himself.

---

60. Note at Tobit 1:4 in *The Oxford Annotated Bible* (NY: Oxford University Press, 1965), p. [63].
61. See the notes at Tobit 1:4, in both the *Oxford* (RSV) and *New Oxford* (NRSV) *Annotated Bible*. The NRSV *New Oxford* comment softens the blow.

Figure 97 - Artifacts of early kings: Shalmaneser V (726 - 722 BC) and a bas-relief of Prince Sennacherib (704 - 681 BC) with his father, Sargon II (721-705 BC)

"Tobit" claims he served under king Shalmaneser, who he says conquered the northern tribes of Israel. But Shalmaneser died *before* the northern tribes were taken! Tobit listed *the wrong king!* The conquering king wasn't Shalmaneser. It was *his younger brother, Sargon II.* But Sargon II isn't even in the book of Tobit.

In Tobit 1:2, 13-16, it says that Tobit served under Shalmaneser in Nineveh until Shalmaneser died in 705 BC and Sennacherib his son took his place. Impossible. Shalmaneser had been dead 17 years. And besides, Sennacherib was not Shalmaneser's son. He was the son of his younger brother and successor, Sargon II, the guy missing from Tobit.

And after serving for 17 years under a king, you'd think he'd know his name. Either Tobit forgot, didn't know the name of the conquering king he served under for 17 years, or Tobit is a fake. So those are a few of the problems of the story —history and chronology.

Now let's see just some of the errors of geography. I have a theory, after going over this a few times. The text in Sinaiticus might have been invented to smooth over some of the glitches in Vaticanus and Alexandrinus.

For instance, in Tobit 6:9, Vaticanus and Alexandrinus say the man Tobias and the angel Raphael in disguise were approaching Rages, but Sinaiticus says they were getting close to Ecbatana. But Rages is over 175 miles past Ecbatana, as the crow flies.

What's Wrong with Tobit? 239

Figure 98 - Rages is 176 miles past Ecbatana, "as the crow flies."

Many study Bibles will only tell you about locations just like that, "as the crow flies." But people aren't crows. We're talking about distance for people to walk on a journey. They walk, and they need roads to make the way easier and safer for them.

See, "as the crow flies," it's 176 miles from Ecbatana to Rages, and it's 320 miles from Nineveh to Ecbatana. But the walking distance is more than that. Using David Barrett's Bible Mapper, that's the one I used to create the GPS-correct maps in our deluxe RVG Spanish Bibles, I could find the actual trade routes. That gives a different picture.

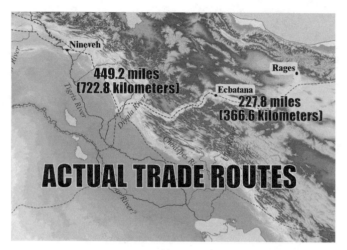

Figure 99 - Rages is actually 228 miles past Ecbatana by trade route

Now we can see it is actually 449 miles from Nineveh to Ecbatana.

And it's another 228 miles from Ecbatana to Rages!

That's a huge trip! And it makes me question whether what the angel said in the Sinaiticus in 5:6 was possible, that they could walk to Rages in just two days. Then again, in Sinaiticus, Raphael also says that Rages is in the mountains but Ecbatana is in the middle of the plain. Actually, it's the other way around. Obviously, whoever wrote that never walked it!

Of course, the Vulgate and Douay-Rheims are way worse, saying that Rages is in the mount of Ecbatana. Ecbatana is 176 miles away. They can't move the mountain.

You see, nobody really knew how to check this stuff before the advent of modern archaeology. So you could say anything was anywhere, and people would believe you. How could they check?

So let's go back to the difference between Sinaiticus and Vaticanus. Which are they standing outside of: Ecbatana, the home of the family where the angel was leading Tobias, or Rages, 228 miles past where Raphael was taking Tobias? If it's Ecbatana, at least that makes sense.

But that puts Catholics in a huge bind. From at least 405 AD to the 1900s, for 1500 years, the Catholic Bibles have all claimed they went to Rages.

You only have three choices:

1. The Catholic Bible was wrong for 1500 years.

2. The Catholic Bible has been wrong for the last 50 years. Or

3. The story of Tobit is a fake.

And now that they are just switching to Sinaiticus, do they trust Sinaiticus? They can't! Trusting Sinaiticus causes other problems. You see, it's ***missing 12 entire verses*** of Tobit's moral advice to his son Tobias, skipping from verse 4:7a all the way over to 4:19. And the Catholic Bibles have to have them, because of a doctrine that is stated in two verses I'll show you, in Tobit 4 and 12.

There is also another section with missing verses, in 13:7-9. Some, like the Common English Bible, fill the space with a translation of a Latin retelling of Tobit. Others, like the New RSV, use the Vaticanus and Alexandrinus to fill in the missing spots. I guess they picked whichever text made the translators feel good. That's not a good technique, by the way. Scriptures are about truth, not feeling good.

Then again, Tobit isn't scripture. Do you know how the American Bible Society described those 12 verses missing from chapter 4? You can see it in The Good News Bible with Deuterocanonicals/Apocrypha: They said "The translation of verses 7b-19b" was "accidentally omitted in the Greek manuscript that this translation normally follows...."[62] I don't know why they didn't just say "the Sinaiticus."

The CEB Study Bible with Apocrypha calls it "a gap." Isn't that interesting? When they want the verses, like here, they call them "a gap" and they say that Sinaiticus "accidentally omitted" them, as if they knew the scribes' motives.

But when it's another 12 verses, like Mark 16:9-20, the resurrection appearances of Christ, suddenly it's an "Ending added later," and they say, "In most critical editions of the Greek New Testament, the Gospel of Mark ends at 16:8."[63]

Did you catch that? "Critical editions," not "Greek texts." Every single Greek manuscript but 2, Sinaiticus and Vaticanus, **has Mark 16:9-20**. But "critical editions," aren't ancient Greek manuscripts at all. They are scissor-and-paste modern Greek texts that were ***made up*** by Bible critics, putting in what they want, and leaving out what they don't want.

Of course they are missing from "most critical editions." They took them out themselves! But they are in all Greek manuscripts except those two that they like, Sinaiticus and Vaticanus. These guys are tricky. You have to pay attention to the words they use.

So there are huge errors in the dates, the geography, and the text. Why would anyone in his right mind want to hang onto a text so filled with holes that it contradicts almost everything you can think of, including itself?

---

62. Good News Bible with Deuterocanonicals/Apocrypha, footnote at Tobit 4:7, p. 1136.
63. The CEB Study Bible with Apocrypha, note in the text at 16:9.

What's Wrong with Tobit?

Because of what I'm about to show you, the doctrine. There are some doctrines that are in that book that prove very useful for the Roman Catholic religious system of bondage. First, let me show you what they could not leave out from Chapter 4, Tobit's advice to his son Tobias, Tobit 4:11-12.

Douay-Rheims says:

> For alms deliver from all sin, and from death, and will not suffer the soul to go into darkness. Alms shall be a great confidence before the most high God, to all them that give it.

Tobit *is* useful for doctrine —the Catholic doctrine of paying to get out of Purgatory or to lessen one's time burning there.

Now a little about angels. Raphael in the story eventually admits he is one of the seven angels who stand before God. But he doesn't act like the angels of God in the Bible. I have to tell you a little tiny bit of the story.

In Chapter 5, Tobias goes to look for an honest man to help him journey to Rages to retrieve for his dad —get this— ten talents, 570 pounds of silver, a king's ransom, from a guy he never met, on roads he never traveled, walking 677 miles up and 677 miles back, expecting no trouble along the way. And they never even considered whether the guy's traveling companion would just take it all for himself.

People have robbed and killed each other for far less. The **believability** factor of this story has dropped into negative digits.

So after talking to his blind dad, Tobias walks out his door and almost instantly meets a guy. He claims to be a relative, and claims to need work. Then he claims to know the family

Tobias is going to, when Tobias has not publicly declared any intention of traveling to meet them. He claims to know the roads and the mountains and valleys (but I already told you he got *that* wrong).

On top of that, Tobit, the father, rightly a bit cautious, asks him who he is and where he is from. And this angel, Raphael, first replies, "Why? Do you want a tribe, or do you want a hired man?" So he doesn't actually answer the question. And that didn't raise their suspicions?

Then Tobit asked again who he was and whose son he was. And Raphael says, right here in 5:13 in the Catholic New American Bible, I kid you not, "I am Azariah, son of the great Hananiah, one of your own kindred." So Raphael is not only an angel ignorant of geography. He's also a ***liar***! But the Jesuit CEB commentator says "he has to tell a few white lies." I am ***not*** loving the doctrines I'm getting from this book.

But those lies told by the angel are ***good enough*** for blind Tobit. Now he trusts a stranger with his riches (that he hasn't seen for 20 years, by the way), and his son's life, on a 1,354 mile round-trip. Tobit's wife is dubious and Tobit actually rebukes her!

Apocrypha is stranger than fiction. But I can only mention a couple more points. I could go on doing this for several pages.

Back to Raphael. He does all this prophesying and telling what is going to happen to Tobias, who just doesn't have a clue. He never says, "Hey, wait a minute. How do you *know* all this stuff?" He just trusts a stranger he's never met with the weirdest of things.

What's Wrong with Tobit? 245

One of them is killing a fish that attacked his foot, saving the heart, gall and liver in his bag for the next few weeks. (Eww!)

Then he's told he must burn the heart and liver on coals to chase off the demon Asmodeus, who killed the seven men in a row who tried to go to the marriage bed with some lady named Sarah, who just happens to be his relative, as well. And the angel knows ***all*** this. (You know, there are witches and sorcerers who do rituals like that.)

And in chapter 12 come the most serious doctrines. The Douay has the angel Raphael saying this, in Tobit 12:9:

> For alms delivereth from death, and the same is that which purgeth away sins, and maketh to find mercy and life everlasting.

No! There is just ***one*** way to purge away sins: Hebrews 1:3 says of the Lord Jesus "... after he had by himself purged our sins, sat down on the right hand of the Majesty on high;"

And Hebrews 9:22 says: "And almost all things are by the law purged with blood; and without shedding of blood is no remission." Only the shed blood of the Lord Jesus Christ takes away sins! No good work we sinners can do, not even the best of alms, could take the place of the finished work of the Lord Jesus Christ on the cross.

The Common English Bible, approved by my former seminary, Fuller, reads like this in Tobit 12:9: "Giving to the poor saves from death, and it washes away every sin."

No! No! Revelation 1:5 says of the Lord Jesus Christ: "... Unto him that loved us, and washed us from our sins in his own blood," It couldn't get any clearer than that. This book, Tobit is not only "not useful for doctrine," but it has ***doctrines of devils!!***

Finally, Raphael, having now revealed his lying self to be an angel of God, says this in 12:12 of the Vaticanus-Alexandrinus-type text: "I did bring the remembrance of your prayers before the Holy One…" And in verse 15: "I am Raphael, one of the seven holy angels, which present the prayers of the saints, and which go in and out before the glory of the Holy one."

Doesn't God hear prayers directly? Psalm 65:2 is as clear as crystal as David says to God: "O thou that hearest prayer, unto thee shall all flesh come." And 1 Timothy 2:5: "For there is one God, and one mediator between God and men, the man Christ Jesus;"

We do not need the mediation of angels. We only need our God, the Father, and His Son, the Lord Jesus Christ, and the Holy Ghost, so we can pray in the Spirit to the Father in the name of the Son.

So why is this book, or any apocryphal book, in a Bible?

*It **was** in the King James, but only because the bishops of the Church of England forced the translators, against their will. But they had the last say, sticking them into the Twilight Zone of the Apocrypha, not in either New or Old Testament.*

It was put in Catholic Bibles, because it supported the Catholic doctrines of Purgatory and Indulgences (paying money to get out of punishment for sins) and the doctrine of angels as mediators. They also used it to teach the doctrine that Christ's shed blood wasn't enough, but human effort was needed in order to be saved and go to heaven.

It was put in ***ecumenical Bibles***, for one big reason: to bring confusion. In effect, it lifts up the apocryphal books and puts down the actual books of the Bible. Look at these comments from the Common English Bible: "The book is best understood as a historical novel,"[64] meaning it's set in a historical time, but it didn't actually happen.

Later the writer says: "... the author was more interested in entertaining and encouraging than in reporting historical facts. Thus, the book should be read alongside *other historical novels* like the books of *Ruth*, *Esther*, and Judith."

Did you catch that? It's written like history, but it didn't happen. So it's claiming Ruth and Esther *also never happened!* That's what you get when you trust a Catholic to interpret the Bible for you. Oh, and remember: the editor of this book, Tobit, in the Common English Bible, is a Jesuit priest —Daniel J Harrington, SJ from Jesuit Boston College.

And the general editor is Joel B. Green, the newest Dean of Fuller's School of Theology! Nine Fuller professors contributed to this study Bible. So it *must* be "Fuller-approved."

So the purpose of the Apocrypha is to bring confusion. When you're confused, where do you go? They want you to go to a priest —or a scholar!

Do you get it? It just happened in the CEB. All the rationalizations and suggestions and doctrinal explanations, were made right there, by a Jesuit priest!

It doesn't matter how old a story Tobit is. It is just a story. And it is a very *dangerous* story at that. This is a perfect example of why the King James translators rejected the Apocrypha from being part of either the New or Old Testaments.

---

64. "Tobit Introduction" by Daniel J. Harrington, S.J., in *The Common English Study Bible with Apocrypha* (Nashville, TN: Common English Bible, 2013), p. 5 AP.

This is why they were willing to use the Vaticanus-Alexandrinus-type Alexandrian text to translate the Apocrypha into English.

But anyone who would include any Apocryphal books as part of the Bible is putting man's corrupt words alongside God's holy words.

So the King James translators could use a text like Vaticanus for the Apocrypha.

But they totally rejected it for any ***real*** scriptures, in either Testament.

SECTION IV: THE BIBLE VERSION CONSPIRACY

27

The Evidence

Have you ever played the board game Clue? You are trying to figure out who the murderer is, and how and where he or she did it, in a mansion. As you walk into each room, you are given a new clue. Then you make a "suggestion." If no one has evidence to prove you wrong, then you make an "accusation." If you're right, you win the game! If you're not, you lose and are out.

In September of 2014, producer Chris Pinto interviewed me outside Nashville. At that time I didn't have a 50th of the information I have now regarding Sinaiticus, Tischendorf, or Manly P. Hall; nor did I have high-resolution photos of Sinaiticus and Vaticanus, thanks to Steven Avery and Mark Michie; nor did I have the actual facsimiles of them, thanks to Brother Jack McElroy.

And most of what I showed online from December 2015 had been brand-new information to me, as I learned, received or figured it out. On YouTube, you had a front-row seat to my discovery process.

Some of my viewers asked me about my conclusions. What is the Sinaiticus, really? Where did it come from? And why is the Roman Catholic church suddenly interested in the Alexandrian Greek texts?

Before, it was only interested in the Roman Catholic Latin Vulgate. Why did the Catholic leadership start giving accolades and commendations to Greek textual critics, starting in the 1800s? And finally, where's it all heading?

In other words: What *IS* the Big Picture? I will now put facts in evidence that lead toward an accusation. This is Part One: the Evidence. Part Two will be My Accusation. Shall we play Clue together?

Figure 100 - The great end time conflict: NWO vs KJV

In April of 2015 I pieced together writings by New World Order (NWO) occultist Manly P. Hall, for what became Chapter 6: Why the NWO Hates the KJV. But a few months later, some words he had said caught my eye. He wrote these words for his article in spring of 1944:

> To make things right we will have to undo much that is cherished error. The problem of revising the Bible shows how difficult it is to do this. For the last hundred years we have been trying to get out an edition of the Bible that is reasonably correct; but nobody wants it. What's wanted is the good old King James version, every jot and tittle of it, because most people are convinced that God dictated the Bible to King James in English.

Suddenly it hit me: 1944? 100 years earlier was **1844**. And the only Bible version-related event was the so-called "discovery" of the Sinaiticus, starting in 1844. I showed how I got to this point in what became Chapter 7: ***KJV, Sinaiticus and the NWO***.

Was the Sinaiticus important? And who was this "we" that Hall talked about, anyway? They weren't Bible-believing Christians. It seems he hated them. They were the "problem" to be solved. And since he was a high-level occultist, with connections to major political figures, like 33rd degree Masonic President Franklin Delano Roosevelt, it seems the "we" included some pretty high-up people.

Hall believed ***only two things*** stopped the New World Order before it started: the King James Bible and the thinking of the people. You take out one, the King James, and the other (the thinking of the people) goes with it.

Please let that sink in. Don't let go of your King James for anyone, not even a turncoat former King James believing professor or preacher.

Hall had two solutions to get the NWO ball rolling. The first was indoctrinating the people like the Nazis did. Start in kindergarten, teaching psychology and "mental and emotional tolerance." Sound like today?

The second was doing whatever had to be done, to get people to *let go* of their belief in every "jot and tittle" of the King James Bible.

He figured it could be done in five generations. We are in generation four, and already most of what Hall wanted has been done, almost to the letter.

Figure 101 - For Bible believers, the choice is clear

A year before this, in December 2014, I made Vlog 92: This Is Not a Conspiracy Theory. I showed how the former head of Planned Parenthood, Richard Day, revealed many plans of a group he belonged to, called "the Order." Their big plan included lots of social change that has already happened to us by the second decade of the 21st century.

But he also said they had *to rewrite the Bible* "to fit *the* new religion," changing meanings of words, one word at a time. Soon the Bible would become *flexible enough* to embrace that new world religion.

So the King James Bible has been on a lot of people's hit lists. And the Sinaiticus, it turns out, was the Greek Codex that set the ball rolling against the King James and toward the Alexandrian stream of manuscripts. This includes Codex Vaticanus, housed at the Vatican (of course).

So I turned my focus onto the Sinaiticus. Researcher Steven Avery had shown me actual photographs of Sinaiticus in March 2014.

Figure 102 - Constantine Simonides —creator of the Sinaiticus?

He was willing to consider the idea that a guy named Constantine Simonides had actually put together the Codex Sinaiticus around 1840. Chris Pinto had fronted that theory in his Bible video: ***Tares Among the Wheat***.

I told Steven that I had "a very, very, very hard time believing" that Constantine Simonides, a peddler of what he said were ancient manuscripts, had anything to do with the Codex Sinaiticus.

Even if Sinaiticus were not an ancient codex, I believed what Scrivener and others had said, that Simonides was a con man. It seemed he kept finding the most gullible people, and sold many counterfeits to them.

But it seemed he could sell something even to the hardened critics. They became convinced that "The others may be fakes, but mine is genuine." The only problem was, every "expert" disagreed on which was the "one genuine one"!

As I saw it, Simonides did both short and "long cons." Long cons take longer to develop. Sometimes it involves a third party, who sells to or "discovers" something for the target guy. Then later, Simonides would show up, and claim he could check authenticity on anything, and the target would naturally show that artifact, even if he didn't know a paper was carefully rolled up or hidden inside it.

Then voila! Simonides would "discover" it and validate it, or he'd suddenly say, "You have a priceless artifact!" and then the guy, not seeing any connection between the first guy and him, would trust Simonides to sell him other "ancient" stuff.

So I didn't believe Simonides' story of assembling the codex now called Sinaiticus as a gift for the Tsar of Russia, when Simonides was a late teen. The story went that it was a gift, because the Tsar was the guy who financed the monasteries, so it's good to keep him happy. Well, okay, that much of the story was true. But he also said that Tischendorf was either deceived or a liar.

Figure 103 - Constantin Tischendorf —Deceived or a Liar?

I had no reason to doubt Constantin Tischendorf, who claimed that in 1844 he saved a bunch of sheets headed for the fireplace to keep the monks warm. I even wrote it in my book.[65] Then years later, in 1859 a monk gave him hundreds more pages of this same Greek Bible, that he soon called Codex Sinaiticus. I'd believed that story for over 30 years. So did every professor I ever spoke to. I'd need good reason not to believe Tischendorf's story, with his sterling reputation.

So now I was back to square one. I had reasons to focus on Sinaiticus, not Simonides. I needed solid facts. So...

Fact #1: Someone darkened Sinaiticus! Steven Avery showed me codexsinaiticus.org, where I could actually see high-quality photographs of Sinaiticus for the first time! I was looking to see if someone whitened the 43 folia of

---

65. See *Answers to Your Bible Versions Questions*, editions through 2010.

animal skin that Tischendorf brought from St. Catherine's monastery in the Egyptian peninsula to Leipzig. This was called the Codex Friderico-Augustanus, or CFA.

After hours of looking, I could see that the CFA wasn't lightened. The rest of the pages were darkened! Someone had spilled tea or coffee or something and spread it on the pages.

Then I found out that a Russian religious official, Porfiry Uspensky, the very next year, 1845, saw all the rest of what we call Sinaiticus and said it was all white.

The dates given make it clear. The majority of Sinaiticus was darkened sometime after 1850, Uspensky's last visit, and before 1860, when people began to see it in Russia. But if it were between 1850 and 1860, Tischendorf would have known it was changed, and should have cried foul, if he was innocent.

That means either Tischendorf knew who did it, or he was an accomplice, or Tischendorf darkened Sinaiticus. Tischendorf no longer had a sterling reputation with me.

Then came the next bombshell.

Fact #2: Tischendorf lied about how he got the Sinaiticus! In reading *The Bible Hunter*, a few things became clear:

1. Parchment doesn't burn nicely. It smolders and stinks.

2. The basket for burning parchments was actually a standard way of storing them.

3. That means the whole conversation Tischendorf had with the librarian was a lie, since it involves 1 and 2.

4. That also means that the reason Tischendorf gave for bringing home the 43 folia of Sinaiticus was also a lie. Now

I had no idea why or how he brought them to Saxony.

All I knew for sure was that my 30 years of believing Tischendorf were in flames. He was a liar and a con and a counterfeiter —because it turns out that the only reason for darkening or yellowing pages was to make them look older than they were, usually to sell them, since ancient manuscripts were extremely popular. It is even said that monks engaged in counterfeiting, for money for their monasteries.

Fact #3: Sinaiticus is not even a trustworthy copy! It is more like a draft paper before the rewrite. Now it was time to look more carefully, more closely, at the Sinaiticus facsimile sent by Jack McElroy. What I found astounded me. On a single page the copyist managed to skip from 1 Chronicles 19:17 to Ezra 9:9. It was done by the one called Scribe A. And he didn't miss a beat! He just went on copying Ezra, as if nothing had happened.

So it was clear he was copying something, got to the bottom of one sheet and then looked up at another sheet, totally out of order. Then on the very same line, he kept copying. That makes it look like he wasn't reading what he was copying, or he would have seen the radical difference.

This made me think that there were multiple source documents, put together, and then they were being rapidly copied, maybe in a rush. If they had been identical, the skip wouldn't have happened in the middle of the column. It would have been at the bottom of the page. So something that didn't have four columns was copied onto something that did have four columns.

Oh, and Sinaiticus is about the only manuscript of the Bible in four columns. Alexandrinus is in two columns.

Vaticanus is in three columns. Only Sinaiticus is in four columns. So whatever the scribe copied from was not the same. And it was probably in less than four columns.

But the fact that this wasn't proofread, and such a massive, glaring mistake was made, told me that this wasn't a final copy. It was maybe a draft. Maybe the people were calligraphers, but couldn't actually read Greek! Or maybe a proofreader, who could read Greek, forgot to check this one before it was bound and made into a book. In fact, after this page, the corrector does start correcting again, so it is a possibility.

This shot the idea that either

1. The scribes were the brilliant people I was always told, or

2. That the Sinaiticus was a reliable copy of the scriptures —even of the Alexandrian stream.

Fact #4: Sinaiticus sections were colored differently. Fellow researcher Mark Michie and I downloaded high resolution photos of Sinaiticus. When I created a collage of all 823 pages together, it became clear that whoever colored Sinaiticus did it in stages. I've enhanced the colors to show you on a photo.

The Evidence 259

Figure 104 - Montage of Sinaiticus pages showing white and darkened sections[66]

The white is the CFA, exactly the pages Tischendorf brought to Saxony. Then there is a certain color to the rest of

---

66. Photo has been adjusted in black and white, to show the differences you can easily see in color (see cover for full-color image). We recommend you view the originals at *www.codexsinaiticus.org*.

the Old Testament. Then there is a third color group in the New Testament. It is unmistakable.

But the people who made the printed 2010 facsimile of Sinaiticus said they made "sensitive adjustments" to the color and voila! All those differences disappeared! The facsimiles do *not* show you the real colors. They even make the white pages of the CFA look just as dark as the rest.

This means that someone in charge of printing the facsimile deliberately changed the colors, so they would match. Why? Didn't they want people to see what I saw on codexsinaiticus.org in plain sight? What were they afraid of? That led to even more questions.

Fact #5: You can't tell by looking which is and isn't scripture. Modern scholars are inconsistent in picking which rewrites are scripture, and which are not. There is scribbling and erasing and rewriting, by multiple people. Then which one is scripture? How come in the Old Testament the extra writing is added to the text, but in the New Testament it is usually taken out of the text?

It looks like Tischendorf just picked and chose a Bible with what he wanted in the text, not what God wants in the text.

Which scribe gave us the true scripture? A? B? C? D? Which corrector fixed the mistakes right? A? B? C? D? How can you tell?

We already know Tischendorf was a liar and a con. So how can we trust which words he decided to put in his specially printed facsimile of Sinaiticus, as the actual scripture? Answer: We can't.

Fact #6: Some whole sections were changed. There are

three sheets that, when folded, make four pages each, that Scribe D used to cancel out Scribe A's mistakes. One of them is right where Mark ends and Luke begins. The letters are squeezed together in Luke 1 and spread wide in Mark 14:54 to Mark 16:8. Then it just stops, leaving a large space. That tells me that they are trying to cover for some big, empty space.

But it would have been bigger, if they didn't spread out the letters. So it was made so that there would *not* be room for Mark 16:9-20. Leaving it out makes Sinaiticus, then, like Vaticanus, which was the only other Greek manuscript in the world that didn't have Mark 16:9-20. That seems planned.

Fact #7: Sinaiticus could *not* possibly be one of the Bibles made for Emperor Constantine in the early 300s AD. According to his lapdog Eusebius, Constantine wanted 50 well-written Bibles. There is no way the Sinaiticus would even be accepted as a term paper, much less a Bible for the emperor.

Fact #8: Sinaiticus had unique mistakes in place names. One was 1,200 miles off the mark, saying "Gaul" instead of "Galatia." This mistake was only found in four lower-case manuscripts, called "minuscules," and Codex Ephraemi Rescriptus. One was seen by Tischendorf and a second, in the codex, was first deciphered by Tischendorf.

Amazingly, some rare and unusual readings found in Sinaiticus do match manuscripts that Tischendorf either found or examined before Sinaiticus. Tischendorf used to tell about these journeys in magazines and journals, and made a little money on the side that way.

Could Tischendorf, himself, have had something to do with the Sinaiticus? Or rather, is it possible someone custom-made a Bible that had things Tischendorf was looking for?

Fact #9: Sinaiticus can't be as old as they say it is. Porfiry Uspensky, who knew Alexandrian manuscripts, said it couldn't have been made before the 5th century, at least 446 AD, because of the space-wasting four columns. But that would make Sinaiticus the same age that they say Alexandrinus is. It's 120+ years after anything Constantine could have ordered. And it loses its authority as "oldest and best."

That also means Vaticanus, with its three columns, also couldn't be before 446 AD. So it can't be "oldest and best," either. Both would be the same as Alexandrinus, and in the Gospels, Alexandrinus is way more like the preserved text than like the Sinaiticus or Vaticanus.

But there's more. By the 1800s, the oldest copy known that had some unique Latin readings that matched the *Shepherd of Hermas* at the end of the New Testament of Sinaiticus, was the Latin Palatinus 150 in the Vatican library, from the late 1300s. But by 1855 people became aware of another one, in Greek, that had those unique readings. It came from a monastery in Mt. Athos, in northern Greece.

The guy who came to sell it (or a copy of it) was none other than Constantine Simonides! So could Sinaiticus have simply back-translated the Latin of a late 1300s manuscript in the Vatican? Or could Simonides have had a part in putting together *Hermas* in the Sinaiticus? Either way, it didn't look like the Sinaiticus was so ancient anymore. Now, almost any date was possible.

On another note, throughout the centuries, lots of copies of scripture were found, which were quite different from the Sinaiticus. But starting after the "discovery" of Sinaiticus, suddenly the vast majority of 20th century finds mostly matched Sinaiticus. Is that a coincidence?

Or could counterfeiters have just gotten much better — maybe trained to do just that, and paid to do this by some big group with a big goal in mind?

Fact #10: Sinaiticus and Vaticanus do not agree —so they could not be what Constantine wanted. Constantine wanted 50 Bibles, maybe. But he didn't want 50 different, disagreeing Bibles! He just wanted multiple copies of **one** text.

Fact #11: The text-critical scholars accepted Tischendorf's early date for Sinaiticus, no questions asked. In exchange, they get a text-critical gold mine, with enough problems to employ them writing papers on Sinaiticus for the rest of their lives.

So they in turn teach their students to doubt the true Bible and accept this counterfeit without question, and reward them for those doubts. So one zombie-scholar churned out another. A perfect example is Bart Ehrman, who believed his professors, and doubted his God.

Fact #12: Bible making is big business. Bible making is well over a billion dollar a year business. And it employs thousands upon thousands of people, in all walks of life. If they were to admit right now that Sinaiticus is a fraud, or that there is only one line of preserved Bibles, many of them would be instantly out of a job. Even if they knew the truth, they have a vested interest in maintaining the lie, to keep their careers. Chapter 20, *It's a Job*, gave a glimpse at how big this issue truly is.

Fact #13: It is a bold-faced lie that "none of these [changes] affect any basic doctrine of the Christian faith," as Jesuit-educated Norman Geisler and most professors have said. The resurrection of Christ is a basic doctrine. Sinaiticus and Vaticanus do not have Mark 16:9-20.

Then scholars claim that Mark was the 1st Gospel and that Mark wasn't written until Mark was dead —in the 80s AD! Therefore the resurrection appearances of Christ were added later, and the bodily resurrection is treated as a later addition to Christianity.

The ascension of Christ into heaven is a basic doctrine. But in addition to Mark 16:19, Luke 24:51, about Jesus' ascension to the right hand of God, is also missing from Sinaiticus. This is the *only* other verse in the Gospels that mentions Christ's ascension.

So if you trust the Sinaiticus and the text scholars, then you may end up believing that the physical resurrection and the ascension into heaven are not original Christianity, and may not have happened at all!

So the Sinaiticus in two places alone can be used to topple two of the most basic doctrines of Christianity.

Fact #14: All the top Greek scholars were fooled into trusting Category I Codex 2427 of Mark's Gospel, until it was proved to be a fake! All the way through Nestles 27th edition Greek New Testament, scholars accepted that Codex 2427 was a top-level Greek text, even though they dated it in the 1300s. That is because it very largely backed up readings in Codex Vaticanus and Sinaiticus.

It turned out that it was a copy of a bad copy of Mark in Vaticanus, made some time between 1874 and 1917. They never would have been so wrong, if they had looked for just two things:

1. Provenance —where it came from, what it was like, and proof of it.

2. Chain of Custody —where did it go, who had it, and proof that it wasn't tampered with.

Here's what's true about Sinaiticus to this day:

1. Sinaiticus has *never* been chemically tested. They canceled the April 2015 testing.

2. There is no master copy that has been found for Sinaiticus. Nothing looks like it, anywhere.

3. It has no provenance. It just "showed up" in St. Catherine's monastery about 1844. There is no record of its existence before 1844.

4. It has no chain of custody. And the only ones who claimed to witness Tischendorf after he got the Sinaiticus, claimed that he aged the text to make it look older! And the guy who stated this was a friend of —Constantine Simonides.

I found out after this that the monks at St. Catherine's monastery told one manuscript explorer in 1815 that they only had **three** Bibles.[67] Thirty years later in 1845, when Porfiry Uspensky came, they said they had **four** Bibles. That fourth was the Sinaiticus.

Fact #15: Until 2004-2009, almost nobody saw actual pictures of more than a single page of Sinaiticus. That means almost everybody who told stories about Sinaiticus

---

67. See Chapter 30 for more information.

was trusting someone else, who also had not seen Sinaiticus, all the way back to 1862.

That also means that everybody *was trusting his or her professor* to be telling the truth, when **nobody** really knew what Sinaiticus even looked like. But trusting the professors meant doubting the King James.

So thousands of students and pew sitters threw away their King James Bibles for a blind trust in a manuscript that not even their pastors or teachers had seen, much less examined!

*They threw away their faith for a mess (and I **DO** mean a mess) of pottage!*

Go online at codexsinaiticus.org and see it for yourself, while it is available. Psalm 118:8: "It is better to trust in the LORD than to put confidence in man."

Fact #16:[68] **The Greek Old Testament "Septuagint" copied 48 words in a row out of Romans 3:13-18, into Psalm 14:3 (13:3 in the so-called "Septuagint").** This means the Septuagint **as we have it** could not be a BC document, but was made after Paul wrote Romans. And both *Sinaiticus* and *Vaticanus* contain this: Paul's words stuck back 1000 years into Psalm 14:3.

Not only that, even Origen's Hexapla from at least the 230s AD *admitted* they do not belong, and so did the Catholic New American Bible through the 1970s. So the Septuagint, as we have it today in the Sinaiticus and Vaticanus, was written *after* the New Testament, after 100 AD, not 285 BC.

Fact #17: There are no physical copies of a "Septuagint" that is earlier than the 4th century AD. The copies that

---

68. For more on Facts #16, #17 and #19, please see my book *Did Jesus Use the Septuagint?* (2017), available from Chick Publications.

exist have their origin in Origen. People like Eusebius of Caesarea trusted Origen and copied the 5th column of his Hexapla. There are no more than a few lines here and there from any time earlier. You could not make a "Septuagint" out of them.

At the earliest, any copies of the "Septuagint" are from three centuries or more after Jesus, not before. So the only person in between is Origen. And he believed that God lied, the Bible contained lies, and that it was okay to lie to anyone that was not a close disciple. That doesn't give me confidence in the Greek texts that supposedly came from him.

Remember, no Greek Septuagint has ever been found that is just an Old Testament, anywhere. Every so-called Septuagint is a combined book, made of at least pieces of an Old Testament, mixed with some Apocryphal writings, followed by the New Testament and maybe a few extra books.[69] Ultimately, Origen is the origin of modern, doubting Bibles. Even though he didn't create the Septuagint himself, the one that he passed down was the one that people used from then on.

Fact #18: Textual Critics make three big mistakes:

1. *Text Critics judge the scriptures by a rule:* "the harder reading is to be preferred," They didn't get this rule from the scriptures, and it contradicts the way God works.

2. *Text Critics forget the active presence of the Devil,* who wants people to have doubt, not faith —just like their critical text Bibles.

3. *Text Critics forget the power of God,* whose pattern is to give us exact words, and who commands us not to add to them nor take away from them.

---

69. See Appendix A for more information.

And there are *two lessons to remember*:

1. I do not *judge* the scriptures. The scriptures judge me.

2. I do not *change* the scriptures. The scriptures change me.

Fact #19: There was no B.C. Septuagint. It was created before 50 AD, probably by Philo of Alexandria. And the Letter of Aristeas, that claims it was made in the 280s BC, is a fake. You can see this in YouTube Vlogs 166-171, in the playlist "Was There a BC Septuagint?" Or you can read it in the book, *Did Jesus Use the Septuagint?*

Fact #20: The Apocrypha is being added to Bibles all over the world, even though the King James translators gave seven good reasons for keeping them out of either the New or the Old Testament. Even new translations like the Common English Bible and the English Standard Version now have the fairy tales of the Apocrypha available.

Fact #21: The Apocryphal books contain false doctrines that are taught by the Roman Catholic religion, but that contradict the actual scriptures. Tobit is a perfect case in point. It is wrong in history, chronology, geography, and it teaches dangerous doctrines, that make man have to pay for his own sins, literally.

Fact #22: The King James Translators had a Vaticanus-Alexandrinus-type text. They used it for the uninspired Apocrypha, but rejected it for any actual scriptures. Brenton's Greek-English Parallel Septuagint accurately used the KJV translation of the Apocrypha for 10 whole books of the Apocrypha, instead of making his own translation, as he seems to have done for the rest of the apocryphal books.[70]

These are the 22 facts I learned over a six month period.

---

70. See Chapter 26, *"What's Wrong With Tobit?"*

28

The Beginning to the 1800s

Let me start by saying this:
THIS IS *MY* ACCUSATION!
You are more than welcome to disagree. God bless you, and have a wonderful day.

This is based on piles of facts. But this is what *I* believe. It's open to being changed by new evidence, and I am getting new evidence every day. It's just that the new evidence keeps backing up what I believe.

It has a few optional possibilities along the way, but the general story remains the same. If you want, you can read this through, then think it through on your own. I totally encourage you to check the sources for yourself.

The key is to THINK. Your eternal destiny may depend upon it.

Here is the big picture, from the beginning to the 1800s. The next chapter will deal with 1800 to today. And remember, it is **my** view on the conspiracy. I take full responsibility for the contents.

The first conspiracy mentioned in the Bible was Joseph's brothers in Genesis 37:18: "And when they saw him afar off, even before he came near unto them, ***they conspired against him to slay him.***"

The next two were accusations by King Saul. He accused the people of conspiring to hide from him that his son Jonathan and David were allies against him in 1 Samuel 22:8. And King Saul accused Ahimelech the priest of helping David commit treason against him in 1 Samuel 22:13.

The fourth and fifth mentions are in 2 Samuel 15:12 and 31, where Absalom got his friends to make him king of Judah and rebelled against King David, attempting to kill his own father. This took the help of one of David's greatest counselors, David's own nephew, and the turned hearts of the men of Israel.

So the main type of conspiracy in the Bible is ***people gathering together to take down somebody or something***, that they were *not* able to attempt alone.

The other type is people grouping together to do evil ***against the Lord God***. There are two examples. One is in Jeremiah 11:9-10:

> And the LORD said unto me, ***A conspiracy is found*** among the men of Judah, and among the inhabitants of Jerusalem. They are turned back to the iniquities of their forefathers, which refused to hear my words; and they went after other gods to serve them: the house of Israel and the house of Judah have broken my covenant which I made with their

fathers.

So they broke their covenant with God, **refused to hear His words** and **served other gods**.

Here's the other example from Ezekiel 22:25:

> There is a ***conspiracy of her prophets*** in the midst thereof, like a roaring lion ravening the prey; they have devoured souls; they have taken the treasure and precious things; they have made her many widows in the midst thereof.

So these prophets "***devoured souls***," filling them with false doctrines and took "***treasure and precious things***," being paid well for their false prophecies, and "made many widows," persecuting and destroying those men who stood up against them. Those were seven of the 30 verses mentioning conspiracy. I don't find it necessary to list all the rest here. You can look them up, if you'd like.

The conspiracy I have found involves elements of all of these. It is the attempt by a lot of people to overthrow a king, refuse to hear God's words, put false words in their place, make a lot of money at it, and use their power to destroy all who would come against or expose their conspiracy. And all this would have the effect of devouring souls, eating away at their faith in the Bible, and in the God who gave His words to us.

And their conspiracy has three purposes:

1. To take away God's preserved and trustworthy words from you, in English, the King James Bible,

2. To give you in its place a Bible with so much confusion and contradictions that you must trust a priest to interpret it for you, and

3. To deliver at the end *one world Bible for one world religion*.

Here's how I see it:

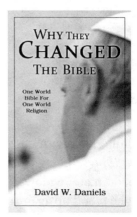

As I wrote in ***Why They Changed the Bible***, Satan has hated God's words from the beginning in Eden. When he could not outright destroy them, he started by getting people to question God's words: "Yea, hath God said…?" This came out in two forms:

"Did God really *mean* that?" and

"Did God really *say* that?"

During the 400 years that God stopped speaking through prophets until John the Baptist, men wrote their own books. Some were legends. Some attempted to be historical. Some were folktales. And some were so far-out that they sound like campfire stories, even claiming to be about famous people.

Of one thing you could be sure: ***none*** of these were, or even ***claimed*** to be, the words of God. These stories were mostly written down in Alexandria, Egypt. But some were changed and rewritten by various people and in other languages. A few stories even made it into Israel, but as stories, not as scripture. What harm could campfire stories do?

But Satan had a sinister, serpent-y thought: "Why don't I get people to ***add*** these stories into a Bible?" That brings us to Alexandria, Egypt. Alexandria, Egypt, was a pagan city that had numerous religions and philosophies.

The Alexandrian Jewish people were pulled away from the

Hebrew Scriptures and corrupted by those pagan philosophies. But they had no official Greek text of the Old Testament.

In the first century AD, a well-off guy with major Roman and Jewish connections, named Philo, paid for people to create a Greek Old Testament. Before he died in 50 AD, Philo put out a story in the form of an "ancient" *Letter of Aristeas,* to make it sound like the Greek Old Testament was written hundreds of years earlier.

That phony pedigree would make people think this Greek Old Testament was worthy to use and compare with Greek philosophy, which Philo liked to do. However, from Philo's writings, it appears that he only wrote about the Law of Moses in Greek, not the Prophets or Writings. So it is ***possible*** that he only got the five books of Moses translated into Greek, before he died. If so, then the Prophets and Writings were composed after he died in 50 AD.

Then sometime later, around the end of the first century, some other people took those Jewish folktales, legends and far-out stories, though ***they never even claimed to be inspired***, and added some of them to that Greek Old Testament. Regardless, by sometime in the 2nd century, they called this whole mess, containing the Law, Prophets, Writings and the Apocrypha mixed together, —***The Septuagint***. [71]

That name connected it to the fake legend that Philo made up, (and that 40 years later Josephus pushed), about 72 translators from all 12 tribes who supposedly lived over 300 years before, that miraculously translated the Old Testament from Hebrew into Greek, when they barely would have known Greek themselves. Then Alexandrian Greek philosophers could compare Moses and other Hebrews to Plato and other

---

71. See Appendix A for more information.

Greeks, to their heart's content.

Colossians 2:8 was given by God to warn us about people like this:

> Beware lest any man spoil you through philosophy and vain deceit, after the tradition of men, after the rudiments of the world, and not after Christ.

Satan had a field day. Then you know what?

This is admitted by about everybody, ancient and modern. It's beyond dispute. People from Alexandria, who called themselves Christians, **changed** that messed up Old Testament Greek. They stuck Christian, New Testament words, that prophesied of Christ, into verses where they didn't belong! God never wrote any such thing in those places. So ***they just wrote it in themselves!***

For instance, here in my 2006 *Septuaginta*, it admits that where it says in *Psalm 96:10* (95:10 in Greek): "Say among the heathen *that* the LORD reigneth," the Septuagint that Justin Martyr had, added words. We find them in his *Dialog with Trypho, a Jew,* Chapter 41.

"Say among the heathen, the Lord hath reigned ***from the tree***," meaning the Lord Jesus reigns from the cross of Calvary. This makes a *fake* prophecy about Jesus in Psalm 96:10.

And Justin Martyr (100-165 AD) actually accused the Jews of maliciously **removing these added words**. But David **didn't write** those words. There's even a parallel verse that David wrote in 1 Chronicles 16:31b. Check it for yourself.

As I showed you in the book, *Did Jesus Use the Septuagint?* (2017), Justin Martyr is unreliable.

KJV Acts 13:29
And when they had fulfilled all that was written of him, they took *him* down <u>from the tree</u>, and laid *him* in a sepulchre.

απο του ξυλου
apo tou xulou
from the tree [cross]

KJV Psalm 96:10
Say among the heathen *that* **the LORD reigneth**: the world also shall be established that it shall not be moved: he shall judge the people righteously.

Septuagint (LXX):
The LORD reigneth ***<u>from the Cross</u>***...

απο   ξυλου
apo   xulou
from [the] cross/tree

Figure 105 - The words 'from the tree' taken from Acts and added to Psalm 96

The words "from the tree" (*apo xulou*) added to the Septuagint version of Psalm 96:10 actually come from Acts 13:29. They were not written by the Psalmist. They were written by someone with the New Testament.

Those added words just happen to **match Paul's words** in Acts 13:29, where he said they took the Saviour, Jesus,[72] down **"from the tree,"** *apo tou xulou*, "and laid him in a sepulchre."

Who changed Psalm 96:10? It couldn't have been Alexandrian Jews who did this. They wouldn't add the cross to a prophecy of the Messiah. The cross was a **stumbling block** to them (1 Corinthians 1:23).

So it had to be so-called "Alexandrian Christians." By the time of Origen, these words were already taken back out of Psalm 96:10. We only know about them because early writers talked about those added words, and Roman Catholics and text critics still write about them.[73] What were they **thinking**?

It's the age-old problem: **once you start to change God's words, where do you stop?**

Back to the Alexandrian Jewish community. In the 2nd century, about 120-200 AD, some Alexandrian sort-of-Jewish men, some say apostates, abandoned using Hebrew and made their *own* Old Testaments in Greek.

---

72. See Acts 13:23, "Of this man's seed hath God according to *his* promise raised unto Israel a Saviour, Jesus:"
73. Pope John Paul II both referred to those words and titled a homily "The Lord Reigns from the Cross," which is described as his "Address at the General Audience on September 18, 2002, in the Paul VI Audience Hall. In his 50th catechesis on the Psalms, the Pope commented on Psalm 95[96]."

Hebrew.	Hebrew Transliterated.	Aquila.	Symmachus.	LXX.	Theodotion.	Variants.
לַמְנַצֵּחַ	λαμανεσσηα	τῷ νικοποιῷ	ἐπινίκιος	εἰς τὸ τέλος	τῷ νικοποιῷ	εἰς τὸ τέλος
לִבְנֵי קֹרַח	βνη κορα	τῶν υἱῶν κορέ	τῶν υἱῶν κορέ	ὑπὲρ τῶν υἱῶν κορέ (τοῖς υἱοῖς)	τοῖς υἱοῖς κορέ	
עַל־עֲלָמוֹת	αλ· αλαμωθ	ἐπὶ νεανιοτήτων	ὑπὲρ τῶν αἰωνίων	ὑπὲρ τῶν κρυφίων	ὑπὲρ τῶν κρυφίων	
שִׁיר	σιρ	ᾆσμα	ᾠδή·	ψαλμός	ᾠδή	ψαλμός
אֱלֹהִים לָנוּ	ἐλωειμ λανου	<ὁ θεὸς ἡμῖν>	ὁ θεὸς ἡμῖν	ὁ θεὸς ἡμῶν	ὁ θεὸς ἡμῶν	
מַחֲסֶה וָעֹז	μαασε· ουος	ἐλπὶς καὶ κράτος	φενοίδησις καὶ ἰσχύς	καταφυγὴ καὶ δύναμις	καταφυγὴ καὶ δύναμις	
עֶזְרָה	ες	βοήθεια	βοήθεια	βοηθὸς	βοηθὸς	
בְצָרוֹת	βσαρωθ	ἐν θλίψεσιν	ἐν θλίψεσιν	ἐν θλίψεσι	ἐν θλίψεσιν	
נִמְצָא מְאֹד	νημσα· μωδ	εὑρεθεὶς σφόδρα	εὑρισκόμενος σφόδρα	ταῖς εὑρούσαις ἡμᾶς σφόδρα (εὑρεθήσεται ἡμῖν)	εὑρέθη σφόδρα (ταῖς εὑρούσαις ἡμᾶς)	
עַל־כֵּן	αλ· χεν	ἐπὶ τούτῳ	διὰ τοῦτο	διὰ τοῦτο	διὰ τοῦτο	
לֹא נִירָא	λω· νιρα	οὐ φοβηθησόμεθα	οὐ φοβηθησόμεθα	οὐ φοβηθησόμεθα	οὐ φοβηθησόμεθα	
בְּהָמִיר	βααμιρ	ἐν τῷ ἀνταλλάσσεσθαι	ἐν τῷ συγχεῖσθαι	ἐν τῷ ταράσσεσθαι	ἐν τῷ ταράσσεσθαι	
אֶרֶץ	[α]αρς	γῆν	γῆν	τὴν γῆν	τὴν γῆν	
וּבְמוֹט	ου βαμωτ	καὶ ἐν τῷ σφάλλεσθαι	καὶ κλίνασθαι	καὶ μετατίθεσθαι	καὶ σαλεύεσθαι (μετατίθεσθαι)	
הָרִים	αριμ	ὄρη	ὄρη	ὄρη	ὄρη	
בְּלֵב	βλεβ	ἐν καρδίᾳ	ἐν καρδίᾳ	ἐν καρδίᾳ	ἐν καρδίᾳ	
יַמִּים:	ιαμιμ	θαλασσῶν	θαλασσῶν	θαλασσῶν	θαλασσῶν	

Figure 106 - Origen's Hexapla shows the earlier Greek OT versions

These were: Aquila, very wooden, unnatural-sounding Greek, Symmachus, a little better, and Theodotion, closer to a paraphrase. But Theodotion also included those *folktales*. We call them *Apocrypha*.

That takes us to the 200s AD. Satan brewed up leaders who were two-faced. Both Clement and Origen believed in *lying* to everyone but their closest disciples about their true beliefs. So *in public*, they could *look like* they were Christians who believed the Bible.

But *in private*, they were connected to the *occult* and were God and Bible *doubters*. And in private, Origen put together that giant, 6-column Old Testament in Hebrew and Greek, called the *Hexapla* (see Figure 106,) paralleling Hebrew, beside the Greek of Aquila, Symmachus and Theodotion, along with his own special column.

Asterisks and Obelisks

In Hebrew?	In Greek?
Yes	No

Added Greek to Origen's column to match the Hebrew
(usually from Theodotion).

In Hebrew?	In Greek?
No	Yes

Marked the Greek in Origen's column, that it wasn't in the Hebrew.

Figure 107 - Origen's symbols mark discrepancies in manuscripts

And yet in private, he also correctly wrote that the Hebrew text was the correct text for the Old Testament. What was in the Greek text, but not in the Hebrew, was wrongly added to the Greek. But what was in the Hebrew text, but not in the Greek, was missing from the Greek and needed to be added. And he wrote symbols that noted what belonged and what didn't.

Origen knew that the Apocrypha didn't come from the Hebrew, but from the Greek, so he knew that the Apocryphal books weren't really Bible, either. But in public, he defended those apocryphal books. He even said the whole Septuagint was given by God!

Over time people got confused, trying to figure out Origen's symbols, so they pretty much just accepted Origen's whole modified text as if it was from God, no questions asked. But remember, the Jewish people in Israel ***never*** fell for that ***Alexandrian lie***. They trusted the words preserved through the Levitical priests that were known to be scripture.

The real test is easy, to find out what is Old Testament scripture.

*What the Jewish people received as scripture, **is** scripture. What they did not receive as scripture, is **not** scripture. That is how Bible believers from the early church through the King James Bible believed it. And Bible believers today still do.*

But what about the Dead Sea Scrolls? In caves in the desert of Judaea near the Dead Sea, people found parts of books written in scrolls, most of which broke into thousands of tiny scraps. Some are from books of the Bible. Some are scraps of apocryphal and pseudepigraphal books (faked writings of prophets). And most of those writings ***nobody has ever even claimed*** to be scripture of ***any*** kind.

There are a few scraps of Greek apocrypha that pretty much have the same words as some Alexandrian Greek Old Testament apocryphal books. But all these, aside from being found in a cave, have:

1. No ***provenance***. That means we do not know ***where*** they were from, ***who*** made them, or ***why***. And they have

2. No ***chain of custody***.

We have no idea ***who*** got hold of them after they were

written, or *why* they were put in caves in the first place, other than keeping them from being destroyed by the Roman army.

And even though there are scraps of apocryphal stories, nothing says they belonged in a scroll *with* the Hebrew scriptures. They are completely separate writings of men.

Explorers also found some religious sect's rules in the caves. But nobody believes those rules and beliefs were considered scripture. Neither were the apocryphal stories:

1. There is *no provenance.*

2. There is *no chain of custody.* And

3. There is *no verified history* to indicate that the scribes or Levites would have stored their own, commanded by God, carefully-copied scriptures there.

So when we find a scroll of Isaiah that turns out to be almost identical to the Masoretic text, that's because the guy who copied it did a pretty good job. It *doesn't* make the Dead Sea *scraps* any better than, or a substitute for, God's holy, preserved words. God's words have:

1. provenance, and

2. chain of custody, and

3. verified history, being passed down by Bible believers, both Jewish and Christian.

Real Bible believers through history have had the same 39 books in the Old Testament (The Hebrews grouped them as 24) that we have in non-Catholic Bibles today.

But Origen's modified Greek Old Testament, together with a corrupted New Testament, got copied and spread around by the Alexandrians. In the 300s, Latin gradually became the next world language. God had already prepared Bible-believing Christians for that.

By the 150s, the Bible had been translated into both Syrian (Aramaic) and Old Latin, from preserved texts at Antioch of Syria (where the disciples were called Christians first, Acts 11:26).

But by 325, Constantine had combined paganism with a thin Christian covering, and called himself "***Bishop of Bishops***," as well as the ***Pontifex Maximus***. Starting in 330, the empire started to shift power toward the spawning Roman Catholic religion. And 50 years later in the 380s, an early pope told Jerome to make an official Latin Bible.

*Now the Devil wants **everyone** to question God's words. The most efficient way is to **add to** and **take away from** God's words, then **mix in** men's fake stories. The Alexandrian Greek with the Apocrypha was perfect for that plan. In 405, Jerome presented an official Roman Catholic Latin Vulgate Bible.*

The Catholic Vulgate (which contains the Apocrypha) gave support to the false doctrines being set up through the Catholic system, like purgatory, angels as mediators, paying for your own sins —literally.

It also changed *meanings* of important words, like changing "repent" to "do penance," —do works that a priest commands to get forgiven of sins… as if you could ***earn forgiveness***.

And they had the nerve to call this lying garbage *Biblia Sacra*, "The Holy Bible." Then persecutions began. For nearly 900 years they persecuted and killed Bible believers to stamp out the true Bible and force people to use their Roman Catholic Latin Vulgate.

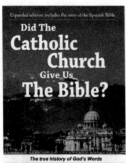

I tell about this in ***Did the Catholic Church Give Us the Bible?*** Catholic leadership said all education had to be in Latin, and nobody's native language. Rome had separated from the Eastern, Greek empire, about 1000 AD.

But in 1453, the Greek curtain was ripped open, when the Muslim Ottoman Empire invaded Constantinople, now called Istanbul. Greek speakers flooded the eastern Roman Catholic countries, and suddenly Greek literature spread all throughout Europe.

The Catholic institution wanted to control the flow of information. So eventually, they allowed people like Erasmus to learn Greek, in order to translate the Greek manuscripts and documents for them into Latin. That way the Roman Catholic system could take control, and keep a lid on the spread of ideas contrary to Catholicism.

God used Erasmus to create a Greek and Latin New Testament starting in 1516 that switched Jerome's Latin back to agree with the preserved scriptures he found as he went from library to library. And because the pope was flattered by the fluff dedication page he wrote, an amazing thing happened:

Roman Catholics started using Erasmus's Greek and Latin! Satan must have been so upset!

Figure 108 - Erasmus' 1516 Greek-Latin NT, Hebrews 13 to James 1

Of course, one man who was influenced by the text that Erasmus published was the monk, Martin Luther. He found out we are justified before God by ***faith*** and ***not works for salvation***. And the Protestants, who left Roman Catholicism, were born.

The Jesuits came into popularity as an army against the Reformation, a Counter-Reformation. They were officially blessed by Pope Paul III in 1540. Then they helped arrange the *Council of Trent*, starting in 1545, to try to stop these Protestants and other Bible believers from ruining everything and rejecting the Apocrypha.

The Jesuits raised the Apocrypha to "Deuterocanonical," which meant they were a "second canon," or a second part of scripture, instead of the inaccurate, dangerous words of men that they were.

The Jesuits *empowered the Inquisition* like never before. Over the next century Jesuits got the Dominicans to torture and kill many Bible believers, including the Vaudois who preserved the Old Latin, Protestants who left Catholicism, and the Anabaptists who were never Catholic.

Now the lines were drawn: Protestants, Anabaptists and other Bible believers on one side, the Roman Catholic hierarchy on the other.

Satan's *first* strategy had been to *kill* the Christians and *destroy* their Bible. This didn't work. They continued to thrive and spread and God helped them preserve the words of scripture for the next generation.

Satan's second strategy was to *substitute a fake Bible for the real one*. That didn't work. Anyone who compared them could see they were completely different. Again, God kept preserving His Bibles for the next generation.

Then Satan came up with a *third strategy*. He went back to the first thing that ever worked for him. Four little words: *"Yea, hath God said?"* And Satan began a plan to get Christians to believe their own preserved Bible had to be *FIXED*. Here's how he pulled it off.

During the 1500s, Bible believers kept working at translating God's words. But in 1604-1610, God blessed a final English translation. It was an open translation project, where the Bible was gone over no less than 14 times.

Every translator had the opportunity to convince the rest of his idea for translating a word. Over 50 people is a lot to convince. Personal opinions get left by the wayside. That helped safeguard the translation.

The few disagreements that a translator clung to all the way through the process got put in the margin, with an "Or." The text itself is what all 50 plus people agreed on. That is the preserved text. Not the notes, references, "or," "that is," or word definitions or literal renderings —just the text. That result is God's preserved words in English, the King James Bible.

Faith is its fruit. People can read, believe, and act upon it, and they have fruit for the kingdom of God! It's amazing!

The Devil had to get people to turn away from **God's preserved words**, and the Reformation Greek New Testament. Remember, from the early 1500s, Catholics used Erasmus' Greek and Latin text, just like the Protestants! They couldn't get Christians to switch from the preserved Greek text to that corrupt Catholic **Latin** Vulgate.

So Catholics had to switch Protestants to their corrupt **Greek** text, like the Vaticanus. Starting in the 1600s, Satan had to get Catholic scholars to switch from Latin to Greek, because he had a plan using Greek.

Figure 109 - Hug's Latin book *On the Antiquity of Codex Vaticanus*

Now before 1810, a Roman Catholic named Johann Leonhard Hug (1765–1846) spent a few years going over a certain Greek text. He wrote a book about it in Latin, called *On the Antiquity of Codex Vaticanus*.

Erasmus had already recognized in the 1520s-30s that the Codex Vaticanus was ***not*** the early document it claimed to be. It was either created or modified after the Council of Florence (about 1435). Erasmus knew it was untrustworthy and refused to use it in his Greek New Testament.

I found verification of that in an online article written by Chris Thomas and in the 1856 book he referenced.[74] Erasmus said Vaticanus couldn't be that old, because it was influenced by the Latin, which came later. Even Hort (of Westcott and Hort) ***admitted*** the Latinisms. In fact, Hort thought Vaticanus might have been written in… ***Rome***.

But Hug argued that the Vaticanus was not a later text. He said it was one of the earliest. He said that in the search for the truest Bible text, we had to go to the ***Egyptian*** Greek manuscripts, like Vaticanus.

---

74. See the online article, Erasmian Myths: Codex Vaticanus by Chris Thomas, found at http://confessionalbibliogogy.com, dated May 16, 2016. See also *An Introduction to Textual Criticism of the New Testament* by Thomas Hartwell Horne, revised and edited by Samuel Prideau Tregelles (London: Longman, Brown, Green, Longmans, & Roberts, 1856,) pp. xv – xvii.

The Beginning to the 1800s 287

Figure 110 - Annotations to the NT with Hug's Latin *Antiquity* included

Hug's book spread quickly. The entire text was stuck into other books, so all the scholars could see it. Suddenly, palaeographers (people who determine the age and genuineness of texts) were scrambling to get a view of the Vaticanus!

I had just written the above words, and guess what? Chris Pinto texted me and told me about an article by the president of the American Historical Association, James Westfall Thompson, written just before he died in 1941. In his article, "The Age of Mabillon and Montfaucon," he tells us that palaeography itself was invented in the Counter-Reformation by Rome through the Benedictines.

And the very guys who set up the so-called science of deciphering ancient manuscripts, palaeography, were anti-Protestant priests. These are the same guys I wrote about in

Did the Catholic Church Give Us the Bible.

Mabillon —said that we should "criticize" the Bible just like any other book, and

Montfaucon —started "lower criticism" and said that the text Christians had used for centuries was inferior to Origen's.

Those are two of the guys behind every scholar who tries to figure out how old documents are! All the text critics learned their stuff from Roman Catholics or people taught by Catholics, who were trying to destroy the Reformation and get rid of the Greek behind the King James Bible!

Thompson wrote, "…the historical attack became so effective that Rome was compelled to fight history with history, to combat fire with fire." They had to invent a way for Protestants to think that the Catholic texts they were finding were better than the traditional text used for centuries by Christians. They called it "palaeography."

They invented this "science" of palaeography to make people think they were wise. But they were foolishly being duped into turning toward Catholicism. All those text critics you've heard of? They were set up, starting in the 1600s.

This means that Franklin Logsdon, who helped interview translators for the New American Standard and later denounced it, was right, when he said the Jesuits were trying to get Protestants away from Erasmus' text, to undermine and supplant it, and the King James Bible, that it leads straight to.[75]

So all the great text critics who figured the age of

---

75. You can hear Logsdon yourself, in the movie *Bridge to Babylon* (2016), available from Chick Publications.

manuscripts, like *Tischendorf* and *Tregelles*, learned their craft from Catholic or Catholic-taught teachers! These Benedictines, the Maurists, were part of the *Counter-Reformation*, just like the Jesuits were.

Do you trust their scholarship? I don't. The Bible is *not* like any other book. It should never be treated like any other book. And the preserved texts are *not inferior to Origen's*.

I trust the tried, tested and proved, preserved text, God's holy words in English, the King James Bible.

You have just heard my Background Story. What was the end game? That's in the next chapter.

29

1800s to Today

Now we come to the most controversial part: what I believe happened in the 1800s and 1900s. Are you ready? Fasten your safety belts.

After J. L. Hug's book claiming Vaticanus was oldest and best, the carefully-prepared palaeographers bought the Vaticanus and other Egyptian Bibles hook, line and sinker. They believed the lie that Vaticanus had to be one of the oldest and best, if not the oldest and best. If it was, we needed to change all our Bibles to match it. Vaticanus became the prize to seek. Everyone who was anyone wanted to get a look at it.

But who had control over it? The Vatican. So anyone who wanted to see it had to make nice with Rome, and not say anything or do anything that would upset them, in hopes of seeing Vaticanus.

It was a race. And everything went to Rome. Now you have to be nice to the pope. So none of these guys are going to try to rescue any Catholics from their bondage to Rome, say that the pope is Antichrist, preach or teach against Rome in any way. Ironically, they have to act better than Catholics if they want to be allowed a glance at what they now believed was "oldest and best," —Codex Vaticanus.

One guy was totally enamored with that Catholic French monk, Montfaucon, and his science of palaeography, "deciphering ancient manuscripts." That guy was anxious to see the "oldest and best," and admitted that he hoped that it would bring him money, a good position, and the highest praises of man.

That guy was Constantin Tischendorf.

At that time, according to the scholars there were three known Egyptian manuscripts: Alexandrinus, Ephraemi Rescriptus and Vaticanus. Tischendorf was too late to study Alexandrinus. That had been done already. He needed something new to put his own name on.

The Catholics sponsored him to spend two years working on the Ephraemi Rescriptus, an erased and rewritten-over codex. They awarded him for that. And he got some scholarly recognition. But the public *still* didn't know who he was. It wasn't enough.

Tischendorf also spent a few years doing favors for various Catholic leaders, deciphering Greek documents. Then he asked them to write letters to the pope, for the pope to let Tischendorf see the Vaticanus, the goal of his life.

But as the 1800s went on, scholars started to see that it wasn't enough to have just Vaticanus. They needed *something else* to justify the unusual readings in it, the words that were missing and the words that were changed.

Then, as if by magic, POOF! In 1844 suddenly the Sinaiticus appears. It has no provenance, no history of any kind. It has no chain of custody.

It just showed up in a monastery that 29 years earlier in 1815, only said it had three Bibles.[76] Now they suddenly said that they had FOUR.

Sinaiticus was the magical fourth. I'd spent a lot of time gathering facts. But I hadn't simply spilled the beans of what I believe really happened.

Tischendorf was set up.

From his favorite teacher in college, they picked him out. They knew what sort of person he was. They saw his pride, his ambition, and decided to make it work for them.

So they gave him the plum of sole access to the Ephraemi Rescriptus —for two years! Then they rewarded him for his work. In 1843 Tischendorf was granted an audience with the pope. He was mostly silent about the meeting, but there are a lot of details coming out now in books from many different sources, including Catholic ones, about what happened.

Tischendorf got to see Jesuit Cardinal Mai's personal work on Vaticanus, ***before it was published.*** He might have taken notes of it home with him. Regardless, he learned about certain unusual readings, and he was now on the lookout for them in any manuscripts he would find. Remember, he is credited as having "found" more manuscripts than almost anyone else. I wonder how many of them were fake, or set up for him to find?

In that papal audience, ***they told him he should go to the East to find manuscripts.*** We know that after this, he raised money and made a beeline to Cairo, then to St. Catherine's monastery. It's pretty obvious that they "tipped him off" that there was something to be found there.

---

76. See Chapter 30 for more information.

1800s to Today 293

Somehow the Catholics got wind of this special, Vaticanus-favoring text. But they were in a hurry. They needed for an outsider to get hold of it, while it was still available.

Somehow those were set up for Tischendorf to find. That's why we have found some of them only at Mount Athos.

They had worked up Tischendorf's reputation. They had taught him what to look for to judge a manuscript "ancient." He was totally set up for this.

Somehow they had a made-to-order manuscript there for Tischendorf to find.

They started with the Old Testament, and then moved to the New at the last. We know for sure it was finished in the form that we see today by 1845. They could have moved down to St. Catherine's and tried to finish stuff up in the last year or so. I say that because scraps of Sinaiticus were tossed into a little hidden chamber and only found in 1975.

They seem to have cut out huge chunks of the Bible that didn't have major doctrinal stuff or many alternate readings. It will take more study to figure out why someone cut them out.

Many monks were paid good money to come up with ancient Greek manuscripts after the fall of Constantinople in 1453. There were only so many to go around. So there were many counterfeiters.

Maybe Constantine Simonides was a counterfeiter. But maybe he was just a good calligrapher. Someone could have employed him to work on this text, which was corrected and rewritten in various ways by other people. That way he, and his friends —maybe Benedict? maybe Kallinikos?— a number of correctors worked on this rush job of a text. Then it was sent down to the monastery in the Egyptian desert for Tischendorf to find. If Tischendorf got his finances together for his trip really fast, it would make it necessary to get the manuscript down there even faster. That could force some short cuts.

I mentioned mistakes. There are many. They would put up texts to copy, but they would have to go from single-column documents most likely, and copy into four columns. That is very tricky. So they set down one manuscript and turned to another, and kept writing. They didn't have time to read it. That's how they skipped from Chronicles to Ezra and kept on writing. Not till later did someone catch it and write a couple creative notes.

But all these mistakes actually worked for Rome. There were so many layers, palaeographers could read Sinaiticus for a lifetime and never run out of theories. And they'd be indebted to Rome for it all!

And did anyone notice, they abandoned the preserved Bible for all this?

Protestant scholars had a vested interest in believing Tischendorf's date of 350 AD. Then they could teach it to their students on down to today, deceiving Christians into thinking that God didn't actually preserve His words. They led their students to think that we have to have priests —I mean "textual scholars"— to tell us which words ***might*** be God's, and which words ***might not*** be.

I think Tischendorf didn't know he was duped… at first. He may have seen the book (yes, book, just like it was clearly described the next year) and cut out two portions, just like an ordinary thief, thinking he got away with something. He didn't know he was falling into Rome's plan.

Then after he realized what he had taken, he didn't let people get too close to the pages he removed. They had such errors! So he just typeset his own Codex Friderico Augustanus (CFA), printing up which Greek variants he thought belonged in the text. Then he put all the stuff he rejected into end notes that told why he thought they didn't belong. People didn't get to see the CFA. They only saw Tischendorf's book, so they simply read *it*, and believed *him*.

Rome was delighted! They awarded him, as well as every palaeographer who agreed that these were indeed ancient manuscripts.

I have to skip a lot here. So let's jump to the third visit, in 1859. I think he thought he had a great find, maybe through the 1840s. But at the latest, when he got the Sinaiticus to Cairo in 1859, he figured out it was a fake. It was too new. The parchment was supple. It was ... white, too fresh to *really* be old.

So he came upon a plan. He darkened Sinaiticus with, maybe lemon juice, like Simonides' friend says he did. I have to say, if Simonides made it all up, and his friends are imaginary, it is amazing that they claimed specific events that I only discovered starting in 2014, and people in general could only check starting in 2009.

Either Simonides or one of his friends saw Tischendorf claim he was "cleaning" the pages. But actually, he was aging them to look older, before he went to Russia with Sinaiticus, and people could see it up close.

Tischendorf and Simonides knew each other. There's more to that story.

But it's clear that Simonides didn't want Tischendorf taking away his glory. He'd worked on it himself! So he came out and brazenly said he was the author of the Sinaiticus, and it wasn't old, it was a special project and gift for the protector of the monasteries.

Later he clarified the story to say it was more of a draft copy. For some reason that draft copy was not used as the basis for a final copy. The project was never finished. Again, that fit into Rome's plans.

Tischendorf went into one rage after another. Simonides pushed all his buttons. Tischendorf responded that he was the expert, and Simonides was a con man. (However, the evidence leads me to the conclusion that the opposite is closer to the truth.)

It was said that Simonides disappeared in 1867, with a story that would make nobody want to look for him, saying he died among lepers.

That's enough on them for now. What was the result?

Tischendorf's analysis and date were pretty much accepted by the scholars. Sinaiticus was now the "oldest and best." He got award after award. He got some money, some position, and he got to spend more time with Vaticanus. In 1867 he published Vaticanus, his prize.

That was just what Westcott and Hort needed. They took both Sinaiticus and Vaticanus and made them the determiner of their magical "oldest and best" Greek Text.

Despite all the protesting about changes, Westcott and Hort's text is still pretty much the same as the newest one you find out today. That became the Revised Version, and the Bible version mill was started, which still churns out

1800s to Today

new, disagreeing Bibles, to this day.

What does Rome get out of all this? They want people believing the Alexandrian texts are the best. And Alexandrian texts have the Apocrypha. So the "oldest and best texts," they say, have the Apocrypha.

A Bible with the Apocrypha switches you to a Bible with so many contradictions that you MUST TRUST YOUR PRIEST.

That sets the stage for the one world Bible. The one world Bible will have: an Alexandrian critical Greek text, a Critical Hebrew text modified by other "ancient discoveries," including Septuagint readings. (The Hebrew Masoretic text will be put down and maybe taught to be worse than the Septuagint!)

And one world Bible will have the Apocrypha, with the contradictory, unscriptural doctrines that are so important to Roman Catholicism.

By the way, that is already happening, right now. So the stage is set. That's why it was so important in 1966 for the United Bible Societies to require that any new Bible translation project in the world can be stopped and the Apocrypha added, simply by Catholics in the area asking for it.

Satan got what he wanted. "But it's a Bible!" Yes, but it's not GOD's Bible. It's man's Bible. Satan has gotten everyone to come over to Rome's Bible. Everyone but the stick-in-the-mud, jot-and-tittle King James Bible people (and a few other translations in other languages)

Satan doesn't care what Bible you read in English, as long as it isn't the King James Bible.

To add insult to injury, Satan has started pushing the King

James Apocrypha, giving it false importance, and pushing it on King James Bible believers, to get them to accept the Apocrypha —anything to get them away from God's words, to lower God's words, and to lift up man's words.

This is a conspiracy. The Catholic system and the text critics have conspired to take down a king, the King James Bible. They ridicule anyone who trusts the King James, and are happy to try to destroy the reputation of anyone who turns from the so-called Critical Text.

The goal is to get everyone to let go of the King James Bible. They want them to accept a contradictory and confusing text. They want you so confused that you have to ask a scholar —or a priest— to tell you which to believe and which to doubt.

Ultimately, they want you to accept a new Bible that is coming, a Bible that all the scholars will agree on, complete with Apocrypha: One world Bible for one world religion.

30

The Sinaiticus Smoking Gun?

Who really wrote Sinaiticus? Where? When? Let's see where —and to whom— the evidence leads us.

Let me sum up: in 1844 Constantin Tischendorf claims he found 129 folia of vellum, in a wastepaper bin to be burned, at St. Catherine's monastery in the Egyptian Peninsula. He took with him 43. Then he claims that by 1859 he got hold of where they came from: a huge codex he called Sinaiticus, with parts of the Old Testament, all of the New Testament, plus the *Epistle of Barnabas* and the *Shepherd of Hermas*.

In 1862 he published the Codex Sinaiticus, and it became the game changer in Biblical criticism. It was paired with Vaticanus and its unusual readings. And suddenly, almost all Bibles to this day were changed away from the historical, traditional text to the modern form. But there was a cost: faith was replaced with doubt.

In 1862, Constantine Simonides, who had sold documents to Tischendorf before, claimed that Tischendorf had made a huge mistake. The so-called "Sinaiticus" was actually a project that he himself had done, 20 years earlier, as a gift for the Tsar. Of course, Tischendorf was outraged.

I have shown over time that Tischendorf and perhaps Simonides lied about various things. So let's think about this. Is there a way to find out who was telling the truth, if anyone, and what the real facts are about the Codex Sinaiticus? This chapter may give you the smoking-gun facts that influence your decision.

Who really wrote Codex Sinaiticus? Where? And when?

I've just found some evidence —and verified some evidence— that's starting to make me think I know where Sinaiticus came from. And it fits into the big picture so well, that it's starting to settle the story of the move to create one world Bible for one world religion.

When the evidence starts to make sense and the puzzle pieces begin to fit together, then it will also expose some of the lies and other doubts placed in our path.

I really want you to track with me, so I want to summarize some past information and show how it fits in with what I just discovered. After this, you may never look at the "oldest and best" Codex Sinaiticus in the same way again.

First, as you have seen in this book, you know very well that it seems that both Constantines, Constantin Tischendorf and Constantine Simonides, lied at one time or another.

Tischendorf lied about parchment documents, scraped animal hide, being in a wastebasket to be burned. First, you don't burn parchment. You burn wood or paper. Animal skin is a stinky, smoky, smoldering mess.

According to a book by a Tischendorf supporter, a monk named "Father Justin" informed him that:

> "... it was positively ridiculous to claim that the sheets would have been burnt. Parchment is

scraped animal hide, and hide burns badly. Unlike papyrus, its predecessor as a writing material, it was almost imperishable and thus, as Tischendorf must have known from personal experience, reused rather than destroyed. If an ancient text became redundant it was scraped off and the parchment written on afresh. The whole thing was then called a palimpsest, and Tischendorf himself had won fame for deciphering one such. Parchment had remained in use for binding books even when it was superseded by paper. Father Justin said that no modern expert gave credence to Tischendorf's claim that he had saved the Sinai Bible sheets from the flames in the nick of time."[77]

Second, the "wastebasket" was really a storage bin for parchments, widely used for 2,000 years at least.

Third, that means every conversation Tischendorf claimed to have had about that with Kyrillos the librarian was a lie, totally made-up out of Tischendorf's imagination.

So much for his sterling reputation. And I've shown you the evidence that someone darkened Sinaiticus. I've had the theory it was Tischendorf, to make Sinaiticus look older, because Steven Avery showed me the website, codexsinaiticus.org, where I could see it for myself back in 2014.

And when I looked online at the 43 folia that Tischendorf took from St. Catherine's monastery in the Egyptian peninsula and gave to the king of Saxony, they are clearly white.

---

77. Jürgen Gottschlich, *The Bible Hunter: the Quest for the Original New Testament* (London: Haus Publishing, Ltd, 2013), pp. 96-97.

They still are, today. But the rest of Sinaiticus looks like someone darkened it with some kind of juice.

So I suspected that what Tischendorf said about his three visits to St. Catherine's in 1844, 1853 and 1859, were lies.

But what about Simonides?

What I read about Constantine Simonides was that he could take any group and split it in half. Half of the people would agree that the documents he was selling were ancient originals. And he could take most of the doubters, and get them to admit that at least what he sold ***them*** was real, even if the ***others*** were fake. And he did that numerous times.

Simonides also claimed that Egyptian hieroglyphics were all wrong, and that ***he alone*** could decode their metaphysical meaning. This was at a time when they were first deciphering hieroglyphics, over 150 years ago, and not everyone was convinced on how to do it. History shows Simonides was either deceived, taught incorrectly, or just lying about that.

On top of that, it seemed he did ***everything***. He was a patriot, he was a scholar with a doctorate, he was a calligrapher, he was a palaeographer who could date ancient documents, and he was an amazing copier of manuscripts. Many people said that, actually, he was a forger.

And to top it all off, Simonides claimed that he wrote the Sinaiticus with his own hands, starting when he was about 19 years old, in 1839-40. If so, Sinaiticus couldn't have been the "oldest and best," because it wasn't the oldest. It was a brand new replica in the form of some older manuscripts, for the collection of the Tsar of Russia. And he penned it all, not in Alexandria, Egypt, but in his uncle's monastery, at the beautiful Mt. Athos in Greece.

The Sinaiticus Smoking Gun?

So Tischendorf claimed he found and dated the oldest complete New Testament in a Greek Bible ever discovered. And we should change our Bibles to match it. But Simonides claimed that that Bible is really what remains of the first draft of a project he began two decades before, that was intended to become a gift to the Tsar of Russia.

So now in the 21st century we have to ask, who is telling the truth? Who is lying? Both? Neither? Or parts of both?

What do you do with people you suspect are telling a lie? Simple. You stop believing anything you cannot verify.

So we do not let anything we cannot verify, or that we can prove to be wrong, enter into the equation. We just set it aside and don't even consider it. It doesn't matter why they may have lied at this point. It's just a distraction. We want the truth.

So we can only trust what we can verify. The rest is open to our best understanding and interpretation of the evidence. Does that sound fair to you?

Here are the basic elements of Simonides' story: In 1839-40 Simonides, a 19-year-old, came to Mt. Athos to make a single Bible from a compilation of a bunch of old texts, and make it look like an ancient manuscript.

He wanted to send it to the Tsar of Russia, the rich patron supplying money to support the monasteries around Mt. Athos, in the hopes that the Tsar would pay for a printing press for his uncle's monastery of Panteleimon. He wrote it, overseen by his friend, the monk Kallinikos Monachos.

But while Simonides was away, busy with other things, his working copy of that Bible was sent —without corrections— to St. Catherine's monastery. Then later, when Kallinikos was at St. Catherine's in 1844, he saw Tischendorf all excited about the codex.

Kallinikos knew that Tischendorf stole small parts of it. Then at a later time Kallinikos saw Tischendorf, who claimed he was cleaning the manuscript, but actually, he was aging it.

What can we verify of this story?

Simonides claimed that he created the Sinaiticus himself, on Mt. Athos, for his famous uncle Benedict.

So let's start with Mt. Athos. Is Mt. Athos a real place?

Is it a mythical place, like the myth of Mt. Olympus? Sure, there is a mount Olympus in Greece, but there aren't gods on the top.

So what's the truth about Mt. Athos?

Here's what I found out. Mt. Athos is at the northeast tip of Greece, just south of Bulgaria. It's on the third peninsula that looks like a 3-fingered glove. It's on your Bible maps.

Mt. Athos is a peninsula. But it's also a single mountain. It is also an autonomous, self-governing state full of monks, with 20 monasteries. And it has no roads around it, so you can't drive there. They will only allow you to go by boat.

And not just anyone can go there, not even on a visit.

No women can enter at any time, ever.

Unless a monk has invited you himself, you have to be at least 18 to come to Athos.

If you want to stay for more than one day, you must have permission from the monastery. Then you can, with the proper paperwork and permissions, stay up to four days, three nights.

The Sinaiticus Smoking Gun?

And they really want pilgrims, who come to pray, etc., not just tourists. So there is a tightly limited tourist trade for visitors today, but in the 1800s it was much tighter.

The only way to find out what was on Mt. Athos was to find out from someone trustworthy who had been there. In the late 1800s to early 1900s, there was just such a man: Spyridon Paulou Lampros.

Figure 111 - Spyridon Paulou Lampros

He studied literature in Athens, then got his PhD at the University of Leipzig. From 1890 to 1913 at least, Lampros became professor of history and classical literature at the University of Athens. Twice he was Dean of the University. And he even founded a historical magazine about Greek philosophy and culture, and researched Medieval Greek.

Lampros made a two-volume catalog of books he found on Mt. Athos, and told who wrote or copied them. And I found a copy of that catalog.[78]

Among the names he listed, three are important to us: "Holy deacon and teacher Benedict," Simonides' uncle; Constantine Simonides; and Kallinikos Monachos. The next two pictures have certain words underlined.

| Κ' ΒΙΒΛΙΟΘΗΚΗ ΜΟΝΗΣ ΠΑΝΤΕΛΕΗΜΟΝΟΣ | 381 |

5999. 492.
Χαρτ. 8. (0,20 × 0,14). XIX. (φ. 219).
1 (φ. 1 β). Τυπικὸν "Ἐνθύμισις τι μεγάλι τεσαρακοστί."

2 (φ. 3 α). Εὐχαὶ κατ' ἀλφάβητον, ἐν εἴδει οἴκων, εἰς τὸν Χριστόν.
Ἄρχονται ἀπὸ τῆς Θεολογίας καὶ τελευτῶσιν εἰς τὴν Δευτέραν τοῦ Χριστοῦ παρουσίαν. Περιέχουσι δὲ κατὰ τάξεις Δοξολογίας, Εὐχαριστίας, Ἐξομολογήσεις καὶ Αἰτήσεις.

3 (φ. 16 α). Ἰωάννου τοῦ Δαμασκηνοῦ
Εὐχὴ εἰς τὴν Θεοτόκον διὰ στίχων κατ' ἀλφάβητον.

4 (φ. 23 α). Ἰωσὴφ τοῦ ὑμνογράφου Κανὼν εἰς τὸν τίμιον Σταυρόν.

23 (φ. 161 α). Οἶκοι Μακαρίου τοῦ νέου ἀρχιεπισκόπου Κορίνθου κατ' ἀλφάβητον.
24 (φ. 169 α). Ἀκολουθία τῆς ὁσίας Ἀθανασίας Αἰγινήτιδος.
Μένει ἀτελὴς ἐν ταῖς λέξεσι· καὶ ἀνδρείας τὸν πύργον Ἀθανασίας σή....
Γέγραπται τὸν XIX. αἰῶνα χειρὶ Ἰακώβου διδασκάλου.
25 (φ. 185 α). Ἀπολυτίκιον Φωτεινῆς τῆς Σαμαρείτιδος.
26 (φ. 186 α). Κανὼν εἰς τοὺς θεοπάτορας.
27 (φ. 192 α). Ἀκολουθία τῆς Ζωοδόχου πηγῆς.
Ἐπιδιορθωθὴ παρὰ τοῦ διδασκάλου Βενεδίκτου.
28 (φ. 200 α). Χαιρετισμοὶ τοῦ τιμίου Προδρόμου.

Figure 112 - One of the pages showing Benedict's name

Χαρτ. 8. (0,21 × 0,155). XIX. (φ. 10).
"Κανὼν τῆς ἁγίας καὶ μεγάλης Κυριακῆς τοῦ Πάσχα, ἤτοι λαμπροφόρου Ἀναστάσεως Κυρίου. Ποίημα ὄντα τοῦ ἐν ἁγίοις πατρὸς ἡμῶν Ἰωάννου τοῦ Δαμασκηνοῦ."
Ἐν τέλει· Χεὶρ Κωνσταντίνου Σιμωνίδου. 1841. Μαρτίου 27.
Ἴδε καὶ 6406 (899), 6407 (900).

6406. 899.
Χαρτ. 4. (0,25 × 0,17). XIX. (σ. 22).
Ἰωάννου τοῦ Δαμασκηνοῦ "Κανὼν τῆς ἁγίας καὶ μεγάλης Κυριακῆς τοῦ Πάσχα, ἤτοι λαμπροφόρου Ἀναστάσεως τοῦ Κυρίου."
Ἐν τέλει· Χεὶρ Καλλινίκου μοναχοῦ.
Ἴδε καὶ 6407 (900). *Ἔστι δὲ ἀντίγραφον τοῦ* 6405 (898) *ὡς καὶ ὁ εὐθὺς* 6407 (900).

6407. 900.
Χαρτ. 4. (0,25 × 0,17). XIX. (σ. 22).
Ὅμοιος τῷ ἀνωτέρω.
Διὰ χειρὸς τοῦ αὐτοῦ Καλλινίκου μοναχοῦ. *Ἔστι δὲ ἀντί-*

*6411. 904.
Χαρτ. 8. (0,21 × 0,15). XIX. (φ. 288).
Ἀνθολογία.
Ἐν ἀρχῇ εὔσημα διὰ κινναβάρεων.

6412. 905.
Χαρτ. 8. (0,19 × 0,14). XVIII. (φ. 188).
1. Γερμανοῦ Νέων Πατρῶν Ἀνθολογία τοῦ Στιχηραρίου (Δοξαστάριον).
2. Τοῦ αὐτοῦ Ἑτέρα ἀνθολογία τοῦ Στιχηραρίου.

*6413. 906.
Χαρτ. 8. (0,205 × 0,15). XIX. (φ. 368).
Ἀνθολογία ἤτοι νέα Παπαδική.
Ἐν φ. 364 β'. Ἐγράφη ἡ παροῦσα ἀνθολογία παρὰ τοῦ μουσικολογιωτάτου κυρίου Γρηγορίου Λαμπαδαρίου τῆς τοῦ Χριστοῦ μεγάλης ἐκκλησίας μέχρι τῶν τασαντοαρίων τοῦ Εὐαγγελίου ἀπὸ δὲ τούτων ἄχρι τέλους παρ' ἐμοῦ Θεοκλήτου ἱεροδιακόνου τοῦ Πελοποννησίου ἐν ἔτει ͵ϛωιϛ' κατὰ μῆνα Ἰουνίου (=1816).
Ἐν ἀρχῇ εἰκὼν τοῦ προφήτου Δαβὶδ διὰ χρωμάτων καὶ χρυσοῦ.

Figure 113 - Catalog page showing the names of Simonides and Kallinikos

---

78. Spyridon Paulos Lambros (or Lampros), *Catalogue of the Greek Manuscripts on Mount Athos: Edited for the Syndics of the University Press*, Vol. 1 (Cambridge: University Press, 1895); and Vol. 2 (1900).

The Sinaiticus Smoking Gun? 307

Simonides is only listed in a single record of a minor project. But because of this entry, we know for sure that on March 27th, 1841, Constantine Simonides was on Mt. Athos, at Benedict's Panteleimon monastery. And so was Kallinikos Monachos.

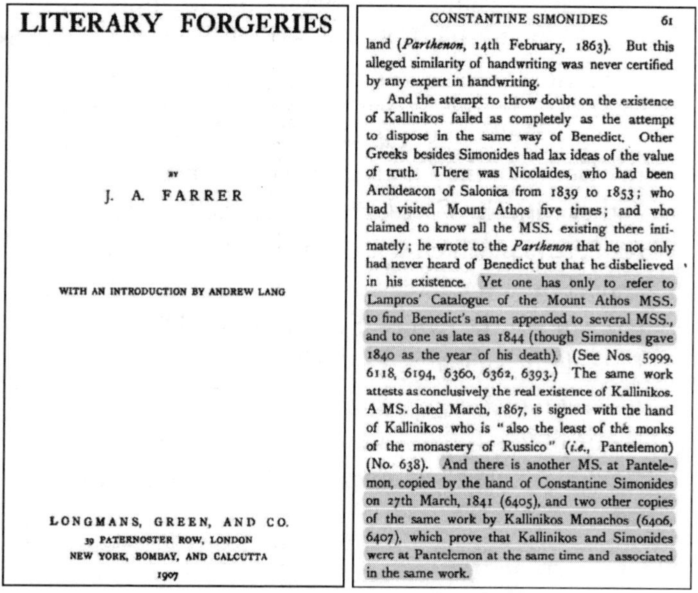

Figure 114 - Title Page of Farrer's book, *Literary Forgeries* (1907) and page 61, stating Kallinikos and Simonides were both on Mt. Athos

In his 1907 book, *Literary Forgeries*, J.A. Farrer wrote that these entries in the catalog "prove that Kallinikos and Simonides were at Pantelemon [*sic*] at the same time and associated in the same work"[79]

---

79. J.A. Farrer, *Literary Forgeries* (New York: Longmans, Green and Co., 1907), p. 61

This is important, because Simonides said Kallinikos was his friend. In 1862, London journals recorded the battle between Tischendorf, who said Sinaiticus was from the 300s AD, and Simonides, who basically said "No, I wrote it myself, 1839-40."

Then, a letter came from Alexandria, Egypt, written on October 15th, 1862. It was signed, Kallinikos Hieromonachos. Here are three of the many statements in that letter:

> ...I do myself declare to all men by this letter, that the Codex of the Old and New Testaments, together with the *Epistle of Barnabas* and of the *Shepherd Hermas*, which was abstracted by Dr. Tischendorf from the Greek monastery of Mount Sinai, is a work of the hands of the unwearied Simonides himself. Inasmuch as I myself saw him in 1843 … in the month of February writing it in Athos." This is one of two times Kallinikos mentioned seeing Simonides. Further down he wrote "22 years ago," which was 1840.

Here's a second:

> ...Dr. Tischendorf, coming to the Greek monastery of Sinai in 1844, in the month of May (if my memory does not deceive me), and remaining there several days, and getting into his hands, by permission of the librarian, the codex we are speaking of, and perusing and re-perusing it frequently, abstracted secretly a small portion of it, but left the largest portion in the place where it was, and departed undisturbed.

And here's the third:

> ...And I know yet further, that the codex also was cleaned with lemon-juice, professedly for the purpose of cleaning its parchments, but in reality in order to weaken the freshness of the letters, as was actually the case.[80]

It was signed: "Kallinikos Hieromonachos, Alexandria, October 15, 1862."

Some people think that Simonides made up Kallinikos. But we know from the catalog that he actually existed. We know he was with Simonides on Mt. Athos one year after Simonides claimed he made Sinaiticus, with Kallinikos watching him.

Let me remind you again, how in 1845, Sinaiticus was a **bound book** examined by Porfiry Uspensky of Russia.

It's pretty clear that Tischendorf cut out parts secretly and snuck them back to Saxony, to Leipzig, in 1844. And Tischendorf either darkened Sinaiticus himself, or he knew who did and kept silent, because *anyone* can see the difference between white pages and dark pages.

As far as I know, nobody else made these claims that Kallinikos' letter made. And I came to my conclusions just by looking at the evidence. There are three possibilities: Simonides found out all these facts; or Kallinikos was actually there; or one of them knew somebody who was, because these three statements match the facts.

Whatever way, it adds up. So far, it seems logical that Tischendorf at first thought the codex was genuine, and

---

80. See *The Journal of Sacred Literature and Biblical Record*, Vol. 3, (1863) pp. 211-212.

stole parts when he couldn't get somebody to let him have the whole thing. He had to justify the expense of going down there, and he wanted the reputation that he would get from discovering an ancient codex. At this point Tischendorf was deceived.

I was informed that J. Michael Featherstone was writing a book, and for the first time he was translating Tischendorf's private letters to his family. We know from biographies that Tischendorf wrote personal letters to his fiancée, then wife Angelika, and to his brother, Julius. Here is one interesting point from those letters.

Please note, the author turned the letters into the 3rd person, probably to protect his copyright on the finished product, so imagine that Tischendorf is talking about himself.

Tischendorf wrote in 1844 that he:

> …has come into possession of 43 parchment folia of the Greek Old Testament which are some of the very oldest preserved in Europe. He believes they are from the mid-fourth century, and they are remarkable not only for their age but also other reasons.

Sounds like he bought the story, at first. And "come into possession of," not "someone gave them to him." As I said, I think he's admitting that he stole them.

Anyway:

> He must cut his trip short: he wants to go to the patriarch in Constantinople in order to obtain the rest of the folia (beside the 43 he has) which remained at Sinai; thus he has suspended making

The Sinaiticus Smoking Gun?

a public announcement of his find. ***That his trip to Sinai was of interest to him in thousands of other ways his brother will certainly understand.***[81]

The next year, 1845, Russian religious leader and researcher Porfiry Uspensky came to St. Catherine's.

Jurgen Gottschlich, in his 2010 book (English in 2013), *The Bible Hunter: The Quest for the Original New Testament*, made it sound like Uspensky was a manuscript novice. Let me quote just snippets here:

> Uspensky had twice been to St Catherine's between Tischendorf's first and second visits in 1844 and 1853, and that he had personally examined the 86 sheets of ancient manuscript Tischendorf so sorely missed. What was more, Uspensky had actually seen far more of them, but, just like Tischendorf, had made no mention of this when reporting on his travels.

Are you with me so far?

Gottschlich is right that Uspensky came to St. Catherine's twice. He did, in 1845, the year after Tischendorf's first visit, and 1850, three years before the 2nd visit.

He's also right that Uspensky saw far more than the 86 folia Tischendorf claimed to see. I'll show you in a minute.

Then Gottschlich wrote:

> Uspensky was no manuscript expert, had received far less academic training than Tischendorf, and

---

81. J.M. Featherstone, *The Discovery of the Codex Sinaiticus as Reported in the Personal Letters of Konstantin Tischendorf*, (unpublished book, 2011), pp 83-84. Emphasis mine.

did not belong to the exclusive inner circle of European palaeographers,...

Then: "... he had failed to detect how old the manuscript was, and, consequently, how valuable."[82]

Uspensky was no manuscript expert? And he couldn't tell the age? Is Uspensky really not qualified? How can we know?

Figure 115 - Uspensky's original book describing his 1845 visit to the monastery

Uspensky wrote books on his travels! *The First Trip to Mt. Sinai Monastery in 1845*, was published in Saint Petersburg in 1856, in Old Church Slavonic. But a missionary friend of

---

82. Jürgen Gottschlich, *The Bible Hunter: The Quest for the Original New Testament* (London: Haus Publishing Ltd, 2013), pp. 104-105.

ours in the Ukraine got a man who had ability to translate what Uspensky actually wrote, from the original language, to Russian, to English. He did that for us.

I'll show you that in a bit.

But first, here is a tiny quote from the book, *Secrets of Mt. Sinai*, that Chris Pinto suggested I get. Notice the date, 1815:

> William Turner who visited the monastery in 1815 reported, 'To my enquiries after manuscripts and a library the priests answered, that they had *only three Bibles*, and I took their word more readily, as [Richard] Pococke [in the mid-1700s] states they had *no rare manuscripts*.'[83]

In 1815. Only three Bibles. They had no rare manuscripts.

So now, here is the Archimandrite Porfiry Uspensky's description of what he found in 1845:

> The best Greek manuscripts are stored in the priors' cells. There are only *four* of them, but they are very precious for their antiquity, rarity and handwriting features, for their content, for the elegance of the beautiful faces of the saints and entertaining drawings and paintings.

In 1815, there were *three* Bibles, nothing rare. But in 1845, 30 years later, there were *four* Bibles. And that one, a Greek Bible, was very rare. It was, and still is, one of a kind. POOF! There it is:

---

83. James Bentley, *Secrets of Mount Sinai: The Story of Finding the World's Oldest Bible—Codex Sinaiticus* (New York: Doubleday & Company, Inc., 1985), p. 45.

> The first manuscript, containing the Old Testament which was incomplete and the entire New Testament with the *epistle of St. Barnabas* and the book of *Hermas*, was written on **the finest white parchment** ....

So the entire manuscript was what color? "the finest **white** parchment." Just like the 43 folia now in Saxony, the Codex Friderico Augustanus, that Tischendorf took the year before, in 1844. But not like all the rest of Sinaiticus today, which is yellowed and darkened in color.

> All the sacred texts were written in four and two columns ..." [It turns out that Sinaiticus is **the ONLY ancient Greek codex written in four columns**.] "Such a formulation of letters without ... versification [with no verse markings] and the way of the writing of the sacred text, invented by the Alexandrian deacon Euthalius about 446 AD, and soon abandoned due to the many gaps between the columns on the expensive parchment, prove that this manuscript was published in the fifth century [the 400s AD].

So as I said before, Sinaiticus couldn't be from the 300s. It had to have been made after 450 AD. And yet that's the date they give to Codex Alexandrinus, which they don't regard as reliable, because it's such a late date!

Uspensky continues:

> It is notable in many ways. It comprises: a special order of the sacred books, intelligible presentation of Psalms and the Song of Solomon, many differ-

ent readings on the margins of the New Testament texts, and ***the particular dialect.*** [In another place, Uspensky says it's the Alexandrian dialect.]

Then he listed the books in the same order and form that we find them in today.

It looks like Uspensky knew exactly what he was talking about. He clearly described the Codex Sinaiticus, as a bound book.

In February 2016, Steven Avery contacted Dirk Jongkind, author of the 2013 book, *Scribal Habits of Codex Sinaiticus*. Listen to what he says about Tischendorf:

> It is still fascinating how Tischendorf got away with the part published in Codex Friderico Augustanus, and whether or not he had seen the New Testament part already, in 1844.
>
> He [Tischendorf] only speaks about the 130 leaves of the Greek Old Testament, but I would not put it beyond him to ***consciously suppress his knowledge of the wider manuscript*** (which would mean that between Tischendorf and Uspensky [between 1844 and 1845] the manuscript was not reunited at all, as it ***had been*** together).

So as of February of 2016, Dirk Jongkind was open to the idea that Tischendorf "got away with" the 43 folia. That sounds a lot like Kallinikos' claim, that Tischendorf secretly cut out and stole those 43 folia. And so Tischendorf also ***hid*** the fact that it wasn't a bunch of loose sheets, but a bound book.

That would link together the testimonies of Uspensky, Kallinikos, Constantine Simonides, and my accusation. ***And that would make Tischendorf a bold-faced liar***.

Figure 116 - Title page of an 1856 *Shepherd of Hermas*, edited by Tischendorf

In Chapter 17 you saw how the *Shepherd of Hermas* very largely matched the copy of *Hermas* that Simonides sold in 1855. It was published twice in 1856: one by Anger and Dindorf;[84] and an edited version by Tischendorf himself, despite criticisms of its Latinisms and late date.[85]

Did you get that? Simonides' 1856 *Shepherd of Hermas*, even the one edited by Tischendorf, is basically the same as the one in the Codex Sinaiticus.

But just before Chris Pinto released his new movie, "Bridge to Babylon," he asked me what I thought about **the other book** at the end of Sinaiticus, the *Epistle of Barnabas*.

84. *Hermae Pastor Graece, Primum Ediderunt et Interpretationem Veterem Latinam, ex codicibus emendatam,* addiderunt Rudolphus Anger and Guilelmus Dindorf (Leipzig: T.O. Weigel, 1856).
85. *Hermae Pastor Graece ex Fragmentis Lipsiensibus, Instituta Quaestione de Vero Graeci Textus Lipsiensis Fonte,* edidit Aenoth. Frid. Constant. Tischendorf (Leipzig: J.C. Hinrichs, 1856). After Tischendorf saw Sinaiticus, he decided it was old, after all!

I prayed about it. And then I made a chart with columns. I copied the text of *Barnabas* from Sinaiticus into one column, right off www.codexsinaiticus.org, and then made a blank column for notes. Then I opened another copy of *Barnabas*.

Figure 117 - Simonides' 1843 book, compiling eight versions of the *Epistle of Barnabas*

Chris Pinto had shown me that Constantine Simonides published his **own** book of the *Epistle of Barnabas*. (See Figure 117, where it shows you "Konstantinou Simonidou" as the author.)

He published it in 1843, the year ***before*** Tischendorf even set foot at St. Catherine's, the same year that Tischendorf had his audience with the pope. It had a main text, compared with seven other Greek versions of *Barnabas* in the footnotes: Karakallou, Onesimou, Iveron, Aniktetou, Gaspareos, Mavrikiou and Lavra.

Figure 118 - Front page of the Star of the East, October 17th, 1841 (Microfilm)

The Sinaiticus Smoking Gun?

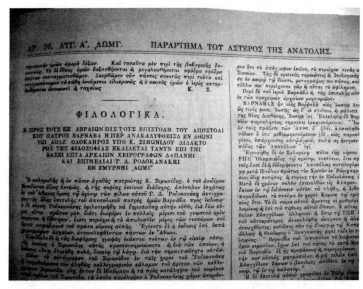

Figure 119 - Review of Simonides' *Barnabas* in the Star of the East, Number 26, August 1st, 1843

It was published in Smyrna, Turkey, and was reviewed in the Greek publication, *The Star of the East*, in the same year. The review was on August 1st, 1843.

That's when I checked all my info on *Barnabas* again. And I found out that until Sinaiticus showed up, the Western world had **never** seen a Greek original for the first 4-plus chapters of *Barnabas*, 1:1 to 5:7a.

So I wondered, how would Simonides' first four-plus chapters of *Barnabas* compare to the Sinaiticus? Is the Sinaiticus version of the first four chapters the real one? Remember, *the Sinaiticus version is the one that became the model for every copy of Barnabas right up to this day*.

Or would the Sinaiticus be like Simonides' book? If so,

then only TWO known documents in the world had the first four plus chapters in Greek: Simonides' **and** Sinaiticus.

Simonides' *Shepherd of Hermas* is already almost just like Sinaiticus. And Simonides had two versions of them. But I've only seen one.

If *Barnabas*, though, was also the same, then that would really push my thinking that Simonides helped make Sinaiticus, like he said.

But if Simonides' *Barnabas* was different, then we could just say that Simonides **made up** the first four chapters in his copy, and that would be the end of that.

It took a while to get used to the way they spelled some words. The copy I found was low-resolution, from the Aristotle University of Thessaloniki Library (Thessalonica), so my eyes had to adjust. And I had to play with the graphics, too.

But eventually I figured it out and I compared the text.

Let me just summarize what I found.

The Sinaiticus Smoking Gun?

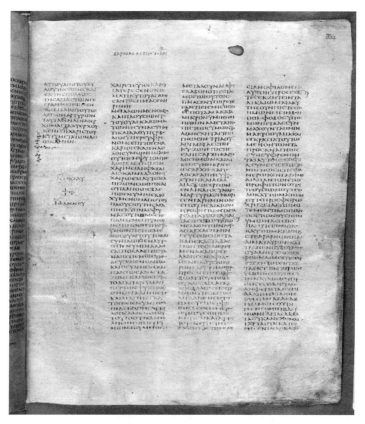

Figure 120 - Q91 F2r, the end of Revelation and beginning of *Barnabas* in Sinaiticus. Note the blank space between them.

First, look at the Sinaiticus version of *Barnabas* in Figure 120. The first column has the end of Revelation. And *Barnabas* starts in the next column. It's literally connected on the same page.

So whoever wrote Sinaiticus intended that *Barnabas* be connected to Revelation, as part of the New Testament.

Barnabas ends in a partial quire, of only 1 folded sheet, which is 2 folia, four pages. So it looks like they wanted to end the New Testament there. The *Shepherd of Hermas* actually starts in a brand new quire, after *Barnabas*. So we don't yet know whether it was originally intended to be part of Sinaiticus. But we know that *Barnabas* was supposed to be part of their New Testament.

Now the **main** text of *Barnabas* in the Sinaiticus is not **exactly** the same as the **main** text in Simonides' 8-version *Barnabas* book. There are some differences. So at this point, Simonides' *Barnabas* is close, but no match to the Sinaiticus *Barnabas*. At this point, we have no reason to believe that he wrote it.

But Simonides' *Barnabas* is more than just the main text. It also has footnotes. I mentioned that there are 7 other versions. Any place that any of those 7 versions said something different from the main text, it was noted in a footnote, along with whose text it was.

So I looked at each of those seven different versions of *Barnabas* listed in the footnotes. Three of them are named after monasteries on Mt. Athos. Others are named for specific people. As I carefully compared the Sinaiticus version of *Barnabas* to each of these footnotes, something amazing happened.

What if **one** of those seven versions in the footnotes had the words to correct Simonides' text to match the Sinaiticus? Then it would mean that we are getting close to the source of the Sinaiticus *Barnabas*. Remember, no one in the Western world had ever seen a Greek copy of chapters 1:1-5:7a.

Well, guess what? If I take Simonides' text, then correct

The Sinaiticus Smoking Gun?

the differences between it and Sinaiticus with the Gaspareos version, the result is almost identical with the text of Sinaiticus! Any variations I found between the two were just ordinary copyist's errors, such as switching "ei" for "i," etc.[86]

That means Gaspareos' manuscript of *Barnabas* **could actually have been** the source of Sinaiticus *Barnabas* —and we know that Simonides later made use of it by 1843.

But there's more.

As I showed you, Codex Sinaiticus is a text with a lot of corrections. What would happen if I "corrected" Sinaiticus *Barnabas* with all those notes scribbled all around the text? (You can do it yourself, on www.codexsinaiticus.org.)

You guessed it. It ends up looking just like the main text of Simonides' *Barnabas*! Ask yourself: what are the chances of that happening, so exactly? And in four-plus chapters no scholar had ever seen before?

Because no other copy reads like Gaspareos and Sinaiticus *Barnabas*, I think we have found evidence of one of the many manuscripts used to create Sinaiticus. And it was there in the hands of the only guy who ever claimed to have written Sinaiticus: Constantine Simonides himself.

So, Simonides' *Barnabas* main text + Gaspareos variants = Sinaiticus *Barnabas*.

And Sinaiticus *Barnabas* + marginal corrections = Simonides' *Barnabas* main text.

In other words, Gaspareos' text of *Barnabas* is the *Barnabas* of Sinaiticus.

Now consider this. As I learned about Mt. Athos, I found

---

86. Switching "ei" to "i" or vice versa is called *itacism* or *iotacism*. It was very common throughout the Sinaiticus.

out that it was pillaged over the centuries by pirates. And this led to a practice of hiding valuable manuscripts. Also, I found out that there are many more ruins of monasteries than are visible on any map. In any one of them monks could have hid valuable books, to prevent them from being stolen. Then, as it is also a practice of monks, before one would die, he would entrust the location of the hiding place to a younger monk.

Simonides said that another monk, Gregory, revealed on his death bed just such a hiding place to his Uncle Benedict. In it was a valuable library. Benedict then sent for young Simonides in order for the budding calligrapher to make copies from it.

All this makes perfect historical sense. In fact, it's making it harder and harder to disbelieve Simonides. He gives too many verifiable historical details that critics, even in the 1800s, refused to investigate. And yet here we are in the 21st century and the evidence keeps siding with Simonides.

So it is likely that the stash of manuscripts Benedict showed to Simonides included those 8 versions of *Barnabas*. We know for sure that Lampros never saw any of them in the public archives, when he created his catalog of Mt. Athos monastery libraries.

And remember, Gaspareos IS Sinaiticus *Barnabas*. Yet nobody has seen any of those versions except in Simonides' book.

Guess what else this indicates? Walk with me through this scenario. Sinaiticus was created from various documents between 1839-1840. So that came first. The story goes that Simonides was supposed to take that Bible, with

The Sinaiticus Smoking Gun?

its corrections, and make a brand-new, clean Bible, without any corrections in it.

Where is the evidence that he wanted to make a corrected Bible? We have one book of that corrected Bible right in front of us: *the Epistle of Barnabas*. Simonides clearly took the Sinaiticus *Barnabas*, with all its corrections, as you can see online, and from it created the main text of his own book of *Barnabas*. Then, to show his work, he listed the variants in the 7 other versions he had, in the footnotes.

But remember also, Gaspareos IS Sinaiticus *Barnabas*, so that is the very manuscript Simonides used to make the original text of *Barnabas* in Sinaiticus. Simonides started out, simply copying Gaspareos. Then the monks around him put in their corrections, all over the text. Then Simonides took that corrected text, made a new "main text" out of it for his own book, and published it with the other versions in footnotes, in Smyrna (now called İzmir), Turkey, in 1843.

We have the evidence that the newspaper he claimed reviewed his *Barnabas* existed, despite the British journals claiming it didn't. We have the review in *The Star of the East*, though British journals claimed it was fake. Everything makes sense if Simonides' story is true. But I have no way to explain the evidence if he simply lied.

If you assume that Simonides lied, what are you going to do with all these facts? But if you accept that he told the truth, at least in these verifiable details, then all the facts fit the story.

What about Simonides' scholarship?

When I began reading Simonides' *Barnabas* book, with all his detailed footnotes, I had to admit that he did a very good job. He had this reputation as a mere forger and con man. But what I found was the work of a studious, careful scholar. For the first time in this investigation, I began to have respect for the man Constantine Simonides.

I cannot think of a better way to do what he did. I have many Greek texts, critical editions, commentaries, and the like. And his book was at least as good as all of them. And yet it was all done by one person, not a committee.

I think he actually cared about what he was doing. This is a different man from whom I expected to find, based upon his tarnished reputation. So Tischendorf was looking like the con, and Simonides was looking like the real scholar! It was a mind-blower!

This is a smoking gun. Here are my conclusions:

One: Simonides' wrote or dictated at least *Barnabas* and the *Shepherd of Hermas*. But he was a master calligrapher. So he really might have **written** them with his own hand, as Kallinikos stated, and as the evidence made plausible. Both Simonides and Kallinikos were there. Kallinikos **knew** stuff that no one else **knew, and no one else said,** that just happened to match the facts. I think Kallinikos saw Tischendorf.

Two: Now if Simonides wrote the main text of *Barnabas*, then he wrote the whole New Testament. Aside from the three sheets of corrections, the 12 pages, the entire New Testament with *Barnabas* has the same handwriting all the way from Matthew to *Barnabas*. (Some claim someone else wrote *Hermas*.)

Three: Tischendorf was a lying liar who lied. But he thought he got away with a genuine ancient document, and then eventually he figured it out. It wasn't old at all. But he still wanted the gold and the glory.

So, either in 1853 or 1859, to make them ***look*** old, Tischendorf ***darkened all the rest of the pages*** that he did not take out in 1844, those snow white pages he sent to his patron in Saxony, the CFA. Then he told more lies to cover up his earlier lies, over and over again. He wanted fame and fortune. He got them, but he didn't live to enjoy them. He died in 1874, before he even finished the thing he prized above all else: his master project on Vaticanus.

Four: Simonides' motive was to make a Bible that looked ancient and would please the Tsar enough to buy an expensive printing press for Simonides' Uncle Benedict's monastery, Panteleimon. But for some reason, he designed that Bible in a four-column format, unlike any Bible anyone had ever seen before. It makes me think someone else told him to use that design.

Five: Someone pulled strings behind the scenes: Instructing Simonides to make a four-column manuscript, and guiding Tischendorf to go to St. Catherine's. I think it was done that way to make Tischendorf think it was the fulfillment of his interpretation of Constantine's order to Eusebius, to make a Bible "in threes and fours." (See Chapter 18.)

Vaticanus, in ***three*** columns, suddenly appeared in the Vatican library in 1475.

Later Sinaiticus, in ***four*** columns, showed up at St. Catherine's monastery, between 1815 and 1844. But more likely it was around 1841-43. And it was put there, according to Kallinikos, by the Patriarch Constantius (or a helper of his). It looks like this happened while Simonides was busy publishing the corrections to Sinaiticus *Barnabas* in his own edition, in Smyrna.

Six: The evidence suggests that this Bible found by Tischendorf in 1844 is what occultist Manly P. Hall was referring to, when he said, in 1944:

> ***For the last hundred years*** we have been trying to get out an edition of the Bible that is reasonably correct; but nobody wants it. What's wanted is the good old King James version, every jot and tittle of it.

Seven: This messed up, corrected, rushed text called Sinaiticus was suggested to Simonides ***by someone***. Maybe it was someone secretly working for the pope, like a Jesuit. Kallinikos sure is an interesting character. He seemed to always show up wherever Simonides or Tischendorf had contact with the Sinaiticus through 1859.

Then when questions about Simonides' involvement with Sinaiticus came up, Kallinikos emerged again in 1862-3, writing letters in support of Simonides. And those letters detail historical facts that I've been able to verify. Or maybe Simonides told the truth, and his Uncle Benedict asked him to make the text, and Kallinikos was simply in the right place at the right time.

Eight: This Bible fulfills the palaeographer's dream. It gives him stuff to work on and guess at for the rest of his life. And it led the scholars straight to the Codex Vaticanus, a manuscript nobody really cared about before the 1800s, because there really wasn't anything else like it. And it was nothing like the historically preserved text that you find in the King James Bible.

The Sinaiticus Smoking Gun?

And most importantly, Sinaiticus, with Vaticanus, led the world away from the King James Bible, God's preserved words in English.

Because, if you can be pulled away from the King James, history shows you can be led into just about anything else, even one world Bible for one world religion.

Finally, I heard that Simonides claimed that he had written little identifying marks in various places in the Sinaiticus, in the form of acrostics and special markings, that showed that Simonides was the author of the book.

In all my searching, I could only find one reference to these special marks. Only one such identifier was listed in all the books I've read. And that was Genesis 24. When I found out that one part of Genesis was found, I was so happy to see that it had Genesis 24! It was finally reunited with the main text! Now I could look into the margins and see for myself. If the acrostic was in the margin, it was proof that Simonides wrote it! If it was blank, then it was proof that he didn't.

Take a look for yourself.

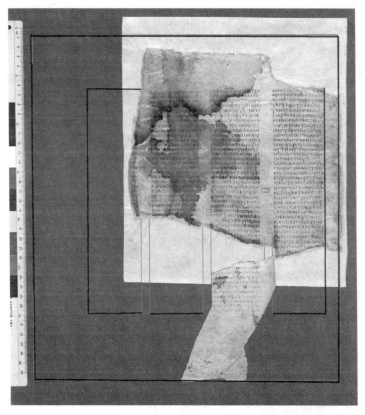

Figure 121 - Fragments of an uncolored Q3 f4v from Sinaiticus, Genesis 24:23-24:46. Note the missing margins.

What's missing?

Someone cut out two parts of the main text, and ***threw away the margins.***

Now why do you suppose **that** happened?

Do you suppose someone might have wanted to cut away the evidence of an acrostic in the margin?

The Sinaiticus Smoking Gun?

I'm so glad I can just trust God's preserved words in English, and place my complete faith in it. Then I can leave the doubting to others. I hope after this, you will, too.

31

Conclusion

So, there you have it. Satan didn't give up when he couldn't burn all the Bibles in the world. He simply moved to plan B: destroy faith, and introduce doubt. It wasn't a new plan. It was his original plan, all the way back to Eden when he whispered to Eve, "Yea, hath God said?" And it still works, at the end of time.

Only in the last ten years has modern technology handed us the tools to strip the smug mask from this monstrous plot against God's words. What was done in secret can now be shouted from the laptop, and posted on the internet!

As you can see, all the evidence points to a completely fake Sinaiticus. But where is the rest of the story? We can't stop here. This book identifies some of the characters in this plot, but what was the interplay of their motives? And how does that affect our modern Bibles?

The answer to these questions is best explored in another book. You may walk along with me as I dig for the truth by following my YouTube videos which will be the basis of the next volume: ***Who Faked the Sinaiticus?***

In my earlier books you can follow my research journey as I discovered the two streams of manuscripts in ***Did the Catholic Church Give Us the Bible?***

Then, in ***Look What's Missing***, I cataloged 257 places in the Alexandrian-based Bibles that were missing words, verses, and even whole paragraphs, in over 40 different Bible versions, compared to the Antiochian manuscripts.

The next book, ***Why They Changed the Bible***, began to discover the grand scheme behind these changes. But what about the foundational documents that created the modern versions? This book, ***Is the 'World's Oldest Bible' a Fake?***, examines one of the two supposedly "oldest and best" manuscripts that tipped the balance and caused the changes you find in modern Bibles.

The outline for the next book is coming into focus.

Here's a bigger picture. Someone gave the Protestants and Baptists the big idea that they had to "fix" the over 250 years tried, tested and proved English Bible. The enemy then proceeded to make or find faked documents and taught the scholars to think they were older and better. Then they taught Christians the wrong way to translate the Bible. Leaders were persuaded to reject the historically preserved Bible and "prefer" one that the scholars liked, instead. God's preserved Bible was put down in every conceivable way, and laughed at, even though it was a source of faith and growth for millions of believers. It became popular to reject the Bible with its solid, faith-building history and buy one with doubting notes and even the fairy tales of the Apocrypha added in. And that's on top of the contradictory Bible verses that lower Christ and the Godhead and add works to salvation.

And once again, Satan whispers: "Yea, hath God said?"

God bless you, and have a wonderful day.

Appendix A: Comparison Chart of Books Containing the Apocrypha

The following charts compare contents of the King James Old Testament with the Vaticanus and Sinaiticus Old Testaments. The Apocrypha that the KJV translators were pressured to consider are included in the KJV column. However, they were included in a separate section at the end of the Old Testament in the King James Bible, because the translators refused to mix them with the preserved books.

By this comparison, you can see the missing parts of the other two manuscripts in relation to the preserved text of the the KJV. You can also see the varying sequences of the books of each document. The familiar sequence of books that we learned in Sunday school becomes impossible to follow when the apocryphal books are scrambled with the regular OT books. This greatly adds to the confusion when trying to use these Bibles for group study.

These lists demonstrate the difficulty of determining which part can be trusted to be what God wants us to know. For example, all of Genesis is in the Vaticanus, but almost all of it is missing from Sinaiticus. If you trust the Sinaiticus to be the Word of God, then maybe He didn't want us to have the creation story of "In the beginning..."? In the same way, are Esther and Ruth really on the same level as the apocryphal folktales of Judith and Susanna?

Appendix A 335

WHAT IS IN THESE BIBLES?

King James OT + Apocrypha	Vaticanus OT + Apocrypha	Sinaiticus OT + Apocrypha
Genesis	Genesis	Genesis 21:26-24:46 (parts)
Exodus	Exodus	[Missing Exodus
Leviticus	Leviticus	Leviticus 20:27-22:30
Numbers	Numbers	Numbers 5:26-7, 16-20, 23-26:2 (parts)
Deuteronomy	Deuteronomy	Deuteronomy 3:8-4, 28-30:16 (parts)
Joshua	Joshua	Joshua 12:2-14:4
Judges	Judges	Judges 4:6-11:2
Ruth	Ruth	[Missing Ruth
1 Samuel	1 Samuel	[Missing 1 Samuel
2 Samuel	2 Samuel	[Missing 2 Samuel
1 Kings	1 Kings	[Missing 1 Kings
2 Kings	2 Kings	[Missing 2 Kings
1 Chronicles	1 Chronicles	1 Chronicles 17:14-18:11
2 Chronicles	2 Chronicles	1 Chronicles 9:27-19:17 (duplicate) [Missing 2 Chronicles]
Ezra	Esdras A (Esdrae I)	
Nehemiah	2 Esdras (Ezra & Nehemiah)	2 Esdras (Ezra-Nehemiah) 9:9-23:31
Esther	Psalms	Esther 1:1-10:31
Job	Proverbs	Tobit
Psalms	Ecclesiastes	Judith
Proverbs	Song of Songs	1 Maccabees
Ecclesiastes	Job	4 Maccabees
Song of Solomon	Wisdom of Solomon	Isaiah

WHAT IS IN THESE BIBLES?

King James OT + Apocrypha	Vaticanus OT + Apocrypha	Sinaiticus OT + Apocrypha
Isaiah	Wisdom of Sirach (Ecclesiasticus)	Jeremiah
Jeremiah	Esther (without Apocryphal chapters)	Lamentations 1:1-2:20
Lamentations	Judith	Joel
Ezekiel	Tobit	Obadiah 1:18-21
Daniel	Hosea	Jonah
Hosea	Amos	Nahum
Joel	Micah	Habakkuk
Amos	Joel	Zephaniah
Obadiah	Obadiah	Haggai
		Zechariah
Jonah	Jonah	Malachi
Micah	Nahum	Psalms
Nahum	Habakkuk	Proverbs
Habakkuk	Zephaniah	Ecclesiastes
Zephaniah	Haggai	Song of Songs
Haggai	Zechariah	Wisdom of Solomon
Zechariah	Malachi	Wisdom of Jesus son of Sirach, (Ecclesiasticus)
Malachi	Isaiah	
1 Esdras	Jeremiah	Job
2 Esdras	Baruch	[Missing Baruch
Tobit	Lamentations	
Judith	Letter of Jeremiah	[Missing Letter of Jeremiah
Rest of Esther (10:4-16:24)	Ezekiel	[Missing Ezekiel

WHAT IS IN THESE BIBLES?

King James OT + Apocrypha	Vaticanus OT + Apocrypha	Sinaiticus OT + Apocrypha
Wisdom of Solomon	Susanna [Handwritten] [θ]	[Missing Susanna [Daniel]
Ecclesiasticus	Daniel [θ]	[Missing Daniel [Main Text]
Baruch w/ Epistle of Jeremiah		
Prayer of Azariah & the Song of the Three Jews	Prayer of Azariah & the Song of the Three Jews [after Dan. 3:23] [θ]	[Missing Prayer of Azariah & the Song of the Three Jews [Daniel]
Susanna		
Bel & the Dragon	Bel & the Dragon	[Missing Bel & the Dragon [Daniel]
Prayer of Manasseh		
1 Maccabees	[Missing 1 Maccabees	
2 Maccabees	[Missing 2 Maccabees	[Missing 2 Maccabees
[3 Maccabees not included	[Missing 3 Maccabees	[Missing Hosea
[4 Maccabees not included	[Missing 4 Maccabees	[Missing Amos
	[Missing Prayer of Manasseh	[Missing Micah

θ = from Theodotion's Greek Text (175 - 200 AD)

A comparison of the KJV New Testament with the Vaticanus and Sinaiticus NT illustrates similar discrepancies. Does the book of Revelation belong in the Bible since it is missing from the Vaticanus?

Should the Shepherd of Hermas and Epistle of Barnabas be added to scripture, since they appear at the end of the Sinaiticus?

WHAT IS IN THESE BIBLES?

King James NT	Vaticanus NT	Sinaiticus NT
Matthew	Matthew	Matthew
Mark	Mark	Mark
Luke	Luke	Luke
John	John	John
Acts	Acts	Romans
Romans	James	1 Corinthians
1 Corinthians	1 Peter	2 Corinthians
2 Corinthians	2 Peter	Galatians
Galatians	1 John	Ephesians
Ephesians	2 John	Philippians
Philippians	3 John	Colossians
Colossians	Jude	1 Thessalonians
1 Thessalonians	Romans	2 Thessalonians
2 Thessalonians	1 Corinthians	Hebrews
1 Timothy	2 Corinthians	1 Timothy
2 Timothy	Galatians	2 Timothy
Titus	Ephesians	Titus
Philemon	Philippians	Philemon
Hebrews	Colossians	Acts
James	1 Thessalonians	James
1 Peter	2 Thessalonians	1 Peter
2 Peter	Hebrews 1:1-9:14 [Missing 9:15 - end	2 Peter
1 John	[Missing 1 Timothy	1 John
2 John	[Missing 2 Timothy	2 John
3 John	[Missing Titus	3 John
Jude	[Missing Philemon	Jude
Revelation	[Missing Revelation	Revelation

WHAT IS IN THESE BIBLES?

King James NT	Vaticanus NT	Sinaiticus NT
		Additional Books to New Testament
		Epistle of Barnabas Shepherd of Hermas

Apocryphal books common to all (KJV, Sinaiticus, Vaticanus, Alexandrinus, Roman Catholic Bibles):

Judith, Tobit, Wisdom of Solomon, Wisdom of Jesus son of Sirach (Ecclesiasticus)

The first charts compared the King James with the Vaticanus and Sinaiticus. The following charts compare the Old Testament, Apocrypha and New Testament of the King James with the other supposedly "early" Alexandrian text, Codex Alexandrinus, and with the accepted books of the Catholic religion from the Council of Trent (1546)[87] to the present.

---

87. See the *De Canonicis Scripturis*, from the Council of Trent, fourth session (April 4th, 1546).

WHAT IS IN THESE BIBLES?

King James OT + Apocrypha	Alexandrinus OT + Apocrypha	Roman Catholic OT + Apocrypha
Genesis	Genesis	Genesis
Exodus	Exodus	Exodus
Leviticus	Leviticus	Leviticus
Numbers	Numbers	Numbers
Deuteronomy	Deuteronomy	Deuteronomy
Joshua	Joshua	Joshua
Judges	Judges	Judges
Ruth	Ruth	Ruth
1 Samuel	1 Samuel	1 Samuel
2 Samuel	2 Samuel	2 Samuel
1 Kings	1 Kings	1 Kings
2 Kings	2 Kings	2 Kings
1 Chronicles	1 Chronicles	1 Chronicles
2 Chronicles	2 Chronicles	2 Chronicles
Ezra	Hosea	
Nehemiah	Amos	Ezra
Esther	Micah	Nehemiah
Job	Joel	Tobit
Psalms	Obadiah	Judith
Proverbs	Jonah	Esther
Ecclesiastes	Nahum	Rest of Esther (as 10:4-16:24)
Song of Solomon	Habakkuk	1 Maccabees
Isaiah	Zephaniah	2 Maccabees
Jeremiah	Haggai	Job
Lamentations	Zechariah	Psalms
Ezekiel	Malachi	Proverbs
Daniel	Isaiah	Ecclesiastes

WHAT IS IN THESE BIBLES?

King James OT + Apocrypha	Alexandrinus OT + Apocrypha	Roman Catholic OT + Apocrypha
Hosea	Jeremiah	Song of Solomon
Joel	Baruch	Wisdom of Solomon
Amos	Lamentations	Ecclesiasticus
Obadiah	Letter of Jeremiah	Isaiah
Jonah	Ezekiel	Jeremiah
Micah	Daniel	Lamentations
Nahum	Susanna	Baruch w/ Epistle of Jeremiah (ch. 6)
Habakkuk	Prayer of Azariah & the Song of the Three Jews	Ezekiel
Zephaniah	Bel & the Dragon	Daniel
Haggai	Esther	Prayer of Azariah & the Song of the Three Jews (after Daniel 3:23)
Zechariah	Tobit	Susanna (as Daniel 13)
Malachi	Judith	Bel & the Dragon (as Daniel 14)
1 Esdras	1 Esdras	Hosea
2 Esdras	Ezra-Nehemiah	Joel
Tobit	1 Maccabees	Amos
Judith	2 Maccabees	Obadiah
Rest of Esther (10:4-16:24)	3 Maccabees	Jonah
Wisdom of Solomon	4 Maccabees	Micah
Ecclesiasticus	Epistle of Athanasius of Alexandria to Marcellinus on the Psalms	Nahum

WHAT IS IN THESE BIBLES?

King James OT + Apocrypha	Alexandrinus OT + Apocrypha	Roman Catholic OT + Apocrypha
Baruch w/ Epistle of Jeremiah	Hypotheses of Eusebius of Pamphilius	Habakkuk
Prayer of Azariah & the Song of the Three Jews	Table of Contents for the Psalms	Zephaniah
Susanna	Canons (rules) of the Daytime Psalms	Haggai
Bel & the Dragon	Canons (rules) of the Nightly Psalms	Zechariah
Prayer of Manasseh	Psalms	Malachi
1 Maccabees	Psalm 151	
2 Maccabees	14 Odes (taken from other verses)	
[3 Maccabees not included	Job	
[4 Maccabees not included	Proverbs	
	Ecclesiastes	
	Song of Solomon	
	Wisdom of Solomon	

Appendix A

As we can see, the order of the books of the New Testament is the same in both the King James and Catholic Bibles. Note the different order in the Alexandrinus, as shown on the following pages. But while the books may be the same, the text is quite different. Words in key verses have been changed or removed, to make them more friendly to the pagan Roman Catholic teachings.[88]

Further evidence of the Alexandrian influence can be found in the additional books at the end of the Alexandrinus NT, as you will see in the following chart.

---

88. See my other books, ***Why They Changed The Bible***, ***Look What's Missing*** and ***Did The Catholic Church Give Us The Bible?***

WHAT IS IN THESE BIBLES?

King James NT	Alexandrinus NT	Roman Catholic NT
Matthew	Matthew	Matthew
Mark	Mark	Mark
Luke	Luke	Luke
John	John	John
Acts	Acts	Acts
Romans	James	Romans
1 Corinthians	1 Peter	1 Corinthians
2 Corinthians	2 Peter	2 Corinthians
Galatians	1 John	Galatians
Ephesians	2 John	Ephesians
Philippians	3 John	Philippians
Colossians	Jude	Colossians
1 Thessalonians	Romans	1 Thessalonians
2 Thessalonians	1 Corinthians	2 Thessalonians
1 Timothy	2 Corinthians	1 Timothy
2 Timothy	Galatians	2 Timothy
Titus	Ephesians	Titus
Philemon	Philippians	Philemon
Hebrews	Colossians	Hebrews
James	1 Thessalonians	James
1 Peter	2 Thessalonians	1 Peter
2 Peter	Hebrews	2 Peter
1 John	1 Timothy	1 John
2 John	2 Timothy	2 John
3 John	Titus	3 John
Jude	Philemon	Jude
Revelation	Revelation	Revelation

Appendix A

WHAT IS IN THESE BIBLES?		
King James NT	**Alexandrinus NT**	**Roman Catholic NT**
	Additional Books to NT	
	1 Clement	
	2 Clement	
	18 Psalms of Solomon	

Careful study of these charts gives more evidence that the classic KJV stands high above the confusion of the modern Bibles. With the KJV's solid history of over 5,000 supporting documents, these few, scrambled Alexandrian/Roman Catholic manuscripts seem hopelessly pathetic. Yet, nearly all of "Christendom" has bought into this monstrous plot hatched by a frustrated Lucifer, who wasn't able to burn all the copies of the real Bible, or the believers who protected them.

Appendix B: Spurgeon's Quote

This is from the last sermon that Charles Spurgeon preached to pastors. For a while Spurgeon had drifted into using the English Revised Version. But then he came to a realization, and he preached this sermon.

"Believe in the inspiration of Scripture, and believe it in the most intense sense .... If this book be not infallible, where shall we find infallibility? .... Are these correctors of Scripture infallible? Is it certain that our Bibles are not right, but that the critics must be so? Now ... when you have read your Bible, and have enjoyed its precious promises, you will have, to-morrow morning, to go down the street to ask the scholarly man at the parsonage whether this portion of the Scripture belongs to the inspired part of the Word, or whether it is of dubious authority ....

"All possibility of certainty is transferred from the spiritual man to a class of persons whose scholarship is pretentious ... who do not even pretend to spirituality. We shall gradually be so bedoubted and becriticized, that only a few of the most profound will know what is the Bible, and what is not, and they will dictate to the rest of us. I have no more faith in their mercy than in their accuracy: they will rob us of all that we hold most dear ...

"This same reign of terror we shall not endure, for we still believe that God revealeth himself rather to babes than to the wise and prudent, and we are fully assured that our own old English version of the Scriptures is sufficient for plain men for all purposes of life, salvation, and godliness."

(Charles H. Spurgeon, "*The Greatest Fight in the World*," The Spurgeon Archive)

ALSO BY DAVID W. DANIELS

112 pages, paperback

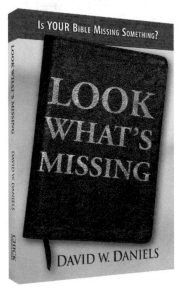

Before you buy another Bible, look at what's being left out!

- See how one left-out word makes Jesus a liar in 19 modern Bibles!
- See which entire verse was removed to leave room for infant baptism.
- See the verses where adultery is removed from God's sin list.
- Does your Bible warn of hell? Many don't!

ALSO BY DAVID W. DANIELS

288 pages, paperback

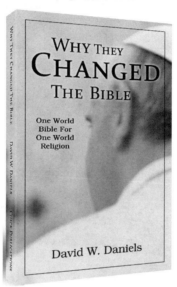

Bible translators, all over the world, are making Bibles that they think are only for Protestant and Baptist believers. But most don't know that Christian translators are being manipulated into helping create a One-World Bible! And all the translation work is paid for by contributions from Bible believers like you. **Who** is behind this? And what do they believe?
Read, as they admit it, **in their own words!**

ALSO BY DAVID W. DANIELS

112 pages, paperback

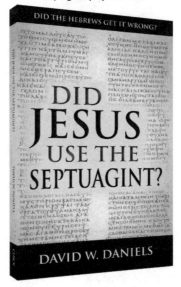

That's what they may have taught your pastor in college. Do you know why?

Simple: the Septuagint contains the Apocrypha, and there are people who want your pastor (and you) to have the Apocrypha in *your* Bible, too. Why? So you will accept Catholic superstitions like:

- Purgatory and prayers for the dead
- Payment to forgive sins
- Angels as mediators

In this new book, David Daniels takes each of the "proofs" promoting a BC Septuagint and shows why they can't be trusted. He shows that Jesus read the same Hebrew Scriptures as other devout Jews. Don't be fooled by the push for "One World Bible for One World Religion".

ALSO BY DAVID W. DANIELS

208 pages, paperback

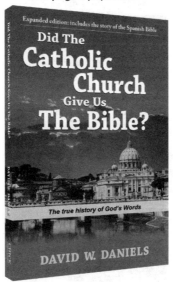

Expanded edition includes history of Spanish Bible.

The Bible has two histories. One is of God preserving His words through His people. The other is of the devil using Roman Catholic "scholars" to pervert God's words and give us corrupt modern Bibles.

Read the history of not one, but two Bibles... One that matches centuries of evidence, and another that has been changed to justify Catholic doctrine.

ALSO BY DAVID W. DANIELS

160 pages, paperback

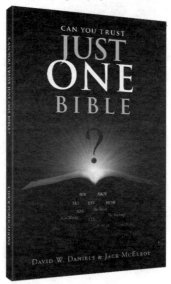

by David W. Daniels & Jack McElroy
Do we need multiple Bible translations?
Or is there one Bible we can simply trust?

Christian leaders tell us we need to compare several, to get as close to the "lost originals" as possible. But that just breeds doubt.

In early 2015, authors Jack McElroy and David W. Daniels recorded two unrehearsed interviews where they answered many anti-KJV accusations. The videos are on YouTube, but this print version has much MORE information.